University of Plymouth Library

Subject to status this item may be renewed
via your Voyager account

http://voyager.plymouth.ac.uk

Tel: (01752) 232323

Korea in the New Asia

Since the late 1980s a number of regional developments have impacted upon South Korea's political and economic standing in Asia. China's spectacular growth and closer integration with its neighbouring economies, along with a tendency toward more assertive political and diplomatic activity, have deeply altered both the economic and political East Asian environment. Simultaneously, the 1997–98 financial crisis catalysed a process of increased regional co-operation in East Asia. China's rise has imposed a leadership problem that may constitute a major obstacle on the road to deeper regional integration, as well as add force to the need for collective action, and it is this paradox that may give South Korea a key role in the reorganization of the region. Moreover, inter-Korean relations and Korea's future security environment may also feel the effects of the rise of China.

Korea in the New Asia seeks to analyse to what extent and how South Korea may contribute to, and take advantage of, the new regional configuration in East Asia. The book represents the first study to address Korea's regional policy responses to the rise of China as an economic power and the regional economic integration of East Asia. Written by an international team of experts, this multidisciplinary study will appeal to researchers, academics and students with an interest in international relations, security studies, economics and East Asian politics.

Françoise Nicolas is a Senior Researcher at the Centre Asie of the French Institute of International Relations (ifri), Paris, and an Assistant Professor at Marne-la-Vallée University (France).

Routledge Advances in Korean Studies

Korea in the New Asia

East Asian integration and the China factor

Edited by Françoise Nicolas

Routledge
Taylor & Francis Group

LONDON AND NEW YORK

First published 2007
by Routledge
2 Park Square, Milton Park, Abingdon, Oxon OX14 4RN

Simultaneously published in the USA and Canada
by Routledge
270 Madison Ave, New York, NY 10016

Reprinted 2008

Routledge is an imprint of the Taylor & Francis Group, an Informa business

Typeset in Times New Roman by
Taylor & Francis Books
Printed and bound in Great Britain by
MPG Books Ltd, Bodmin

British Library Cataloguing in Publication Data
A catalogue record for this book is available from the British Library

Library of Congress Cataloging in Publication Data
Korea in the new Asia : East Asian integration and the China factor /
Francoise Nicolas, [editor].
p. cm. – (Routledge advances in Korean studies)
Includes bibliographical references and index.
1. Korea (South)–Economic policy. 2. Korea (South)–Foreign economic
relations. 3. China–Economic policy. 4. East Asia–Economic integration.
5. East Asia–Economic conditions. I. Nicolas, Françoise
HC467.95.K665 2007
337.5195–dc22
2006101560

ISBN 978-0-415-42006-8 (hbk)
ISBN 978-0-203-94659-6 (ebk)

Contents

Figures

Tables

Contributors

Sophie Boisseau du Rocher is currently a Research Associate at the Asia Centre, Centre études asie, in Paris. She also teaches at the Paris Institute of Political Science (Sciences Po, Paris). Her main research interests are Southeast Asia and regionalization.

Jaewoo Choo is currently an assistant professor in the School of International Relations and Area Studies at Kyung Hee University in Korea. Since his teaching began at Kyung Hee University, Dr. Choo's main research interest has been Chinese oil diplomacy and energy strategy. He is also a contributor on Korean affairs to *Asia Times* online edition since October 2002.

Robert Dujarric is Visiting Research Fellow at the Japan Institute of International Affairs and former Council on Foreign Relations (Hitachi) International Affairs Fellow in Japan in 2004–5. He has written extensively on Korea and has co-chaired the Korea Japan Study Group in Washington (1998–2003) and Tokyo (since 2004). His latest book, co-authored with William E. Odom, is *America's Inadvertent Empire* (Yale University Press, 2004). He is currently working on his next book, *Does Japan Have a Future?*

Sukhee Han is Research Professor at the Institute for Korean Unification Studies, Yonsei University as well as Acting Professor of the China Business CEO Program at Yonsei University. From 1999 to 2001 he was a teaching professor at the School of Government Management, Peking University, and a visiting scholar at the Institute of Asia-Pacific Affairs, CASS. His research interests include Sino-American relations, Sino-Korean relations, Sino-North Korean relations, China's international behavior, power-politics in China.

Changsu Kim is a Senior Research Fellow at the Korea Institute for Defense Analyses (KIDA), a defense think tank affiliated with the Korean Ministry of National Defense in Seoul. Dr Kim is also a member of the Standing Committee of the Advisory Council on Democratic and Peaceful Unification, a Constitutional political body, and Director of

International Affairs of the Military Operations Research Society of Korea (MORSK). His areas of research interest include the Korea–US alliance, security and military strategies, arms control, and multilateral security dialogue and cooperation in Northeast Asia.

Heungchong Kim is currently a research fellow at Korea Institute for International Economic Policy (KIEP). He is now head of the research team for European Studies, and his research interests are broad, extending beyond Europe to East Asia, Africa, and the Middle East. He also teaches at Seoul National University.

Taeho Kim is Professor and Vice President for Academic Affairs as well as Director of the Center for Contemporary China Studies (CCCS), both at Hallym Institute of Advanced International Studies (HIAIS). He is the author and co-author of over 20 books, policy reports, and monographs, including (with Dr. Bates Gill) *China's Arms Acquisitions from Abroad: A Quest for "Superb and Secret Weapons"* (Oxford University Press, 1995) and *The Analysis of the New Party, Government, and Military Leadership in China* (KIDA, 2003 in Korean). His main research interests are Sino-Russian military cooperation, Chinese arms acquisitions, Asian nations' perceptions of China, and Sino-North Korean relations.

Françoise Nicolas is a Senior Researcher at the Centre asie of the French Institute of International Relations (ifri), Paris, and an Assistant Professor in Economics at Marne-la-Vallée University (France). She also teaches at the Institut National des Langues et Civilisations Orientales (Langues' O Paris). Her main research interests relate to development strategies in East Asia, regional economic integration, FDI and growth, and emerging economies and globalization.

Ulrich Volz is a Research Fellow at the Hamburg Institute of International Economics (HWWA) and the Free University of Berlin. He was appointed as Fox International Fellow at Yale University, New Haven in August 2005, where his research focuses on East Asian monetary and financial integration.

Yunjong Wang is Vice President at SK Research Institute for SUPEX Management. He has been formerly Senior Research Fellow and Director of Center for Regional Economic Studies at Korea Institute for International Economic Policy (KIEP) from 1993 to 2004. His main research interests focus on financial integration and exchange rate arrangements in East Asia. His most recent publication is *Financial Governance in East Asia* (RoutledgeCurzon, 2004).

Acknowledgements

The chapters in this volume were originally presented and discussed at a conference on "The Rise of China and Korea's regional Policy" organized by the Centre asie ifri and held at the French Senate (Palais du Luxembourg) in Paris on 24 June 2005. This conference marked the end point of a year and a half research venture involving Korean and European researchers.

This joint research effort would not have been possible without the generous support of the Korea Foundation to which we are extremely grateful. Thanks to the Foundation's support, Sophie Boisseau du Rocher and myself could travel to Korea in order to conduct interviews as well as to co-ordinate the work with our Korean partners. We were both also able to travel to other countries in the region so as to get a better understanding of the perceptions of China's rise by other East Asian players. Thanks to the support of the Korea Foundation Kim Heungchong was also given the opportunity to spend some time in Paris, thus reinforcing the collective dimension of the research effort.

In addition to the Korea Foundation, I would also like to thank the Center for Northeast Asian Economic Co-operation at the Korean Institute for International Economic Policy (KIEP) who hosted me during my research stay in Seoul in the autumn of 2004. During this stay I benefited from fruitful discussions with a number of researchers at KIEP, in particular Heungchong Kim, Chang Jae Lee, Sang-Yirl Nam, and Young-Sook Nam, to whom I am extremely grateful. I would also like to extend my thanks to other Korean researchers for their precious help in my research, in particular Dukgeun Ahn (KDI School of Public Policy and Management), Byungki Ha (KIET), Il Sakong (Institute for Global Economics) and Soogil Young (National Strategy Institute).

Finally, my thanks also go to Stephen Thomsen who edited the volume with utmost care, as well as to Cécile Campagne and Martine Breux who kindly helped prepare the manuscript for publication.

Françoise Nicolas

Participants in the conference organized by Centre asie ifri and held at the French Senate (Palais du Luxembourg) on June 24, 2005

Korean speakers:

Jaewoo CHOO, Professor, School of International Relations and Area Studies, Kyung Hee University

Suk-hee HAN, Research Professor, Institute for Korean Unification Studies, Yonsei University

Chul-ki JU, Ambassador of the Republic of Korea to France

Taik-Hwan JYOUNG, Minister-Counsellor, Korean Permanent Delegation to the OECD

Changsu KIM, Director, US Studies, KIDA

Heungchong KIM, Research Fellow, Korea Institute for International Economic Policy, KIEP

Taeho KIM, Professor and Vice President for Academic Affairs, Hallym Institute of Advanced International Studies, Hallym University

European Speakers:

Sophie BOISSEAU DU ROCHER, Research Associate, Centre asie Ifri

Hervé DEJEAN DE LA BATIE, Deputy Director, Asia-Pacific Bureau, French MoFA

Robert DUJARRIC, Visiting Research Fellow, JIIA, Tokyo

François GODEMENT, Professor, INALCO and Consultant, French MoFA

Françoise NICOLAS, Senior Research Fellow, Centre asie ifri

Karoline POSTEL-VINAY, Senior Research Fellow, CÉRI-Sciences Po

Pierre-Bruno RUFFINI, Honorary President, University of Le Havre

Xavier DE VILLEPIN, Former Senator

Ulrich VOLZ, Hamburg Institute of International Economics, HWWA, Hamburg, Germany

Special Observers:

Guibourg DELAMOTTE, PhD candidate, School of Political Science, EHESS

Jae-Seung LEE, Assistant Professor, Korea University
Alain NASS, Head, North-East Asia Section, French MoD

In attendance:

Arnaud D'ANDURAIN, Asia Project Leader, Policy Planning, French MoFA

Florence BIOT, Project Co-ordinator, Centre asie ifri

Mihye BLIN, Secretary General, EECCF

Jean-Pierre CABESTAN, Senior Researcher, CNRS

Laurent CHEMINEAU, Journalist, La Tribune

Odile CORNET, International Reporter, MOCI

Éric DUPONT, Head, Office for Asia, French MoD

Jérémie FORRAT-JAIME, Intern, in charge of Asia Studies, French MoD

Richard HERD, Head, China Desk, OECD

Diana HOCHRAICH, Economist in charge of Monitoring Asian Emerging Countries, French MINEFI

Christine KARABOWICZ-RIVET, Researcher in Chinese Law, University of Paris 1/Director, Karasia China

Cléa LE CARDEUR, Analyst for the Korean Peninsula, Directorate for Asia and Oceania, French MoFA

Ravi MATHUR, First Secretary, Embassy of India in France

Claude MEYER, Professor, Sciences Po Paris and University of Paris 1 Panthéon

Christian MILELLI, Economist, CNRS

Margit MOLNAR, Economist, OECD

Pierre MONGRUÉ, Assistant to the Economic Analysis Desk for Emerging Countries, French MINEFI

Valérie NIQUET, Senior Research Fellow, IRIS

Céline PAJON, Intern, North America Bureau, DAS, French MoD

Guillaume PARMENTIER, Director, French Center on the United States

Sung-Hee PARK-CHOO, Student, University Paris 8

Marianne PERON-DOISE, Asia Analyst, French MoD

Anne-Cécile VIOLIN, In charge of Non-Proliferation, DAS, French MoD

Thibaud VOÏTA, Sciences Po and INALCO PhD. Candidate

1 Korea in the new Asia

*Sophie Boisseau du Rocher and
Françoise Nicolas*

The emergence of a "new Asia"

Over the past decade or so, two major developments have deeply altered
both the economic and political setting in East Asia, giving rise to what can
arguably be called a "new Asia", an Asia that has the potential to dramatically affect world balances. The first of these changes relates to the
apparent shift away from informal "open regionalism" towards an institution-
based form of economic and political co-operation in the region, while the
second is associated with the rise of China as a major actor in the economic, diplomatic, and strategic regional arena.

The shift towards institution-based regional co-operation in East Asia

The first change dates back to the financial crisis which engulfed most East
Asian economies from late July 1997 on. Among its many side-effects,
the financial crisis of 1997–98 has rekindled interest in tighter economic and
political co-operation in the region. While the development of tight
interdependence between the economies in the region had been an integral
part of the East Asia miracle, it turned out to be a lethal weakness as
the financial crisis spread unhindered from one country in the region to the
other. The contagion mechanism and the spillovers underline the level of
interdependence within the region and the need for a collective approach
to address common issues. In the wake of the crisis it thus seemed to be in
the interest of all the countries in the region to opt for a more active cooperation. As argued by Rajan (1998: 60),

> whatever the exact transmission mechanisms, to the extent that eco-
> nomic policy slippages in any one country reverberate rapidly to
> other countries in the region, it is important to ensure that there is
> some sort of peer pressure or club spirit that promotes the pursuit of
> sustainable and prudent macroeconomic policies in each country in the
> region.

In other words, the closer interconnections between East Asian economies have shown that it may be useful to go beyond *de facto* integration, thus reducing traditional scepticism toward a top-down approach to regional integration in this part of the world.

As a result of this change of mindset, a number of concrete steps have been taken in the direction of institutional frameworks to promote economic and political co-operation in East Asia, but in a more limited format than the Asia Pacific Economic Cooperation Forum (APEC). The emergence of the "ASEAN+3" framework (which includes the ten ASEAN countries as well as China, Japan, and South Korea) is one such example. The East Asian Vision Group (EAVG), launched at the initiative of Korea in 1999, emphasizes precisely the need to institutionalize the ASEAN+3 process.

While the economic field, including trade, investment, and finance, was expected to serve as a catalyst in the community building process, recommendations made by the EAVG also encompassed co-operation in political and security issues, as well as in environmental, social, cultural, and institutional matters. For the time being, however, the major achievements have been limited to the financial sphere, with the implementation of the so-called Chiang Mai Initiative which provides for an economic surveillance scheme as well as a set of financial assistance mechanisms. The prospects for an East Asian Free Trade Agreement, in contrast, still appear to be bleak, and the ASEAN+3 has delivered little so far beyond the organization of numerous summits, senior official meetings, and working groups in areas as diverse as security, energy or environmental issues.

On the economic front, a salient feature of the recent move is its "Asia only" orientation which is in sharp contrast to earlier initiatives such as APEC. This change clearly reflects the region's desire to assume a more independent role in the international system and to limit the influence in the region of the United States.[1] In this respect, the conditions are quite different in the security area, where the possibilities for regional co-operation are still heavily constrained by the involvement of the US in the region. Although in theory regional co-operation can serve important regional order-keeping functions, it remains to be seen whether regional security can be rooted more in indigenous institutions and depend less on outside powers (notably the US).

Despite these limitations it is worth stressing that the established perceptions of the region itself have certainly been deeply transformed by the crisis. Asia's nations and societies are coming together in new ways, thus producing, albeit in a still very volatile manner, an emerging perception of togetherness.

The rise of China

At the same time, the economic and political centre of gravity in East Asia has been gradually shifting to China due to its rising political and economic clout.

Since it embarked on its open-door and economic reform policies in the late 1970s, China has grown at a phenomenal rate (at an average of more than 9 per cent per annum over the whole period) to emerge as the fourth largest trading nation and the fourth largest economy world-wide.[2] As the workshop of the world, China has been increasingly integrated with the global trading system and plays a pivotal role in the emergence of regional production and distribution networks in East Asia. While these developments have impacted all countries in the world, the emergence of China has thus been particularly important for its neighbouring economies in the sense that it has helped further fuel the dynamics of private sector-led regionalization. In particular China's trade with neighbouring emerging Asian economies has intensified dramatically.

This new state of play generates both opportunities and challenges for East Asia and for regional community building. On the one hand, strong economic growth is no doubt contributing to a more dynamic and more resilient economy. With the bulk of its imports coming from neighbouring East Asian economies, developed and developing alike, China helps to sustain economic growth in the whole region. On the other hand, however, relocations of production units in China are associated with the risk of "hollowing out" some of the most advanced economies in the region, while rising competitive pressure from China on a number of less advanced economies in the region is perceived as being both risky and potentially destabilizing. Moreover, the speed at which China is supposed to climb the technological ladder is likely to generate new challenges in not too distant a future.

In addition to being at the centre of regional production networks (thus contributing to the growth of intra-regional trade and FDI links and to the overall economic growth of the region), China is also taking advantage of its new status as a regional heavyweight to play an increasingly active diplomatic role in the region. Various initiatives taken by China reflect the country's resolve to become a regional leader instead (or ahead) of Japan. The first initiatives date back to the 1997–98 financial crisis, when China actively publicized its refusal to devalue the renminbi, allegedly in order to protect its neighbours from a new round of contagious devaluations. This "no devaluation" policy for the renminbi was meant to prove that China should be perceived as a responsible and amicable power which could be trusted by its neighbours. At the same time, Beijing also provided some financial assistance to ailing economies such as Thailand and Indonesia, as a way of showing its rising sense of solidarity.[3] China also contributed to initiate the ASEAN+3 mechanism and gave its support to the Chiang Mai initiative (CMI). It is worth stressing at this stage that the latter move reflects a definite shift, compared with China's outright hostility with regards to Japan's proposal of an Asian Monetary Fund in 1997. The shift in China's position may be accounted for by its desire to act either as a leader or collectively, rather than simply as a follower behind Japan; it is thus more politically than economically inspired. More recently still, Chinese officials kept insisting that their refusal to let the renminbi appreciate (vis-à-vis the dollar in particular) was motivated by their concern about the possible negative impact this may have on neighbouring economies.

The China–ASEAN Free Trade Agreement (CAFTA) is probably the latest and most dramatic example of China's new regional policy. The framework agreement on Comprehensive Economic Co-operation was signed in November 2002, one year after the start of the negotiations, formally launching the process of establishing a CAFTA by 2010 for the most advanced ASEAN member countries and by 2015 for the others (Cambodia, Myanmar, Laos, and Vietnam). Through these various moves, China obviously sought to enhance its role and status in regional and international affairs; however, it is worth stressing that China's rising diplomatic activism in the region has also added momentum to the East Asian regionalism highlighted earlier.

Finally, in the political and security arena, while China's economic development could, on the one hand, help reduce tensions between developed and developing countries, on the other hand, East Asian countries are concerned about the possibility of China becoming a dominant power with growing political influence and rapidly expanding military capabilities (a scenario made possible by its economic growth), and upsetting the strategic balance prevailing so far in the region. The risk of a rising rivalry with Japan is also a matter of concern.

In addition China's changing role in the region has far-reaching implications for other partners outside the region and in particular for the US. In this changing context, China's more assertive positioning in the region poses a major challenge and implies new rules of the game.

The implications for South Korea

The new state of play in East Asia constitutes a multifaceted challenge for a middle power such as South Korea.

The first challenge relates to Korea's development strategy. For the past 14 years since their diplomatic normalization in August 1992, China and South Korea have remarkably improved their bilateral ties to such an extent that China is now South Korea's largest trading partner, its largest export market, and its largest trade-surplus source. Although China's dynamism is apparently associated with exclusively positive spillovers, a number of challenges also loom large, in the medium to longer term in particular. As a result, Korea's government may have to design a new development strategy and to set new priorities in its regional economic strategy.

A second dimension of the challenge pertains to China's rising role in regional co-operation schemes and to the possible role Korea may play in the regional community-building process in the presence of two potential and rival leaders. Given its size, Korea has no ambition to be a leader in the region, but it has proven to be particularly active in the regional integration efforts as a "regional broker". Through the "East Asia Vision Group",

Korea has already worked on initiatives concerning the building of an East Asian Community and, thus, greatly contributed to its gradual acceptance. Korea is now a recognised partner in ASEAN + 3. Its status of a middle-sized power probably accounts for its interest in such regional endeavours. A major issue for Korea is to determine the stance to take in response to China's changing role in the regional game. To some extent while the leadership problem that the recent rise of China entails may constitute a major obstacle on the road to deeper regional integration in East Asia, it may as well add force to the need for collective action. It is this paradox that may give South Korea a key role in the regional integration process.

Thirdly, the rise of such a huge economic and political power will inevitably usher in enormous and disruptive changes in its relations with the other nations of East Asia, as well as deeply affect the strategic balance which prevailed so far in the region with the US as a major actor. Moreover, the competition with Japan could lead in particular to aggravated tensions in the region, placing Korea in a delicate position.

From Korea's perspective, the strategic challenge takes on a number of forms. China is likely to have an impact on inter-Korean relations and to change Korea's future security environment. From a geopolitical point of view, the main question to be addressed is the following: despite the heavy uncertainty concerning Korean reunification, how can South Korea develop a new Asian regional partnership with its closest neighbours and with Southeast Asia, and what kind of proposal could Seoul put forward to secure a well-balanced form of regional institutionalization? Moreover, while China's role is essential to any progress in the ongoing Six-Party Talks over the North Korean nuclear issue, there also exists a growing yet little-discussed list of potential problems and issues underlying the otherwise prosperous Sino-Korean relationship. Prime examples include the North Korean "refugees" in China, the history of Koguryo, and the longer-term "China's rise".

Finally, the rise of China and its increasingly assertive positioning in the region may place the traditional US–Korea relationship under heavy strain. To some extent, this question echoes the US/Japan alliance and its compatibility with closer regional cooperation. As far as Korea is concerned a key issue is to decide whether or not it should come closer to China and distance itself from its traditional ally.

The main objective of the book is to examine the impact of the new regional setting on these various aspects of South Korea's policy, and in particular on its regional strategy. To that end it will adopt a multidisciplinary approach and address economic, political as well as security issues.

Outline of the book

While the regional integration process in East Asia, as well as the recent economic and political rise of China, are well-researched issues, they are usually addressed separately. The present book offers to explicitly link the two issues by focusing on the South Korean case. The aim of the book is to analyse to what extent, and how, South Korea may contribute to, and take advantage of, the new regional configuration in East Asia. The following chapters address questions spanning the potential role of Korea in the community-building process, the impact of the recent changes on the Korean peninsular issue, or the impact of China's rise on the Korea–US relationship.

The book is divided into two parts which deal respectively with economic and strategic issues associated with the rise of China and the reorganization of the East Asian region. A first introductory chapter sets the stage and provides an overview of Korea's perceptions of China's rise over the past decades.

In this introductory chapter, Sukhee Han explores the fundamental rationale for Korea's favourable perceptions of China's rise and its possibility for change. He argues that, in contrast to a number of other countries, Koreans have traditionally maintained a positive view of China which they see as a status quo power and as a definite opportunity for Korea's economic recovery.

In the second part of the chapter, however, Sukhee Han explains that China's assertiveness over the past few years has fuelled a growing unease in Korea. He points to a number of recent developments in China's attitude which may account for this change in Korea's perception of its large neighbour. One such development pertains to China's distortions of history over the Koguryo issue. The author argues that these claims are increasingly associated by Koreans with arrogance or even despise on the part of the Chinese, with the risk of arousing strong anti-Chinese feelings in Korea. Recent economic frictions between the two countries give additional substance to this rising concern.

The chapter concludes that if China hopes to become a respected great power, at least in the East Asian region, it is in its own interest to do its utmost to maintain Korea as a consistent pro-Chinese state, be it only because Korea is in a position to exert great influence in shaping international attitudes towards China. In order to be a responsible great power able to play a key role on the regional as well as the international stage, China has thus to tone down its nationalistic assertiveness and learn how to approach countries such as Korea.

Korea, China, and the prospects for East Asian economic integration

The first part of the book focuses on the economic dimension of the challenge posed by the rise of China and on its implications for various co-operative schemes in the region, be they trade or finance-oriented.

In Chapter 3, Françoise Nicolas explores the challenges posed by the economic rise of China to Korean firms and government, with a view to highlighting the implications for their respective regional strategies. The first section of the chapter provides a comprehensive assessment of China's new role in the regional supply chain and of the resulting change in the competitive game being played in the region. It examines in particular the implications for the Korean economy and how both business and government have accommodated their rising neighbour so far. A major conclusion is that Korea has so far largely benefited from the rise of China but that sustained efforts in the direction of structural reform are badly wanted for the positive impacts to persist.

In the second part of the chapter, Françoise Nicolas looks at the changes in China's stance toward its neighbours, focusing on its economic diplomacy moves in the region, which reflect China's resolve to become a regional leader. In the analysis, a particular emphasis is placed on China's and Korea's trade policy. The analysis points to the difficulties still prevailing on the road to an East Asian trade arrangement. As the chances for the emergence of such an agreement appear to be very low and are likely to remain so for some time to come, Korea is shown to be in a position to play a pivotal role in the region through the negotiation of bilateral arrangements with its different regional partners.

The rise of China deeply affects the conditions for regional co-operation beyond trade issues. Because the increasing participation of China in regional production networks has created a complex web of economic linkages and given rise to tighter interdependence within the region, there is a stronger need than ever to push for the deepening of economic policy monitoring, and even to proceed towards exchange rate co-ordination. An interesting point in this respect is that China's stance with regards to regional financial co-operation has clearly shifted over time from sheer hostility, as exemplified in its opposition to the Japanese proposal of an Asian Monetary Fund in 1997, to active support of further schemes such as the Chiang Mai Initiative (CMI) launched in 2000.

In Chapter 4, Heungchong Kim and Yunjong Wang review the process of financial integration in East Asia and assess the prospects for further developments in this area. In the course of the integration process, the role of major countries including China, Korea, and Japan are extensively examined. The chapter provides a critical assessment of the various mechanisms already in place, such as the CMI or the Asian Bond Market Initiative, and suggests possible extensions. In this respect, the chapter stresses the importance of Korea's role given the reservations within the leadership of China and Japan toward deeper regional economic integration. Moreover, unlike China or Japan, Korea has a strong interest in promoting regional integration: in particular given its very specific position in the region, Korea would be most severely hit if a conflict in the Korean peninsula were to occur. Any kind of regional co-operation in East Asia that would help keeping peace in the region would be welcome by Korea. At the same time, Kim and Wang argue that Korea's potential role is hampered by its unclear strategic position on regional financial issues and by questions concerning its capacity to lead on these issues.

Following up on monetary issues, Ulrich Volz explores possible scenarios in Chapter 5, in particular the possibility of a monetary union with
the yuan as the anchor currency, and its implications for South Korea.
While China would seem a natural choice for centre country in a regional exchange rate system due to its size and key role in the regional economy, the author argues that the Chinese yuan will not be able to act as
anchor currency for an East Asian "yuan bloc" unless China overcomes
the deficiencies in its domestic financial system, develops deep and liquid
financial markets, and unless the yuan becomes fully convertible. Instead
of centring solely on China, the region would be well advised to also
include Japan in its exchange rate co-operation efforts. First, Japan, despite
many swan songs, still remains the region's most affluent economy with
highly developed financial markets and extensive trade and investment
linkages with the rest of the region and would thus add considerable economic weight to East Asian monetary co-operation. Second, from a
security perspective it would be unwise to exclude Japan as this could give
ground to future political conflict in the region. As the best way forward, the chapter thus recommends monetary co-operation within the
ASEAN+3 framework. In this, Korea could play the important role of
mediator between China and Japan, as well as between the (economically) smaller Southeast Asian countries and the two Northeast Asian
giants.

South Korea's regional diplomacy

The second part of the book turns to political and strategic issues associated
with the rise of China in East Asia and the reorganization of the region,
using a Korean perspective. Three issues are addressed, namely the possible
role Korea may play in East Asian regionalism in the presence of two
potential regional leaders such as China and Japan, the impact of the rise of
China on the future of the Korean peninsular, and the possible evolution of
the Sino-US relationship and its implications for Korea.

In Chapter 6, Jaewoo Choo and Sophie Boisseau du Rocher examine
the evolution in Korea's involvement in East Asian regionalism. They argue
that while Korea has been traditionally an active promoter of regionalism
in East Asia, it has clearly lost ground in the "new East Asian game" as a
result of China's growing influence in the region. The first part of the
chapter explores the implications of China's rise for regional rules, thereby
contrasting the traditional "ASEAN way" and the emerging "Chinese
way". The second part of the chapter examines the particular influence
Korea may still exert in the emerging regional architecture. It suggests that
in order to avoid dropping to a second-tier member state in "new" East
Asian regionalism, Korea must define an East Asian policy; in particular it
must develop a set of goals and interests that it would like to pursue in its
policy towards the region. Because of newly rising economies in the region,

Korea is bound to develop a policy line that would uphold its regional profile as one of the most advanced democratic states and market economies.

In security terms, the rise of China is an issue of great significance for the future of East Asia as a whole and of the Korean Peninsula in particular. China's current and likely future role and status in inter-Korean relations, Korean reunification and a greater East Asia would in large measure influence the future course of events on the peninsula. At the same time, future developments on the peninsula would in turn affect the rise of China as an up-and-coming leader in the regional order. In Chapter 7, Taeho Kim explores the highly interactive yet under-researched aspects in China's relations with the Korean Peninsula.

The chapter attempts to shed some light on this little-discussed yet highly consequential aspect of the Sino-South Korean relationship not only by addressing their 12-year ties but also by gauging their future ties in a balanced and comprehensive manner. Overall, the chapter poses a critical question: How would the China factor play out in South Korea's future security environment and in the evolving US–South Korean relationship?

Taeho Kim comes to the following conclusions. First, the seeming "convergence" of interests between Beijing and Seoul in many aspects of their bilateral ties does not necessarily mean that the former is supportive of South Korea's major policy goals – especially when they come to concrete issues or longer-term questions on the Korean Peninsula. Moreover, in light of the longer-term Sino-American competition, their likely diverging interests over the peninsula, and China's growing influence over the Korean Peninsula, it is for now inconceivable that both the US and China can cooperate with each other on a host of salient peninsular issues. Under such circumstances and for the foreseeable future South Korea's "strategic prioritization" in its relations with the US and with China would highly likely be the optimal strategic choice, even if South Korea should continuously and systematically pursue a specific set of confidence-building measures with China.

Finally, in Chapter 8, Changsu Kim focuses more specifically on the possible evolution of China–US relations with a view to highlighting the major implications for the whole of East Asia. The chapter starts by examining the so-called rise of China and how the US, in concert with other allies and friends, can manage this rise and maintain prolonged peace and prosperity in East Asia. As a next step, it explores the dynamics of a new power configuration in East Asia for the next twenty years. In the analysis a special emphasis is placed on the reasons why the US and China would rather develop their relations into amicable and co-operative ones that can be found among responsible democracies. Finally, the chapter suggests possible regional policy alternatives for South Korea. It concludes that basic tenets of Seoul's security strategy and regional policy will be centred on the continued alliance with the US, improving security co-operation with all other regional powers including Japan, China, and Russia, and laying the ground for multilateral security dialogue and co-operation in East Asia.

By way of conclusion, Robert Dujarric examines in Chapter 9 what are the factors that are likely to shape Korea's China policy in the coming years. He concludes that although Korea may be gradually "re-Asianized" the trend is in no way irreversible.

Notes

1 For more details on this point see Bowles (2002) or Beeson (2003). In this respect, the recent move is more in line with Malaysia's initiative in the early 1990s to set up an East Asian Economic Caucus excluding the United States.
2 In 2005 China ranks 4th when GDP is measured in current dollars, and 2nd when GDP is measured in purchasing power parity terms.
3 Although the amount may have been symbolic, the gesture was meant to be perceived as amicable.

References

Beeson, Mark (2003), "ASEAN+3 and the Rise of Reactionary Regionalism", *Contemporary Southeast Asia*, vol. 25, no. 2, August, 251–68.
Bowles, Paul (2002), "Asia's Post-crisis Regionalism: Bringing the State Back In, Keeping the (United) States Out", *Review of International Political Economy*, vol. 9, no. 2, 230–56.
Rajan, Ramkishen (1998), "The Currency and Financial Crisis in Southeast Asia: A Case of 'Sudden Death' or 'Death Foretold'?", *IPS Working Paper*, #1, August.

2 Korean perceptions of China's rise in East Asia

Sukhee Han

Introduction

The rise of China continues in the twenty-first century. China's growing economic and military power, expanding political influence, distinctive diplomatic voice, and increasing involvement in regional multilateral institutions are key developments in East Asian affairs. China's stable political succession from the third to the fourth generation of leadership as well as a consistent and balanced growth-oriented development has given new confidence to the current leaders in China. Despite its chronic domestic problems including the reform of state-owned enterprises, unemployment and soaring crime, and disparities between urban and rural areas and between east and west, China's new leaders, with the aim of making their country a great power, have pushed forward to upgrade China's international status. Given the growth of China, neighbouring states in East Asia are keenly interested to see what type of great power China is likely to become and have also struggled with the question of how to live with a growing China.[1]

The international community has so far failed to arrive at a common view on China's great power ascendancy. Since the mid-1990s when the rise of China became conspicuous in the world, a number of international pundits, scholars and politicians have considered the rise of China as a source of concern for international and regional security.[2] The major rationale is China's military build-up and its potential military expansion. Taking advantage of its already accumulated economic influence, they claim, China will challenge the existing international system. Since the early 1990s, China has consistently increased its military budget more than 10 per cent every year and has modernized its military capabilities, especially its naval and air forces.[3] Given China's potential for military expansion, the growing perception of China as a threat among neighbouring states, including Vietnam, India, Singapore, Japan and Taiwan, is understandable. To allay these fears, China has engaged in constructive diplomatic efforts for more than a decade, and subsequently international and regional perceptions of China have changed tremendously. China's active participation in various international institutions and its vivacious diplomatic strategies for regional peace and prosperity have created a new image of China as a status quo power.[4] In particular, China's recent "charm offensive" towards its neighbours has added credence to the belief that China has the potential to become a responsible great power in East Asia.[5]

Regardless of the threat of China or China's charm offensive widely discussed in the international community, Korea, one of its closest neighbours not only in terms of physical distance but also in terms of history and culture, has tended to view the rise of China in a positive light. Its growing dependency on China, particularly in terms of trade and foreign direct investment, diplomatic manipulation regarding North Korea, and procurement of natural resources has pushed the Korean government and people to place tremendous emphasis on its diplomatic and economic relations with China. A dominant share of the Korean population favours China over the United States, a five-decade-old security ally of Korea.[6] On the other hand, Koreans have gradually become concerned about the negative aspects of the rise of China. China's economic rise has been so speedy and comprehensive that Korean companies, including big conglomerates, have struggled to survive the competition with low-priced Chinese products. China's attitude towards Korea's FDI is not as welcoming as in previous periods. Furthermore, China's unprecedented assertiveness – largely stemming from its renewed nationalism – has provided fresh grounds for bilateral unease.

The major objective of this chapter is to analyse Korea's dual response to an economically viable, diplomatically flexible, militarily strong and culturally assertive China. On the one hand, Koreans tend to perceive China as a status quo power and as an opportunity for Korea's economic recovery.[7] On the other hand, Koreans are beginning to be concerned about the potential confrontation with China as a result of China's growing assertiveness. One example of the uncomfortable relationship between China and Korea is the case of China's intentional distortion of 'Koguryo' history. Due to the 'Koguryo' case, the 'Kimchi' dispute, and frequent complaints of Chinese maltreatment of Korean citizens in China, China's image in Korea has been continuously damaged. Based on these backdrops, this article argues that China should be more cautious and careful in dealing with Korea, not only in terms of economy and diplomacy but also in terms of cultural interaction, if it wants to become a real great power in the East Asian region.

Korea's positive perception of the rise of China

Since the establishment of diplomatic relations between Korea and China in August 1992, the Chinese perception of Korea has changed dramatically. Before 1992, China had always supported North Korean foreign policy against the Korean government and recognized only North Korea. But as China has adopted a two-Korea policy instead of its traditional one-Korea policy with the establishment of the normalization,[8] China's national interests have been modified as the international atmosphere has changed. For

Table 2.1 Korea's Trade with China since 1992 (unit: billion dollars)

Year	92	93	94	95	96	97	98	99	00	01	02	03	04
Export	2.7	5.2	6.2	9.1	11.4	13.6	11.9	13.7	18.5	18.2	23.7	35.1	49.7
Import	3.7	3.9	5.5	7.4	8.5	10.0	6.5	8.7	12.8	13.3	17.4	21.9	29.6
Trade surplus	1.0	1.3	0.7	1.7	2.9	3.6	5.4	6.0	5.7	4.9	6.3	13.2	20.1

Source: Korean Import-Export Bank.

China, unconditional support of North Korea's violent unification strategy has remained an untenable diplomatic option, while maintaining peace and stability on the Korean peninsula has become more conducive to China's national interests.[9] Therefore, since the establishment of the Sino-Korean diplomatic relations, China has maintained an equidistant policy towards the two Koreas by keeping its traditional political and ideological linkages with the North and extending its economic and cultural exchanges with the South simultaneously. As China carries on influential diplomatic pressures over both Koreas in order to promote its own national interests of keeping peace and stability on the peninsula, a growing number of people in and out of Korea have perceived China as a status quo power for Korea's security.

Another reason to consider China as a status quo power is that North Korea cannot wage a war against South Korea without China's military and economic support. Given that China currently provides as much as 40 per cent of grains and 90 per cent of the oil that North Korea needs, China has considerable political and diplomatic leverage over North Korea.[10] Despite some counter-arguments that Chinese leverage over North Korea is very much limited, China is the only country that can change North Korea's

Table 2.2 Korea's FDI in China (unit: million dollars)

Year	No. of contracts	Amount
1991	101	65
1992	170	141
1993	381	264
1994	841	633
1995	748	838
1996	734	888
1997	628	716
1998	258	678
1999	454	337
2000	752	380
2001	1,020	493
2002	437	252
2003	1,676	1,510
2004	2,149	2,157
Total	10,350	9,352

Source: Korean Import-Export Bank.

decision-making to suit China's national interests.[11] Furthermore, as China's successful economic reform and open-door policy have matured, China requires a peaceful and stable environment in neighbouring states to maintain its economic development. For China, in this perspective, North Korea is the most important strategic partner.[12] Given its geographical proximity, ideological intimacy and diplomatic interdependence, North Korea is surely the lips to the Chinese teeth and therefore China will do its best to keep stability on the Peninsula. In this process, China is a status quo power from a Korean perspective.

In particular, Hu Jintao and the fourth generation leaders in China emphasize the importance of its regional relations under the new diplomatic strategy called "Peaceful Development" (和平發展)[13] The central theme of Peaceful Development is that China's development does not pose a threat to regional and international security, and a developed China would rather be a constructive superpower contributing to the promotion of peace and prosperity in East Asia and the world. Against the perennial nuisance of the China threat argument,[14] Hu Jintao and the other fourth generation leaders have emphasized Peaceful Development as a platform to nurture China's cooperative image as a status quo power which promotes the existing international order and which has become a responsible great power which manages regional security and stability in a diplomatic manner.[15] The Six-Party Talks hosted by China are a good example of China's Peaceful Development successfully applied to promote regional security. The Six-Party Talks are proof of China's constructive efforts for resolving serious regional security headaches such as North Korea's nuclear programme by way of multilateral cooperation. Although it is an on-going process and has not produced any substantial success yet, the Six-Party Talks are symbols to imprint China as a status quo power in Koreans' mind.[16]

Since the Sino-Korean normalization, the two countries have maintained close and amicable economic, diplomatic, military and cultural relations. But as Table 2.1 indicates, bilateral economic exchange, *inter alia*, has increased remarkably over the past decade. Except for a temporary slow-down between 1997 and 1998 when East Asian countries suffered from the

Table 2.3 Number of Koreans Visiting China (unit: ten thousand, %)

Year	No. of Koreans visiting China	Rates of increase
1992	4.3	186.6
2000	134.5	26.0
2001	167.7	25.6
2002	212.4	32.7
2003	194.5	-8.2
2004	284.5	46.3

Source: China's National Bureau of Travel.

economic crisis, Sino-Korean economic relations have been consistently developed with a steady increase in economic interdependence. In particular, Korea's economic dependence on China is growing.[17] Taking advantage of China's consistent economic development, the Korean government and a number of Korean companies have expanded their foreign direct investment into China and have also increased their volume of bilateral trade. Korea's increased economic dependence on China has proved to be timely by helping Korea's damaged economy to revamp itself successfully from its critical decline right after the East Asian Financial Crisis in 1997. Even to this day, Koreans hope to guarantee a minimum of economic growth by managing their economic relationship with China.

Currently China is Korea's number one trading partner, surpassing the United States, and number one source of Korea's trade surplus.[18] In terms of Korea's outgoing FDI, China has also served as the biggest destination, with both the number of projects and the amounts invested growing quickly in recent years (Table 2.2). There are two major reasons to explain this FDI growth. One is that a number of Korean companies have been lured by China's vast market. Another is that many small and medium-sized firms moved into China mainly due to Korea's aggravated domestic industrial conditions. Sky-rocketing wages, frequent labour unrest, a variety of government interventions, and no vision for the future were major factors pushing Korean firms into China.[19] But overall, it is true that China has served as an economic opportunity to Korea, as evidenced by increased trade and investment between the two neighbours.

Based on close economic interactions between China and Korea, both countries have developed other areas of their relationship. For example, China receives the highest number of Korean visitors, with the number more than doubling over the past five years (Table 2.3). The decrease in 2003 was the result of the widespread SARS epidemic in China. As the number of visitors has increased post-SARS, the number of flights between China and Korea has also increased. There are currently 380 flights between Korea's six cities and China's 22 cities every week.

The fact that more and more Koreans visit China reflects the Koreans' sense of opportunity in China.[20] Following Korea's popular predilection, Korean politicians also stress diplomatic and economic relations with China. After the seventeenth national election for Korea's National Assembly in April 2004, 55 per cent of the members of the majority party confirmed that China is the most important neighbouring great power for Korea's future development and prosperity, while about 45 per cent supported the United States as Korea's most important strategic partner.[21] Koreans in general also believe that the rise of China will provide a good opportunity, not only for the improvement of Korea's economy but also for the consolidation of the peninsula's stability. Regardless of its shaky ties with the United States, the Korean government has for more than a decade maintained its cooperative relationship with China and will extend it in the foreseeable future.[22]

Korea's negative perception of the rise of China

In general, a dominant number of Korean people still believe that China is an opportunity for Korea's economic recovery and a status quo power to help maintain peace and security of the Korean Peninsula. But recently concerns about the rise of China have started circulate within Korean society. The major motivation largely stems from China's push for the "Northeastern Project" (東北工程). The key issue is whether an ancient dynasty called Koguryo was included in Korean history or in China's border history. Koreans have confirmed for a long time that Koguryo was a Korean dynasty proud of expanding its territory to a large portion of Manchuria, while China argues that all the histories related to the regions within the contemporary Chinese border should be included in Chinese history, adopting an unconventional way of historical translation, called "United Multi-Ethnicity"(統一的 多民族國家論).[23]

Regardless of which argument is right, the Northeastern Project has the potential to undermine the hitherto smooth and cooperative bilateral relationship. First of all, the Koreans perceive China's inordinate and groundless argument as an intentional diplomatic act. From Korea's perspective, it is obvious that Koguryo was a part of Korea's historical dynasty, as supported by various types of historical documents.[24] A number of scholars, pundits and journalists also confirm Koguryo as a part of Korean history. The most persuasive explanation of China's intention behind Northeastern Project is that China is preparing for the potential collapse of North Korean regime. In the event that North Korea's Kim Jong-il regime is toppled, the Chinese could dispatch the People's Liberation Army to various strategic cities of North Korea, including Pyongyang. At the moment, China needs to suggest understandable justification for its military dispatch and the Northeastern Project would be a valuable source to prove that North Korean territory was historically a part of China. Although China currently does not claim North Korean territory as its own, it would definitely do so if it successfully includes the history of Koguryo as a part of Chinese history.[25] Since Koguryo moved its capital to Pyongyang in its later

Table 2.4 Koreans' most favourite neighbouring power

	United States	North Korea	China	Japan	Russia
2003	44.0	26.5	9.4	10.5	0.7
2004	42.7	29.0	12.0	8.8	1.5
1005	46.4	27.7	11.4	6.2	1.0

Source: *Joongang Daily*, 22 December 2005.

period, China believes that it is legitimate to demand the return of North Korean territory.

Another interpretation of China's Northeastern Project is that China's consistent mobilization of the Project in spite of the massive emotional response in Korea reflects China's growing contempt for neighbouring states. As China gets stronger in its national power, many Koreans complain that China has become less respectful of Korea. A number of Korea's China specialists, economic leaders and Korean residents in China all consider that the Chinese are not as kind, respectful and friendly as before.[26] Koreans tend to regard China's distortion of Koguryo history as stemming from Chinese arrogance. With its successful economic development, Koreans believe, China is beginning to look down on neighbouring countries and dares to project its arrogance to such an extent as to distort other countries' ancient history. In this respect, the Koreans tend to believe that China is no different from Japan, which would influence Koreans' perception of China in a negative direction.

For China, it is very dangerous to see Koreans associate China's distortion of history with its arrogance. Given that the perceived arrogance of the United States is the major reason for flagrant anti-Americanism despite a five-decade strategic alliance and the deaths of many US soldiers defending Korea from communist aggression in the 1950s,[27] Koreans' current perception of China's arrogance could be a source of potential anti-Chinese attitudes in Korean society. Despite anti-Americanism, the US–Korean relationship has still been maintained without any specific signs of separation. Five decades of political, economic and cultural ties between Korea and the United States should be solid grounds for maintaining healthy bilateral relations, but the more important factor is the US–Korean security alliance. The fact that American soldiers are stationed in Korea proves that US–Korean relations cannot be broken without any substantial strategic chasm between the two countries.

For Sino-Korean relations, there has been no strategic lynchpin such as an alliance system to bind the two countries even in case of bilateral miscommunication, political conflict or diplomatic confrontation. Given no solid glue to tie these two countries together, the unexpected emergence of anti-Chinese attitudes in Korea would lead the bilateral relationship into a grave paralysis. As shown in Table 2.4, Koreans' favouritism towards China has recently been declining, while Koreans' goodwill towards the United States has grown. Although the data do not indicate the emergence of anti-Chinese sentiments, they show at least that Koreans have begun to analyse China from a more balanced perspective. At the same time, Koreans seem to realize the crucial importance of US–Korean relations.

In terms of the economy, China has gradually become a less interesting partner. Although China is still Korea's number one FDI destination, a growing number of Korea's middle-to-small size businesses are losing interest in China. For example, Qingdao, a port city in Shandong Province which has attracted the most investment from Korea, recently decided to accept Korean investments only in technology-intensive sectors. Given labour costs as the major rationale of Korea's investment in China, the Qingdao government's decision frustrates Korean businesses in China. Korean conglomerates are also concerned about China's technological improvement. Korea's *chaebols*, including Samsung, LG, SK and Hyundai, calculate that China's technological catch-up could be so fast that Korea's mobile technology could be surpassed by China in two–three years and Korea's semiconductor technology could be exceeded in five–six years.[28] Overall, China still serves as the biggest trade and investment partner of Korea, but its role and contribution counts less and less in Korea's economic development.

With diminished interest in China, there has been soaring Korean interest in Vietnam and India. A number of labour-intensive businesses, searching for an alternative to China, have turned to Vietnam. As a communist country with abundant and cheap labour, favourable investment conditions and relatively little government intervention, Vietnam plays a timely role in absorbing Korean businesses frustrated with China. Along with Vietnam, India has recently emerged as a relevant investment destination. Its advantages include the widespread knowledge of English, a huge population, IT development and lax government control, all of which will induce Korean businesses into India. Reflecting this shift in focus from China to India, a number of advanced educational institutions are preparing to replace their existing special programmes on China with programmes on India. The lack of India specialists in Korea retards further development of Koreans' interest in India, but the fact that India is in fashion in Korea indicates that many Koreans, concerned about Korea's inordinate economic dependence on China, are beginning to search for new investment destinations and markets.[29]

Conclusion

With its rise confirmed, China hopes to become a respected great power at least in the East Asian region. Along with its new leadership group, the fourth generation leaders, China is rushing to enhance its international status as a responsible great power. In order to calm the "China threat argument" and to raise "China's peaceful rise", China has thus far struggled to enmesh itself in international institutions and regional dialogue, and in sustained regional stability and prosperity. China's cooperative behaviour towards regional multinational organizations including the SCO (Shanghai Cooperation Organization), ASEAN (Association of South East Asian Nations), and the Six-Party Talks are proof of China's charm offensive. China's friendly relationship with Taiwan, Pakistan and India would be further evidence to show that China sincerely wants to become a solid member of the international community.

Even before China's charm offensive, Korea was a consistent pro-Chinese neighbour. Due to China's crucial influence over Korea's security and economy, the Korean government and people have continued to favour China diplomatically, economically and emotionally, even at the height of the discussions of the China threat within the international community. Given North Korea's military antagonism against the South and the intimate Sino-North Korean relationship, China is surely a status quo power from Korea's perspective. Given that the volume of trade surpassed that with the United States and Japan and the greatest trade surplus is with China, China is definitely the most important economic partner. In terms of national security and economic interests, a pro-Chinese attitude in Korea is nothing strange.

However, the rise of China and its associated cultural assertiveness have emerged recently as a point of Korean concern. China's distortion of history is proof of its territorial ambitions towards North Korea. China's recent condescending attitude towards Korea and Koreans seems to be viewed as an arrogant gesture by Koreans. And recent economic frictions between China and Korea also seem to be understood by Koreans as China imitating the behaviour of the United States. All in all, China's recent behaviour towards Korea makes Koreans, traditionally pro-Chinese, less enthusiastic about China. At the same time, apprehension of China has gradually been conjured up within Korean society. In contrast to the China threat argument, Korea's fear of China focuses on non-military, including cultural, environmental and economic, issues. Given Korea's search for alternatives to China in economic cooperation, Korea's tendency to avoid China will last for a while.

In this perspective, what China has to do is clear. First, it must recognize the seriousness of changing perceptions in Korea. Korea's favouritism towards China was not based on emotion. For security and economic interests, Korea has temporarily put more weight on its approach to China. Therefore, China has to maintain bilateral relations through diplomatic, security and economic channels. China's recent attitudinal changes have been so premature that it risks losing a loyal supporter in Korea with nothing gained. Second, China's Northeastern Project has no diplomatic advantage and therefore, China should stop the project. What China really needs at this juncture is a sincere friend, not a rhetorical great power. By stopping the project, China is not only able to secure at least one diplomatic friend, but also to use Korea's voice on China as an effective counter-argument against China threat theory.

As a result, it is very important for China to keep Korea as a consistent pro-Chinese state. As a close neighbour, in alliance with the United States, an active economic partner, and a democratized state, Korea's positive relationship with China could exert great influence in shaping international attitudes towards China. For further securing its great power status, China has to tone down its nationalistic assertiveness and learn how to approach neighbouring states like Korea with respect and amity. Without such cautiousness and sensitivity, China can never become a responsible great power.

Notes

1 Regarding the rise of China and its regional and international implications, see Brown 2000, Kokubun and Wang 2004 and Sutter 2005.
2 See Schweller and Ross 2000.
3 For the analyses of China's military budget, see Bates 1999, Ding 1996 and Wang 1996.
4 Regarding China's new image as a *status quo* power, see Johnston 2003. For China's changed relationship with regional neighbours and international institutions, see Medeiros and Fravel 2003 and Shambaugh 2004/2005.
5 See Limaye 2003.
6 For Korea's perception between China and the US, see Chung Jae Ho 2001.
7 For Korea's perception of China opportunity, see Chung Sangun, "Han-Chung Sugyo 10nyon ui Huigowa Chunmang [Retrospect and Challenge of Sino-Korean 10 Years]," *CEO Information*, no. 362 (Seoul: Samsung Economic Research Institute, 2002) (http://www.seri.org).
8 Regarding the historical view of the Sino-North Korean relationship and the Sino-Korean relationship, see Chae-Jin Lee 1996. Victor Cha (1999) explains that Korea's engagement of China was the major cause of the Sino-Korean economic and diplomatic partnership.
9 See Cha 1999, pp. 23–26.
10 See *Time*, 23 December 2002.
11 The academic works on the Sino-North Korean relations are quite limited. It is very difficult to find some sources about North Korea's international relations. But the list of hitherto academic works is as follows: Kim 2001, You Ji 2001, Kim and Lee 2002, Shambaugh 2003, You Ji 2004, Han Sukhee 2004, Scobell 2004.
12 In Korea's history, China has been involved in the Korean Peninsula three times including the Sino-Japanese War in 1592, the Sino-Japanese War in 1904 and the Korean War in 1950.
13 Peaceful Development has been studied and developed from the concept of "Peaceful Rise". For the detailed analysis of the history and concept of "Peaceful Rise", see Hu Jian 2004 and Suettinger 2004. For recent Chinese analysis of Peaceful Development, see Yu Xintian 2004, Liu Chenmin 2005, Guo Zhengyuan 2005.
14 For a comprehensive debate of China threat and regional responses, see Yee and Storey 2002. For a China threat masterpiece, see Bernstein and Munro 1997.
15 Regarding China's *status quo* power debate, see Johnston, 2003, Medeiros and Fravel 2004, Shambaugh 2004/05 and Roy 2003. And for the comprehensive study of China's responsible great power argument, see Yongjin Zhang and Austin 2001.
16 For a detailed explanation of the Six-Party Talks and Chinese diplomacy, see Han Sukhee 2005.
17 Chung Jae Ho 2001.
18 See the data from Korea's Import and Export Bank (http://www.koreaex im.go.kr/kr/file/nation/050607_CR_CHINA_INTRODUCTION.pdf).
19 For Korea's domestic factors to push the firms to China, see *CEO Information*, no. 438 (Seoul: Samsung Economic Research Institute, 2004) (http://www.seri.org).
20 For the sources of data, see the official site of the Korean Embassy in China (http://www.koreaemb.org.cn/contents/information/information_info.aspx?id=15 58&type)=policy&bm=3&sm=6).
21 See *Dong-a Ilbo*, May 3, 2004, available at: (http://www.donga.com/fbin/out put?rellink= 1&code=ap_&n=20040503 0336).

22 US think tanks are the leading institutions initiating research on these topics. These institutions maintain their research topics to reflect contemporary issues of interest. See official homepages of CSIS (Center for Strategic and International Studies), the Brookings Institution, and the Rand Corporation: http://www.csis.org; http://www.brookings.edu; http://www.rand. org.
23 Northeastern Project was researched, analysed and implemented by the Center for China's Borderland History and Geography Research at the Chinese Academy of Social Science. Please refer to the official site of the center: http://www.cass.net.cn/webnew/yanjiusuo/bjzx/more_news_dbgc.asp?class_id=221.
24 For an academic analysis of China's Northern Project in Korea, see Chun Byong-gon 2004.
25 For Koreans' general response to China's Northeastern Project, see an official site of the National Institute of Korean History (http://www.history.go.kr/front/index.jsp).
26 Although Korea's mass media are reluctant to carry articles touching on Korea's nationalistic emotion, Koreans in general perceive China's attitudinal change in recent years. For the explanation of Korea's emotion on China, see *Weekly Donga*, 4 March 2004.
27 For a detailed analysis of Korea's anti-Americanism, see Kim Seung-Hwan 2002/2003.
28 See comments from Jin Daejae, Korean minister of the Department of Information and Telecommunication, *Chosun Daily*, 28 January 2003.
29 Park Bun-soon 2005. Regarding SCO, see CICIR (Chinese Institute of Contemporary International Relations), *Shanghai Hezuo Zhuzhi: Xin Anquanguan yu Xinjizhi* [Shanghai Cooperation Organization: New Security Concept and New System], Beijing, Shishi Chubanshe, 2002.

References

Bernstein, Richard and Munro, Ross, H. (1997) *The Coming Conflict with China*, New York: Alfred Knopf.

Brown, Michael E. (ed.) (2000) *The Rise of China*, Cambridge, MA: Mit Press.

Cha, Victor D. (ed.) (1999) "Engaging China: the View from Korea", in Alastair Iain Johnston and Robert S. Ross (eds) *Engaging China: The Management of an Emerging Power*, London and New York: Routledge, 23–56.

Cha, Victor D. and Kang, David C. (2004) "The Debate over North Korea", *Political Science Quarterly*, vol. 119, no. 2 (Summer), 229–54.

Chen, Jian (2003) "Limits of the 'Lips and Teeth' Alliance: An Historical Review of Chinese-North Korean Relations", *Asia Program Special Report*, no. 115 (September), 4–10.

Chenmin, Liu (2005) "Dangdai Guoji Zhixu yu Zhongguo de Heping Fazhan Daolu [Contemporary International Order and Future Trend of China's Peaceful Development]", *Guoji Wenti Yanjiu* [Journal of International Studies], no. 1, 6–9.

Chun, Byong-gon (2004) *Chungguk ui Dongbuk Gongjung Kwa Uri ui Daeung Chaek* [China's Northern Project and Our Preparation], Korean Institute for National Unification, December.

Chung, Jae Ho (2001) "South Korea between Eagle and Dragon", *Asian Survey*, vol. 41, no. 5 (September/October), 777–96.

Ding, Arthur (1996) "China's Defense Finance: Content, Process and Administration", *The China Quarterly*, no. 146 (June), 428–42.

Eberstadt, Nicholas (2004) "Tear Down This Tyranny", *The Weekly Standard*, vol. 10, No. 11 (November) (http://www.weeklystandard.com/Content/Public/Articles/000/000/004/951 szxxd.asp).

—— (2004) "The Persistence of North Korea", *Policy Review*, no. 127 (October & November) (http://www.policyreview.org/oct04/eberstadt.html).

Finkelstein, David M. and Kivlehan, Maryanne (eds) (2003) *China's Leadership in the 21st Century: The Rise of the Fourth Generation*, Armonk, NY: M.E. Sharpe.

Gill, Bates (1999) "Chinese Defense Procurement Spending: Determining Intentions and Capabilities", in James R. Lilley and David Shambaugh (eds), *China's Military Faces the Future*, Armonk, NY: M.E. Sharpe, 195–227.

Guo, Feixiong (2004) "China's Role and Objectives in the North Korean Nuclear Crisis", *China Strategy* (CSIS), vol. 3 (July 20), 11–16.

Han, Sukhee (2004) "Alliance Fatigue amid Asymmetrical Interdependence: Chinese-North Korean Relations in Flux", *The Korean Journal of Defense Analysis*, vol. XVI, no. 1 (Spring), 155–79.

—— (2005) "Yukja huidam kwa Chungguk ui dilemma [Six Party Talks and China's Dilemma]", *Journal of International Politics* (Korean), vol. 45, no. 1, 232–53.

Harrison, Selig S. (2005) "Did North Korea Cheat?", *Foreign Affairs*, vol. 84, no. 1 (January/February).

Horowitz, Michael (2004/05) "Who's Behind That Curtain? Unveiling Potential Leverage over Pyongyang", *The Washington Quarterly*, vol. 28, no. 1 (Winter), 21–44.

Jiang Xiyuan (2003) "DPRK Nuke Problem and New Framework of Multilateral Security Cooperation in Northeast Asia", *SIIS Journal*, vol. 10, no. 4 (November), 24–37.

Jian, Hu (2004) "Peaceful Rising is China's Strategic Decision [Heping Jueqi shi Zhongguode Zhanlu Juece]", *Journal of International Studies* [Guoji Wenti Yanjiu], no. 2, 18 – 70.

Johnston, Alastair Iain and Evans, Paul (1999) "China's Engagement with Multilateral Security Institution", in Johnston, Alastair Iain and Ross, Robert S. (eds), *Engaging China: The Management of an Emerging Power,* New York: Routledge, 235–72.

Johnston, Alastair Iain. (2003) "Is China a Status Quo Power?", *International Security*, vol. 27, no. 4 (Spring), 5–56.

Kim, Samuel S. (2003) "China and North Korea in a Changing World", *Asia Program Special Report*, (Woodrow Wilson International Center for Scholars), no. 115 (September), 11–17.

—— (2001) "The Making of China's Korea Policy in the Era of Reform", in David L. Lampton (ed.), *The Making of Chinese Foreign and Security Policy in the Era of Reform*, Stanford, CA: Stanford University Press, 371–408.

Kim, Samuel S and Tai Hwan Lee. (2002) "Chinese-North Korean Relations: Managing Asymmetrical Interdependence", in Samuel S. Kim and Tai Hwan Lee (eds), *North Korea and Northeast Asia,* New York: Rowman & Littlefield, Inc., 109–37.

Kim, Samuel S. (2001) "The Making of China's Korea Policy in the Era of Reform", in David M. Lampton (ed.) *The Making of Chinese Foreign and Security Policy in the Era of Reform*, Stanford, CA: Standford University Press, 371–408.

Kim, Seung-Hwan (2002/2003) "Anti-Americanism in Korea", *The Washington Quarterly*, vol. 26, no. 1 (Winter), 109–22.

Kokubun, Ryosei and Wang, Jisi (eds) (2004) *The Rise of China and a Changing East Asian Order*, Tokyo: Japan Center for International Exchange.

Kotch, John Barry (2005) "Six-Party Talks: The Way Forward", *Korea Observer*, vol. 36, no. 1 (Spring), 183–97.

Lampton, David (2001) *Same Bed, Different Dreams: Managing U.S.–China Relations, 1989–2000*, Berkeley, CA: University of California Press.

Lee, Chae-Jin. (1996) *China and Korea: Dynamic Relations*, Stanford, CA: Hoover Press.

Limaye, Sato P. (ed.) (2003) *Asia's China Debate: A Special Assessment*, Honolulu, HI: Asia-Pacific Center for Security Studies.

Lin, Gang and Xiaobo Hu (eds) (2003) *China after Jiang*, Stanford, CA: Stanford University Press.

Liu, Ming. (2004) "Opportunities and Challenges for Sino-American Cooperation on the Korean Peninsula", *The Korean Journal of Defense Analysis*, vol. XVI, no. 1 (Spring), 135–54.

Medeiros, Evan S. and M. Taylor Fravel (2004) "China's New Diplomacy", *Foreign Affairs*, vol. 82, no. 6 (November/ December), 22–35.

Oh, Kongdan and Ralph C. Hassig. (2004) "North Korea's Nuclear Politic", *Current History*, September, 273–79.

Park, Bun-soon. (2005) "Chungguk ui Busang kwa Dong Asia Jiyon Balchon ui Byunhua [The Rise of China and East Asian Developmental Changes]", Samsung Economic Research Institute, November.

Roy, Denny (2003) "China's Reaction to American Predominance", *Survival*, vol. 34, no. 3 (Autumn), 57–78.

Ruggie, John Gerard (ed.) (1993) *Multilateralism Matters: The Theory and Praxis of an Institutional Form*, New York: Columbia University Press.

Scobell, Andrew (2004) "*China and North Korea: From Comrades-in-arms to Allies at Arm's Length*", SSI (Strategic Studies Institute), Monograph, March (http:// www.carlisle.army.mil/ ssi/pdffiles/PUB373.pdf).

Shambaugh, David (2004/2005) "China Engages Asia: Reshaping the Regional Order", *International Security*, vol. 29, no. 3 (Winter), 64–99.

—— (2003) "China and the Korean Peninsula: Playing for the Long Term", *The Washington Quarterly*, vol. 26, no. 2 (Spring), 43–56.

Shen, Dingli (2005) "Accepting a Nuclear North Korea", *Far Eastern Economic Review*, vol. 168, no. 3 (March), 51–57.

Sigal, Leon V. (1998) *Disarming Strangers: Nuclear Diplomacy with North Korea*, Princeton, NJ: Princeton University Press.

Schweller, Randall L. (2000) "Managing the Rise of Great Powers: History and Theory", in Johnston Alastair Iain and Robert S. Ross (eds), *Engaging China: The management of an emerging power*, New York: Routledge.

Sutter, Robert G. (2005) *China's Rise in Asia: Promises and Perils*, New York: Rowman & Littlefield Publishers, Inc.

Suettinger, Robert L. (2004) "The Rise and Descent of Peaceful Rise'", *China Leadership Monitor*, no. 12 (Fall).

Wang, Hongying (2003) "National Image Building and Chinese Foreign Policy", *China: An International Journal*, vol. 1, no. 1 (March), 46–72.

Wang, Shaoguang (1996) "Estimating China's Defence Expenditure; Some Evidence from Chinese Source", *The China Quartely*, no. 147 (September), 889–911.

Wit, Joel S. *et al.*, (2004) *Going Critical: The First North Korean Nuclear Crisis*, Washington, DC: Brookings Institution Press.

Wong, John and Zheng Yongnian (eds) (2002) *China's Post-Jiang Leadership Succession: Problems and Perspectives,* Singapore: Singapore University Press and World Scientific.

Wu, Xinbo (2004) "The Promise and Limitations of a Sino-U.S. Partnership", *The Washington Quarterly,* vol. 27, no. 4 (Autumn), 115–26.

Xintian, Yu (2004) "Renshi he Bimian Dangjin de Hengtu yu Zhangzheng: Zhongguo Heping Fazhan de Zhanlu Xuanzhe [Recognition and Evasion of Contemporary Confrontation and War: China's Selection of Peaceful Development]", *Guoji Wenti Yanjiu* [Journal of International Studies], no. 6.

Yee, Herbert and Storey, Ian (eds) (2002) *The China Threat: Perceptions, Myths and Reality,* New York: Routledge Curzon, 2002.

You, Ji. (2001) "China and North Korea: a Fragile Relationship of Strategic Convenience", *Journal of Contemporary China,* vol. 10, no. 28, 387–98.

You, Ji (2004) "Understanding China's North Korea Policy", *China Brief,* The Jamestown Foundation, vol. IV, no. 5 (March), 1–3.

Zhang, Yongjin and Austin, Greg (eds) (2001) *Power and Responsibility in Chinese Foreign Policy,* Canberra: Asia Pacific Press.

Zhao, Suisheng (2004) "The Making of China's Periphery Policy", in Suisheng Zhao (ed.), *Chinese Foreign Policy: Pragmatism and Strategic Behavior.* Armonk, NY: M.E. Sharpe, Inc., 256–75.

Zhengyuan, Guo (2005) "Zhongguo de Heping Fazhan Daolu yu Qianjing [Future Trend and Prospects of China's Peaceful Development]", *Guoji Wenti Yanjiu* [Journal of International Studies], no. 1, 10–13.

Zhu, Feng. (2004), "China's Policy on the North Korean Nuclear Issue", *China Strategy,* (CSIS), vol. 3 (July 20), 5–10.

Part I
Korea, China, and East Asian economic integration

3 Korea's regional economic strategy in response to the rise of China

Françoise Nicolas[1]

Introduction

The normalization of China's economic relations with the rest of the world and its participation in the globalization process rank among the most important developments of the past decades. The resulting change in the global balance of economic activities has had (and continues to have) far-reaching implications for the world as a whole and for Asia in particular, with Korea as a case in point. The fiercer competition from China in the trade, as well as in the FDI area, has fuelled concerns in neighbouring emerging economies, which tend to perceive China more as a threat than as an opportunity. Although these fears may be partly ill founded, it is worth noting that the necessary adjustments imposed by the integration of China in regional and global production networks constitute a major challenge, which further compounds the difficulties already encountered in the wake of the 1997–98 financial crisis. Moreover, China's rising economic clout is deeply affecting the conditions for institutional economic cooperation in East Asia.

The objective of the chapter is to examine how Korea is responding to the challenges associated with the rise of China. The first section of the chapter provides a comprehensive assessment of China's new role in the regional supply chain and of the resulting change in the competitive game being played in the region. It also examines the implications for the Korean economy and the way both business and government have accommodated their rising neighbour so far.

The subsequent section looks at the changes in China's stance towards its neighbours, focusing on its economic diplomacy moves in the region, which reflect China's resolve to become a regional leader. A particular emphasis is placed on China's and Korea's FTA policy. An important point is to analyse the benefits that could be reaped from the implementation of regional trade agreements, as well as the feasibility of such arrangements given the changing circumstances.

Rising competition from China: implications for Korean business

China as a major trading partner

As a result of its open-door policy, China is now clearly integrated in world trade networks and has become the world's fourth largest trader. The country's exports and imports have surged since the early 1990s, with the US, Japan and the EU (in that order) as major destinations, and with Japan, the EU and emerging East Asia as major suppliers of imports. The pattern of China's trade, with most exports directed to industrial economies and imports originating to a large extent from emerging Asia, reflects the existence of a pattern of triangular trade. As a result, China runs a trade deficit with Asia and a trade surplus with the industrial world, while overall its trade is basically balanced.

Following the normalization of economic relations with a number of its Asian trading partners, China's trade with neighbouring emerging economies has intensified dramatically.[2] Korea has undoubtedly benefited most from this development and is now the second source of imports for China, behind Japan but ahead of the US. The bilateral trade between China and Korea amounted to 79 billion US$ in 2004 (compared to 17 billion in 1995). Korean exports to China rose to close to 50 billion US$ in 2004, while Korean imports from China reached 29 billion US$. From Korea's perspective, China now ranks first among the country's export markets, ahead of the US, and second among its suppliers. This has undoubtedly helped Korea maintain strong growth over the past few years[3] but has also made it more dependent on the fate of the Chinese economy. Moreover, China's chronic trade deficit with Korea has fuelled complaints in the

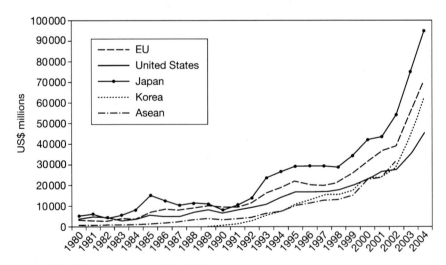

Figure 3.1 China's imports, 1980–2004.

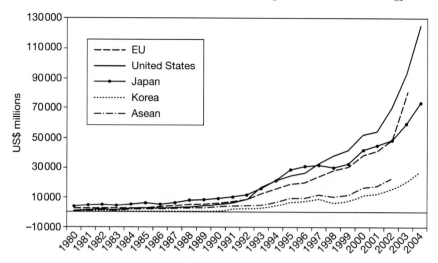

Figure 3.2 China's exports, 1980–2004.

former, leading to the imposition of anti-dumping measures and harming relations between the two countries.

Korea's export pattern to China has substantially changed over time, with a radical shift away from textiles into electronic products, refined petroleum products and chemicals. Moreover Korean electronic exports to China have shifted from consumer electronics to electronic components, telecommunication equipment and more recently computer equipment. More importantly, the bulk of China's imports from neighbouring East Asia are made up of parts, components and raw materials. This holds particularly true for

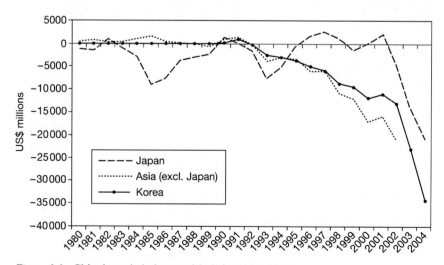

Figure 3.3 China's trade balance with Asia, 1980–2004.

Korea. During the 1997–2002 period, parts and intermediate goods accounted for 69 to 76 per cent of Korea's exports of manufactured goods to China (Lee Chang-kyu 2003).

The rise in East Asia intra-regional trade since the early 1990s has thus been largely driven by rapidly growing trade in parts, components and intermediate products that is a reflection of greater vertical specialization and the dispersion of production processes across borders. This has been described as the "Asian integrated circuit". A major result of China's participation in the regional production networks is that *de facto* economic integration in the region has substantially deepened, giving rise to a higher degree of interdependence.

China as a competitor in third markets

On the basis of the foregoing observations, Korea can be said to have largely benefited from sustained China's growth and from its integration in regional production networks. Yet, the flip side of the coin is that the boom in China's exports to third markets may constitute a threat for neighbouring East Asian economies, which tend to compete in the same categories of production. The fear is that Chinese exports may crowd out Korea's exports to the US and the EU in particular. A number of factors suggest, however, first that the competition from China has been vastly exaggerated and second that this competition, when it exists, should not necessarily be deemed negative. There are a number of reasons for qualifying the Chinese success story and the extent of the competition it imposes on its neighbours.

Since the US is one of the primary export destinations for all Asian economies, focusing on this market seems particularly relevant. Export similarity indices (ESI)[4] suggest that countries such as Indonesia and Thailand may compete head to head with China in the US market while such is not the case for more advanced ASEAN economies such as Malaysia and Singapore, and to a lesser extent for Korea. In the former cases, the ESI exceeds 55, while the index hovers between 30 and 40 in the latter cases. In the case of Korea, the similarity index has been following a downward trend over the period 1990–98 (when it reached a low of 44) before picking up again over the past few years.[5] The absolute value of this index, however, is relatively low in the Korean case, suggesting relatively differentiated structures of exports to the US market.

As rightly stressed by Lall and Albaladejo (2004), however, similarity in specialization and export patterns only shows the potential for competition but it does not prove that competition actually exists.

A casual look at East Asian countries' US market shares suggests, surprisingly enough, that NIEs and Japan were more severely hit by competition from China than ASEAN economies.[6] While Japan's share of US imports dropped from 18 to 9.3 per cent, and Korea's share from 3.7 to 2.9 per cent over the period 1990–2003, Malaysia's share for instance rose from

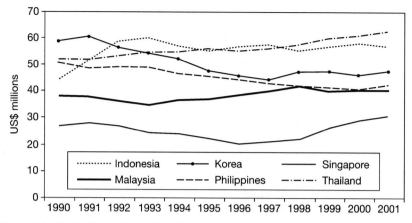

Figure 3.4 Similarity indices with China, exports to the US.

1.1 to 2.0 per cent and Indonesia's and Thailand's shares stayed put. Simultaneously, China's share rose from 3.2 to 12.5 per cent.

These observations require further explanation. First, Table 3.1 merely reflects overall market shares. A look at disaggregated data gives a more precise picture. In particular, while China clearly displaced Korea (and Taiwan) as the major supplier of footwear to the US market, the competition is not as obvious in other sectors such as electronics. Moreover, although China's export performance in electronics may *prima facie* suggest that it is competing head to head with Korea, a look at more finely disaggregated data shows that China and Korea have comparative advantages in different sub-sectors. The evolution in the US market shares shows that China has been displacing Korea in consumer electronics and to a lesser extent in computer equipment,[7] while Korea is still largely dominant in electronic components, together with Malaysia. Interestingly enough, both

Table 3.1 US imports from East Asia, 1990–2003 (in per cent)

	1990	*1995*	*2003*
Japan	18	16.5	9.3
China	3.2	6.3	12.5
Hong Kong	1.9	1.4	0.7
South Korea	3.7	3.2	2.9
Singapore	2.0	2.5	1.2
Indonesia	0.7	1.0	0.8
Malaysia	1.1	2.3	2.0
Philippines	0.7	1.0	0.8
Thailand	1.1	1.5	1.2
Vietnam	0.0	0.0	0.4
Total Asia	32.3	35.7	31.8

Source: Direction of Trade Statistics, IMF.

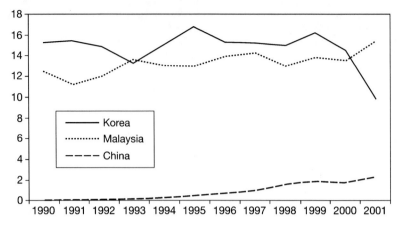

Figure 3.5 US imports of electronic components by country of origin, 1990–2001.

China and Korea have increased their market shares in the telecommunication equipment sector.

Second, as emphasized by Weiss and Shanwen (2003), China's gains of market share in the US market must be assessed in association with the previous observations about the rise in intra-regional intra-industry trade. These gains are to some extent misleading because they are due to exports of some assembled parts and components originally produced in neighbouring East Asian economies. This is particularly true in the electronics sector where China's production and exports of information technology hardware (primarily computer equipment) are based on imports of high value-added parts and components originating from emerging Asia (Korea, but also Taiwan, Singapore, Malaysia or even the Philippines).[8]

The parallel drop in East Asian economies' US market share and increase in exports of these economies to China is indicative of the fragmentation of

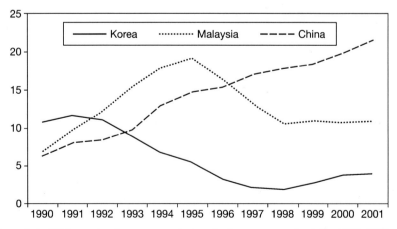

Figure 3.6 US imports of consumer electronics by country of origin, 1990–2001.

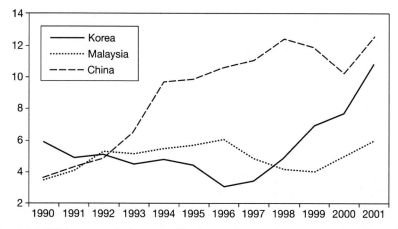

Figure 3.7 US imports of telecommunication equipment by country of origin, 1990–2001.

production processes and of the new regional division of labour, with assembly activities migrating to low-wage countries, while higher wage (and better-skilled) countries specialize in the production and export of components. The close correlation between the fluctuations in Chinese exports to the US and in East Asian exports to China further supports the hypothesis that China is being used as an export-processing zone (Zebregs 2004). At the aggregate level, Chinese exports and East Asian exports appear to be quite closely correlated, suggesting that they may be subject to common shocks but also that their productive structures are complementary.[9] The complementarity assumption is further supported by the observed rise in the complementarity index among Northeast Asian economies, in particular between Korea's exports and China's imports (Sang-yirl Nam 2004).

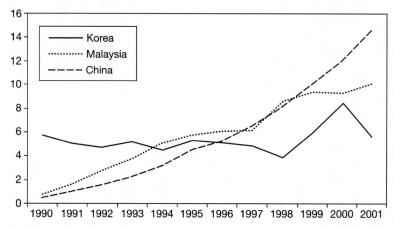

Figure 3.8 US imports of computer equipment, by country of origin, 1990–2001.

Finally, China's gains in market share require a further qualification: the bulk of Chinese exports are due to firms relocating from neighbouring economies which are losing market share. In other words, in addition to being import-intensive, China's exports are mainly driven by FDI, most of which originates from Asia.[10] Indeed, Asian firms rank high among the export-oriented foreign firms, while Western MNCs tend to seek to target the domestic market. This means that while a number of East Asian economies lose direct export competitiveness, their firms preserve and extend their competitive advantage and actually benefit the home country by promoting exports of intermediate products and related design and marketing activities and remitting dividends. This is certainly the case for Korean firms, whose drop in US market shares results to a large extent from the fragmentation of production and from their relocation in China. As a result, these firms now export from their Chinese production bases rather than from their home country's production bases.[11]

Despite these qualifications, in a longer-term perspective, the rising competition from China is likely to intensify in the future for countries such as Korea, as China manages to engage in higher value-added production. This is already a matter of concern, and rightly so, as there is already evidence of deepening of local content and even design and development activity in China. Yet again, this source of concern should not be overblown as local content may be raised thanks to foreign affiliates acting as part suppliers.

The "hollowing out" threat

Another oft-mentioned source of concern relates to the rise of China as a major magnet for FDI. As a result of this new state of play, countries may be faced with the risk either of FDI diversion or of "hollowing out" following massive relocation of labour-intensive production activities. ASEAN countries may be more likely to face the former risk, while the second applies to relatively more advanced countries such as Korea.[12]

While Korea was relatively closed to FDI in the past, the outbreak of the financial crisis in 1997–98 marked a turning point and foreigners are now allowed to enter in basically all economic sectors.[13] Because of its status as a relatively new destination for FDI and because of the discrepancy in development levels between China and Korea, the risk that FDI may flow away from Korea to China is quite slim. Nevertheless, a persistent lack of attractiveness associated with burdensome regulations and a sluggish economic environment may not be to Korea's advantage.

By contrast, Korean investors have been very active in China for a long time, and increasingly so since Korea began to recover from the financial crisis. The resurgence dates back to the year 2000 with a rise of FDI in China of more than 75 per cent compared to the previous year.[14] Korea may merely rank 7th among foreign investors in China, quite far behind the US, Japan or Taiwan, yet viewed from a Korean standpoint China ranks among the top destinations for outward direct investment (ODI). In 2003, China overtook the US as the preferred destination for Korean investors. As a result of this particular situation, rather than losing FDI to China, the risk for Korea is that of industrial hollowing out.[15]

A look at investors' motivations is warranted in order to gauge the potential for hollowing out. While Korean investment in China has resumed, there has also been a shift in the type of investors involved and, as a result, in their motivations. According to Lee and Kim (2004), Korean direct investment to China took place in three stages.[16]

The first stage, from the late 1980s to 1994, was dominated by SMEs relocating labour-intensive activities in China so as to take advantage of cheap labour. It was also characterized by a sharp rise in exports of inter-mediate goods to China, suggesting that FDI and trade were complements rather than substitutes. Moreover, the main objective of these SMEs was to export low-cost manufactures to third markets. They thus contributed to boosting China's exports as they re-exported large amounts of their finished goods to third markets such as the US and the EU.[17] Korean investment in China at that time was primarily intended to help keep afloat firms that were losing price competitiveness. The flip side, of course, is that some jobs may be lost in the process, but they were doomed to be lost as a result of declining competitiveness. This type of FDI cannot be said to be negative but simply the result of adjustment to shifting comparative advantages (Kwan 2004). To some extent, the relocation of Korean firms in China can be seen as the price to be paid, first to maintain the competitiveness of some of these firms, and second for Korea's large trade surplus with China.

The second stage, from 1994 to 1998, featured chaebols' investment in capital–intensive activities targeting both the local Chinese market as well as outside markets. Such market-seeking FDI may be negative (in the sense that it may not give rise to an optimal allocation of resources) if the objective is to jump over tariff barriers for instance.[18] Such investment may indeed result in hollowing out, displacing productive activities, which should have been maintained in the country of origin. In the case of Korean chaebols' investment in China, it seems that the objective was not primarily tariff jumping (even if such may be the case to some extent for car-makers' investments) but rather the desire to get a foothold in a potentially huge market and to be in a better position to penetrate this market by using the advantage of proximity to consumers. As a result, the impact cannot be deemed to be fully negative either.

In the most recent stage, which started with the recovery in 1999, both SMEs and chaebols have been active investors in China, the former acting as sub-contractors to the latter. The SMEs thus choose to relocate to China in order to avoid being squeezed out of the market by Chinese producers. Here again, these moves cannot really qualify as hollowing out, since these firms would have lost their place in the Chinese market if they had decided not to relocate. These firms are, however, encountering a number of difficulties to maintain their competitive edge over their local rivals. As a result, the number of bankruptcies has been on the rise lately.

There are further reasons not to deem the expansion of Korean FDI to China as a negative development. In particular, a number of surveys suggest that Korean firms tend to keep producing at home the most sophisticated intermediate goods and exporting them to their affiliates located abroad. Until now, the share of procurement of intermediate goods from the home country has been sufficiently high for the risk of hollowing out to remain limited. Korean producers tend to relocate those segments of production in which they have lost competitiveness while maintaining higher value-added activities at home. This relocation process is a natural phenomenon, which is perfectly in line with the exploitation of comparative advantages and should thus not be deemed to be negative, provided it is compensated with the emergence of higher value-added production (Nam 2004).[19]

A number of success stories illustrate this situation. As explained by Lee and Kim (2004), large investments in design and development capabilities as well as persistent efforts to establish a brand name account for the success of Aurora World Co., which is the only Korean toy producer exporting under its own brand.[20] The headquarters in Korea are still in charge of R&D and marketing, while they run factories in cheap labour abundant countries such as China. The core of Aurora's strategy has thus been to maximize complementarities between the two economies and even to create new complementarities.

Another interesting success story is Reigncom, one of Korea's MP3 device manufacturers. Struggling as an Original Equipment Manufacturer (OEM) in early 2002, with one of its major contractors in deep financial difficulties, Reigncom realized that being an OEM was a dead end. Moreover, the drop in prices of components and the emergence of cheap Chinese knock-offs had turned MP3 players into a basic commodity. Reigncom thus decided to launch its own brand of flash-memory-based players under the name of i-River. The strategy is based on the idea that MP3 are not mere gadgets but fashion accessories, which implies substantial investments in design and marketing. Reigncom develops its innovative MP3 technologies in Korea, outsources the exterior product design to the US (to the California-based industrial designer – Innodesign) and manufactures its products in China. I-River players now account for about a fifth of all flash-memory players sold in the US. This highly innovative company provides another good example of Korean firms' ability to move up the production and technology chain as China takes over electronics manufacturing.[21]

So far, so good, but what next?

It follows from the foregoing remarks that the rise of China can be deemed for the time being to be more a boon than a bane for Korea. As the fastest and the most steadily growing economy in the region (and even in the world), China has been an important export market and a major contributor to sustained growth in other economies of the region, in particular Korea. Korea should try its utmost to reap the benefits from this new state of play. In the medium term, competition from China may become increasingly fierce as the country climbs the technological ladder, stops importing intermediate products and shifts away from mere assembly activities towards higher value-added activities.

In a longer-term perspective, it is worth stressing that China may be in a particularly good position to take advantage of FDI,[22] in addition to being able to attract large inflows, thus allowing China to raise further its competitiveness. There is thus a risk that FDI can be used by China as a means of upgrading or moving up the technological ladder. Ironically enough, foreign firms can be held responsible both for China's export boom as well as for upgrading its exports. By so doing, they may have created a new Frankenstein's monster, which may gradually be getting out of control.

The sustainability of Korea's former strategy is thus being challenged. Even if the imposed adjustment should be welcomed by Korea as a good incentive to upgrade its industrial basis and to shape up its economy, what may be problematic is the speed at which restructuring has to take place. In particular, an excessively abrupt restructuring process may turn out to be socially extremely costly.

There are a variety of ways in which Korean firms can participate in the regional division of labour and interact with Chinese partners. They can concentrate on R&D or design activities without intervening in the labour-intensive part of manufacturing, they can take advantage of production conditions in China and retain control over the final product through a brand name strategy, or they can act as suppliers for local firms operating in the Chinese market. Another route still is to specialize in process-specific technologies that enable them to provide high quality, low-priced manufacturing and manufacturing-related services. Moreover, Korean firms can seize the opportunity offered by the Chinese challenge to regenerate once traditional competitive sectors such as the textile industry where there is clear scope to capitalize on existing technological capabilities to venture into high-tech products.

In other words, there is more than one upgrading path. The best approach will vary from one industry to the other and, even within the same industry, different firms may opt for a different path depending on their own capacities and assets. What should be clear, however, is that remaining at the same level of competence and technological development cannot be a viable option. Whatever the strategy, it remains key for Korean firms to maintain their price competitiveness and enhance their technological capabilities. In particular even if they continue to make products that will be sold under another label, they have to develop internal capabilities sufficient to invest these products with design and functional features allowing them to command higher prices and to keep an edge on their competitors. The complementary pattern between Chinese and Korean firms is in constant flux, making it necessary for the latter to keep investing in knowledge, R&D and technological capabilities if they want to make the best of these complementarities. The process of upgrading is an open-ended one, which makes it a particularly daunting challenge.

What concrete steps can the Korean government take to help strengthen the capacity of both SMEs and large groups to participate successfully in the new regional division of labour and to be in the best possible position to respond to the Chinese challenge? The most important policies are those whose outcomes benefit all sectors of the economy: macroeconomic stability, a transparent and efficient financial system, confidence in public institutions, a pacified social climate, and a strong foundation of education and training. By contrast, the Korean government should refrain from providing support to declining industries. As emphasized earlier, there is no point in trying to keep afloat labour-intensive activities in which Korea has lost its comparative advantage to China. Moreover, the cultivation of vertically integrated national champions can no longer serve as a primary goal of industrial development policies.

The major goal of public policies should be to create a favourable environment for the expansion of higher value-added activities. In Korea, at present, given the depressed domestic economic context, the real challenge is to design the policies that will help create the appropriate environment to catalyse the private sector. Among the priorities is the need to develop a knowledge-based economy, involving investment in education, human capital development, R&D, and so on. These measures should first help Korea to be better able to attract FDI for instance, and, secondly, be in a better position to make the best of such investments. Also, a sound macroeconomic environment is key for attracting foreign investors. Moreover, it is important to make sure that the financial needs of SMEs can be met adequately. This means that the functioning of the financial system should be further improved, particularly the development of local financial markets. This is the only way that long-term finance for investment can be provided.

Another priority lies in the social sector. The government should take the necessary steps to avoid the widening of the rift between domestically oriented ailing SMEs and export-oriented prosperous conglomerates. There is a definite risk of increased dualism of the Korean economy, leading to social instability as well as a reduction in the potential to adjust to changes.

Beyond these general measures, additional steps can be taken to address the specific capabilities of the supply-base but they should be kept to a minimum and be very precisely focused. In this respect, the government-initiated "Ten next generation growth engines" scheme[23] probably goes in the right direction. These industries are expected to propel the country's economic growth in the future. Under the five-year project, the government and private organizations will invest a total of 3.5 trillion won ($3 billion) into research and development projects for the 10 industries. An important concern should be to ensure that the scheme is consistent with Korea's commitments in various international institutions such as the OECD or the WTO. In other words, the programme should not lead to heavy public subsidization but ensure that private companies undertake the bulk of the R&D effort.

A brief assessment of the Korean government's "hub strategy" is also in order at this stage. Over the past few years, turning Korea into a "hub" in East Asia has become the new national economic mantra. The objective is to make Korea a financial, business and logistical hub for the rest of East Asia. For this strategy to be successful, a thorough overhaul of the Korean economy is needed. In the absence of accompanying measures (including sound macroeconomic policies, structural reforms, pursuit of the reforms of the financial sector, etc.) this strategy is unlikely to succeed. Despite a number of assets, Korea is plagued with problems, which may undermine the feasibility of the whole scheme. The rigid labour market and militant unions, less than transparent markets and corporate operations are often quoted as major stumbling blocks on the road to global competitiveness. As stressed earlier, this is where priorities lie.

China's rise as a regional leader: how can Korea respond?

In addition to being at the centre of regional production networks (thus contributing to the growth of intra-regional trade and FDI links and to the overall economic growth of the region), China has also risen as an active promoter of regionalism, particularly since the Asian financial crisis. Thanks to its stellar economic performances, China has been seeking lately increasingly to play the role of a regional leader, thus shifting the balance of economic power in the region. This implies, firstly a potential rise in the Sino-Japanese rivalry, and secondly a new pattern of possible economic coalitions in the region. The more assertive stance taken by Chinese authorities in the region cannot be ignored by its neighbours.

China's regional strategy

Various initiatives taken by China in a number of economic areas reflect its regional assertiveness and probably the country's resolve to become a regional economic leader instead (or ahead) of Japan.[24] The first initiatives date back to the 1997–98 financial crisis, when China actively publicized its refusal to devalue the renminbi, allegedly in order to protect its neighbours from a new round of contagious devaluations. At the same time, Beijing also provided some financial assistance to ailing economies such as Thailand and Indonesia, as a way of showing its rising sense of solidarity.[25] China also contributed to initiate the ASEAN+3 mechanism (involving the 10 ASEAN countries, as well as China, Japan and Korea) and eventually gave its support to the so-called Chiang Mai initiative (CMI), which provides a general framework for financial cooperation in the East Asian region.[26] More recently, Chinese officials stated that their refusal to let the renminbi appreciate against the dollar was motivated by their concern about the possible negative impact this may have on neighbouring economies. This move was again meant to be interpreted as being not only in China's interest but also in its partners' interest, since a revaluation could be expected to lead to a drop in exports and thus to have a negative impact on the rest of the region as well, given the tight economic relations now in existence in the region. These moves all point in the same direction and are clearly aimed at proving China's amicable stance towards its neighbours.

The China–ASEAN FTA (CAFTA) is probably the latest and most dramatic example of China's new regional policy. Zhu Rongji first proposed the possibility of a CAFTA at the ASEAN+3 leaders meeting in Singapore in 2000, and official negotiations started in November 2001.[27] The framework agreement on Comprehensive Economic Cooperation was signed a year later, formally launching the process of establishing a CAFTA by 2010 for the most advanced ASEAN member countries and by 2015 for the others (Cambodia, Myanmar, Laos and Vietnam).

Under the agreement, the first phase of a free market comprising a quarter of the world's population – 1.7 billion people – and an overall nominal GDP of 2 trillion dollars will be completed within eight years. Under the so-called "early harvest provisions" (EHP), tariff reductions on a broad range of goods[28] are set to begin sooner. The far-reaching commitments made by China to open domestic sectors (such as agriculture and financial services) that are important to neighbouring trading partners should allow them to gain from China's sustained growth. Overall, China can be expected to gain most, be it only because of the imbalance in the partnership.

The official motivation of the agreement is to take advantage of complementarities and build on existing strengths in order to make the region collectively more efficient and competitive and to attract investment, although additional considerations certainly motivated the initiation of the scheme.[29] Through this agreement China is trying to quiet its weakest (and most vulnerable) neighbours' concerns that it is swooping up the lion's share of regional foreign investment by allowing them to export their goods to the expanding Chinese market. At the same time, it may also be seeking to defuse criticisms by industrial countries (and thus potential trade conflicts). The agreement may also be considered as a necessary strategy to preserve outlets for its production. Through this agreement China is also pushing its strategic and political interests in the region. Chinese officials have made quite clear their desire to extend cooperation with ASEAN into the security sphere.[30]

Besides the strategic move to signal China's interest in Southeast Asia, the implications of such an agreement may be far-reaching. For both sides, there should be net trade gains: trade creation is likely to offset trade diversion, with ASEAN getting a slight trade diversion while the same trade diversion would not be obvious for China. With China's strong growth, it seems that China would require more imported inputs and ASEAN could provide an alternative source of inputs for natural-resource based and intermediate inputs in an FTA. Both ASEAN and China's hope to prosper will be intricately linked to their outward orientation and the role of developed countries to open up more opportunities, thus providing a firmer foundation for growth and stability.

Korea's regional strategy

From a Korean perspective, China's attempt to impose a China-centred form of regionalism has major implications. Korea is becoming increasingly isolated as well as more evidently squeezed between two major rivals, China and Japan. This new state of play cannot be ignored by Korea in the definition of its regional policy. As a result, Korean authorities have launched a number of cooperative initiatives with Japan and, more recently, with ASEAN.

Japan–Korea FTA, an obvious, but difficult option

The negotiation of the CAFTA leaves Japan and Korea with little choice but to team up. It is often believed that unless Japan and Korea enhance their competitiveness through a bilateral FTA, they could easily be overwhelmed by China. Japan itself apparently considers an FTA as a possible response to the rise of China (Cho 2004).

Prima facie, however, it may appear paradoxical, from a Korean perspective, to advocate a Japan–Korea FTA since such an agreement can be expected to have relatively negative effects on Korea, at least in the short term, and would thus compound further the difficulties already raised by the rise of China.[31] Korea has a systemic trade deficit with Japan because it is still heavily dependent on Japan for a whole array of high-tech components. The immediate result of the JKFTA is likely to be a further widening of this deficit. All estimations indeed concur that the lifting of trade barriers between Korea and Japan would lead to a surge in Japanese exports to Korea in a number of sensitive sectors such as the automotive, machinery and electrical products. This is because Korean tariffs are still about 7.9 per cent on average against Japan while Japan's tariffs are a mere 2.9 per cent. Korea can be expected to gain in apparel, leather products, agricultural (fishery) products, steel and petrochemicals.

As a result, the scheme is facing resistance from a large fraction of the Korean business sector,[32] especially consumer goods manufacturers, and small and medium-sized parts manufacturers. Smaller industries and consumer products manufacturers will naturally experience erosion in their market share at home as a result of rising imports of Japanese goods of better quality. But in a dynamic and longer-term perspective, the agreement can be expected to yield positive results. In particular, the rising competition from Japanese products will inevitably compel Korean producers to focus their efforts on enhancing the quality of their goods.

It is worth stressing at this stage that for the Japan–Korea FTA (JKFTA) to be beneficial for both countries (particularly for Korea) it has to encompass a broad spectrum of issues, otherwise the only result will be a deepening of Korea's trade deficit with Japan (Ahn 2004). The implementation of a comprehensive agreement would indeed involve other important benefits, in the form of a rise in service trade and dynamic effects through a new division of labour and industrial cooperation. As a result, it is important that the JKFTA should not be aimed only at tariff reduction.

While competition may increase with the implementation of the JKFTA, so will intra-industry trade, with potentially beneficial impacts. Strategic alliances for a more sophisticated division of labour may be possible, as well as restructuring of over-capacity. To some extent, this is what the European economies sought to do with the creation of the Single Market in 1992. At the time, the major objective was no longer to abolish tariff barriers but to create a genuine single market that would allow firms to reap the benefits from economies of scale, thus easing the necessary restructuring of a number of industrial sectors, which had lost competitiveness to foreign, in particular Japanese, rivals.[33]

Another good reason for Korea to go ahead with a JKFTA is that it may provide external pressure to push for reforms and restructuring. Trade liberalization will expose low-productivity sectors to external competition and force them to change. Increased competitive pressure will be brought to bear on consumer goods manufacturers and SME parts manufacturers, compelling them to focus efforts on enhancing quality, efficiency, and so on.

In this respect, Japan and Korea are in similar positions: both countries tend to be plagued with inertia in their economic systems, hampering the progress of deregulation. They thus need the type of external pressure that is brought about by the dynamic cross-border movement of management resources such as people, goods and money under an economic cooperation agreement (Fukagawa 2003).

While going ahead with a Japan–Korea FTA may be a rational and advisable strategy for the reasons highlighted above, the strategy has to be assessed taking into account the regional context and the possible implications it might have on the two countries' neighbours. A purely defensive type of regionalism should be avoided, not least because it would necessarily be associated with the lack of a clear vision. The JKFTA may have started on this basis, but it is important to turn it into a more positive agreement. In particular, the objective should not be to use any kind of regional scheme against China. As a result, it is important for Japan and Korea to design their FTA with a view to opening it eventually to other countries in the region.

The major difficulty facing the Korean government is how to sell the agreement to the public and how to mitigate the short-term (primarily social) impacts. For the time being, the government has apparently failed to find an appropriate strategy. The negotiations have been stalled since the end of 2004, primarily as a result of a lack of commitment on the Korean side. Disagreement about the agriculture issue[34] is a major stumbling block, yet persistent frictions around historical and territorial disputes (over the Dokdo Islands in particular) have also festered bilateral relations and made the pursuit of negotiations close to impossible.

Korea–Asean FTA, a smooth negotiation, so far

In an attempt to diversify export outlets for its producers, the Korean government also contemplates the possibility of signing a FTA with ASEAN.[35] According to a recent survey conducted by KITA, a large proportion of Korean exporters urged the conclusion of such an FTA because they face increasing difficulties due to market integration and the trend towards conclusion of FTAs among major countries in the ASEAN region. Korea's major export products to ASEAN such as passenger cars, plastics, textiles and steel products are indeed burdened by up to 200 per cent customs duties, posing a great obstacle to Korea's exports. Accordingly, if and when a Korea–ASEAN FTA is concluded, exports of these products can be expected to increase substantially. Also, the easing of various tariff barriers through individual FTAs will help increase exports of domestic firms. Korea is also probably fearing the possible negative impact of the implementation of the China–ASEAN FTA as of July 2005.

Negotiations between Korea and ASEAN started in February 2005. Six additional rounds of negotiations were planned throughout the year in order to conclude an FTA in goods whereby at least 80 per cent of products will have zero tariffs in 2009. As of writing (end of 2005), the two sides have been able to reach a substantial agreement on the draft of the framework agreement that encompasses the entire relationship between Korea and ASEAN, thus establishing the basis for signing an FTA in goods at the Korea–ASEAN summit meeting scheduled in December.[36] An agreement on investment and services is planned to be concluded sometime in 2006. Despite the apparently smooth process so far, it is far too early to know whether the negotiation will proceed as timetabled and what will be the exact content of the agreement.

A key concern for Korean authorities should be to make sure that these various FTAs are mutually consistent.

What to do with China?

Even if the possibility of an East Asian FTA has been actively discussed at various ASEAN+3 meetings, concrete steps are still to be taken in this direction. By the same token, the establishment of a Northeast Asian FTA, encompassing China, Japan and Korea has not yet gone beyond the study phase.

For the time being, there are two, to some extent, competing projects, namely the CAFTA and the JKFTA,[37] and a number of overlapping projects involving ASEAN and each of the three Northeast Asian economies. A major issue is to determine how these groupings may relate with one another and how they interact. In this respect, the European experience may hold interesting lessons in store. It suggests that the coexistence of different (and to some extent rival) regional groupings in the same region is unlikely to be long lasting. In Europe, two regional groupings were formed in the late 1950s, the European Communities[38] and the European Free Trade Association (EFTA). Over time the success of the former over the latter led a number of EFTA member countries to seek accession into the EC, while the remaining EFTA member countries eventually established a FTA with the EEC. After a decade and a half, the two groups had collapsed into one, with the most complete and well-structured group prevailing over the other looser grouping. This experience suggests that the modalities of regional arrangements matter.

In East Asia, the nature of the two competing FTAs differs widely. Because Japan and Korea are both members of the OECD, the JKFTA will have to be consistent with the WTO.[39] By contrast, the CAFTA was negotiated under the enabling clause provision rather than Article 24 of the GATT. As a result, the JKFTA is more likely to provide an appropriate starting point for an East Asian FTA than the CAFTA. Two important objectives should thus be kept in mind. First, Japan and Korea should design their agreement with the objective of a future enlargement in mind. This would be a good way of not antagonizing China, and the two countries would eventually be in a better position to attract the other countries in the region. Second, the agreement should be designed to be exemplary. The current stalemate in the negotiations, however, does not augur well for the future of the JKFTA.

As far as the three ASEAN+1 FTAs (China–ASEAN, Korea–ASEAN and Japan–ASEAN) are concerned, a major challenge in the coming years will be how to make them compatible.

It is unlikely that Japan and Korea will engage jointly in negotiations with China in the near future; as a result, it is in Korea's interest to go ahead with bilateral negotiations with China. Actually, for Korea's reform strategy, as described above, to be fully successful, the implementation of a Korea–China FTA would be a further asset. Removing trade barriers with China would contribute to a better exploitation of the market as well as to a better allocation of resources, helping in particular to maintain more sophisticated activities in Korea rather than relocating them systematically in China in order to circumvent trade barriers. Pushing for free trade with China is a promising strategy since it should help enhance production-sharing arrangements. A number of voices indeed advocate the establishment of some sort of preferential trade agreement with China in order to exploit the growing and potentially huge Chinese market and to turn China from an export-processing zone into a large market place. In this respect, the snag is that Korea obviously does not constitute a priority for China. China has launched a partnership with ASEAN and is about to launch a number of other initiatives with a number of resource-rich countries such as the Gulf Cooperation Council economies or Central Asian economies (under the so-called Shanghai Cooperation Organization – SCO[40]). China may have launched a dialogue with Korea as well as suggested further to examine the implications of a China–Japan–Korea FTA, yet one can reasonably argue that these various moves aim primarily at holding the JKFTA in check. According to a number of authors, China is relatively hostile to the JKFTA and it is concerned about the potential negative effects on the Chinese economy (Cho 2004).

Moreover, for Korea the negotiation of a China–Korea FTA would automatically meet a strong opposition from the agricultural lobby. Opening up the Korean agricultural sector to competition from China would prove to be extremely costly for Korean farmers.

Theoretically, the rise of China and the resulting intensification of Sino-Japanese rivalry should have given Korea an edge. The leadership problem that it entails may constitute a major obstacle on the road to deeper integration as well as add a need for collective action. It is this paradox that may give Korea a key role in the regional integration process, but the margin of manoeuvre seems to be extremely narrow. Korea is often considered to be like a shrimp between two whales. Ideally Korea should be able to act as a go-between but it may not be given the opportunity to do so. A Northeast Asian FTA or partnership would probably be the most appropriate solution for Korea, but it seems unlikely to materialize soon.

There are other areas in which Japan and Korea can seek to engage their neighbours so as to deepen cooperation beyond existing *de facto* interdependence. In particular, an important move for Japan and Korea would be to get China to partake in a trilateral investment agreement, encompassing investment protection and liberalization, as well as transparency, national treatment, and so on.

Summary and conclusions

The rise of China has had two major impacts on the East Asian region: first it has substantially changed the competitive setting in the region; and second, it has given rise to the emergence of a potential leader in addition to Japan. These two changes necessarily impose adjustments in other countries' attitudes and policies, particularly for Korea.

As a result of China's active participation in the regional production networks, the degree of *de facto* economic integration has been rising dramatically over the past ten to fifteen years, making the fate of all the economies in the region much more closely intertwined. So far, Korea has managed to take advantage of this new state of play, first by acting as a major supplier (which incidentally has helped the country to continue recording decent export-based growth performances while domestic demand was stagnating), and second, by relocating some activities to the mainland, thus preserving the competitiveness of declining sectors.

From this perspective, the rise of China has been, for the time being, more an opportunity than a threat for Korea. Of course, this is a picture of the past and it is unlikely that this propitious situation will last forever. Even if Korea has resisted better than most other economies such as Taiwan or Singapore, complacency should be avoided. The challenge for the Korean government is to take the appropriate steps to help enhance firms' competitiveness and help them make the best of the potentially huge Chinese market. Beyond specific micro strategies, such as brand name promotion, or niche market strategy, Korean firms also need some public support in the form of a more investment-friendly environment, as well as more comprehensive measures addressing the development of human capital, and the promotion of venture capital. The challenge posed by the rise of China can thus be used as a means of enhancing mobilization for structural adjustment.

Secondly, as a result of China's assertiveness in the region, another challenge for Korea is to remain involved in the regional integration movement currently at work. This involves first going ahead with the JKFTA in order to avoid being isolated and discriminated against. It is important to design the JKFTA not only as a possible benchmark agreement but also as an open agreement. In parallel, it is in Korea's interest to maintain a dialogue with both China and ASEAN, as well as to strengthen existing cooperative schemes at the East Asian level as a whole. In this respect, while the highly publicized CAFTA might prove to be much ado about nothing, it might be instrumental in inducing Japan and Korea to join efforts and hence pave the way to formal economic integration in East Asia.

A final remark provides a further reason for Korea to push for a broad East Asian integration, rather than small competing groups, and for a more wide-ranging form of cooperation. As shown earlier, the increasing participation of China in regional production networks has created a complex web of economic linkages and given rise to tighter interdependence within the region. This new state of play provides a renewed incentive for exchange-rate coordination, but also for the deepening of economic policy monitoring as envisaged in the surveillance mechanisms of the CMI for instance. It also provides a rationale for regional financial cooperation and stabilization (through the creation of regional bond markets for instance). This is particularly important since the risks of instability[41] are far from negligible in China and could easily reverberate on neighbouring economies. This form of cooperation may actually be more urgent than any kind of FTA. From Korea's point of view, the priority should be to strengthen existing cooperative mechanisms in East Asia. Incidentally, this may pave the way for the emergence of a broader East Asian FTA, if cooperation is conducted more systematically in other areas. Moreover, these various schemes would be in Korea's interest as increased financial stability would help Korea with its reform process.

Notes

1 This essay was partly written while the author was a visiting fellow at the Center for Northeast Asian Economic Cooperation (CNAEC), KIEP, Seoul. Financial support from the Korea Foundation as well as from the CNAEC is gratefully acknowledged.
2 This is also reflected in the upward trend of trade intensity indices among the East Asian economies (Ando and Kimura 2003).
3 According to some estimates, exports to China have accounted for about 40 per cent of Korea's export growth over the past few years.
4 We refer here to the Finger–Kreinin index of similarity according to which the similarity of the export structures of two countries a and b is defined by:

$$SIMFK(\mathbf{a}, \mathbf{b}) = \sum_{i=1}^{n} \{Minimum[s_i\mathbf{a}, s_i\mathbf{b}]\}$$

Where $s_i a$ is the share of product i in the exports of country $\mathbf{a}$ and $s_i\mathbf{b}$ is the share of product i in the exports of country b. The index selects the lower of the two values and sums all the values obtained for each of the products. An index of 100 indicates perfect similarity between the two economies, and an index of 0 represents no overlap at all in the branch structure of the two countries. It is calculated on the basis of the CHELEM database (71 product categories).
5 As could be expected, the similarity index between China and Korea based on the two countries' total exports is slightly higher, hovering between 51 and 55 per cent.
6 This finding concurs with Lall and Albaladejo (2004).
7 Actually, China's US market share gains in labour-intensive products should not come as a surprise and should not necessarily be deemed to be negative. It is a simple reflection of the shift in comparative advantages as described in the flying geese pattern of economic development.
8 Electronic components account for more than 40 per cent of Malaysia's and the Philippines' total exports to China, while it accounts for 32 per cent of Singapore's exports to China.
9 As a result of this complementarity, the rise in exports to China may more than offset the market share losses in third markets. See Ahearne *et al.* (2003) or Eichengreen *et al.* (2004) for further evidence on this point. While the former fail to find a statistically significant impact of Chinese exports on East Asian exports, thus concluding that there is no evidence that increases in China's exports reduce the exports of other emerging economies, the latter show, through the use of a gravity model, that the rise in China's exports – and imports – positively affects the exports of its high-income neighbours but negatively affects the exports of less developed countries in the region.
10 This remark concurs with C.-H. Kwan's observation that we need to distinguish between "made in China" and "made by Chinese" or "what China produces" and "what Chinese produce" (Kwan 2004). For a sobering assessment of the China's miracle, see Gilboy (2004).
11 By way of illustration, Samsung now produces about 30 per cent of its PCs in China.

12 In this respect, the Korean situation is comparable to that of Japan. The sharp contrast between the economic performances of Japan and China has led many people in Japan to perceive the rise of China as a threat.
13 See Nicolas (2003) for a detailed account of the evolution of Korea's approach to inward direct investment.
14 The number of Korean firms operating in China has risen from 650 in 1992 to 4920 in 2003.
15 The expression is being used here in a loose way, basically referring to the relocation of industrial activities abroad, leading to massive job losses.
16 See also Shumei (2003) and Fung *et al.* (2004) for accounts of Korean direct investment in China.
17 In this respect, SMEs and large conglomerates seem to differ: while the former are motivated by China's low production costs and seek to improve their export competitiveness, the latter are mainly attracted by the huge Chinese market (Shumei 2003).
18 As pointed out by Kwan (2004), this is the case in the automobile sector where foreign producers are faced with import restrictions hampering their exports to China. With the recent rise in Korean auto-makers' involvement in China, the risk of a similar misallocation of resources is also quite large.
19 In this respect, there seems to be less risk of hollowing out for Korea than for Taiwan for instance. In the latter case, the goods produced in China by Taiwanese affiliates are in direct competition with Taiwanese exports, while such does not seem to be the case in the former.
20 Other successful examples of brand name development is Malaysia's Supermax rubber glove producer, who succeeded in creating a global brand and sells its rubber examination gloves in more than 85 countries, including the US (see *FEER* 9 September 2004). By contrast, Hyundai had to stop marketing its own brand computers in the US because people were puzzled as to why a car maker would want to sell computers (ADB, 2003).
21 As a result of this success story, other Korean groups such as LG Electronics or Samsung, which had missed the MP3 boat at the time, are trying to catch up and investing aggressively in innovative designs.
22 At least in a better position than countries such as Malaysia, which is also quite heavily dependent on FDI. By contrast to Malaysia, the quality of China's human capital is often believed to provide an environment that may be particularly favourable for the development of positive spillovers from FDI. At the same time, however, the poor quality of the financial sector (particularly its fragile banking system) may work in the opposite direction. It remains to be seen whether China will be able to make the transition from a MNC-dominated economy to a technological powerhouse.
23 The ten industries are intelligent robots, future automobiles, non-memory semiconductors, digital televisions and broadcasting, next-generation mobile telecommunications, display devices, smart home networks, digital content and software, next-generation rechargeable batteries and biomedical products.
24 See Hale and Hale (2003).
25 Although the amount may have been symbolic, the gesture was meant to be perceived as amicable. See Vatikiotis (2003) for more details on this point.
26 Interestingly enough, China did not support Japan's proposal for the creation of an Asian Monetary Fund in 1998. The shift in China's stance may be explained by its desire to act either as a leader or collectively, rather than simply as a follower behind Japan.
27 There is disagreement among researchers about the reason for this Chinese initiative. Some authors see it as a defensive move in response to Japan's

proposed FTA with Singapore, while others consider that China acted on its own (See the debate between Tsugami and Lincoln, *RIETI policy debate*, 2003.)

28 These include meat, fish, dairy products, fruits and fresh vegetables.

29 China's entry into WTO clearly makes this strategy less costly.

30 According to some authors, political (or strategic) motivations may actually dominate economic considerations (Sheng 2003).

31 As a result, Japan has shown much more enthusiasm toward the JKFTA than Korea has. The main concern in Korea is that the elimination of tariffs would increase its structural trade deficit with Japan. There may also be the fear of China's reaction. Given the increasing dependence of Korea on China, it certainly cannot ignore its position. The experience of the post-crisis IMF-imposed termination of the import diversification programme (the objective of which was to discourage imports from Japan) and the resulting surge in Japanese exports to the Korean market provides a good reason for the public to be worried. As a result, the deal may be difficult to sell politically to the public.

32 In contrast to what is usually observed with FTAs projects, the main resistance will not come from the agricultural sector but from the industrial sector. The Federation of Korean Industries is particularly active in anti-FTA movements.

33 In the late 1980s, Europe was going through a period of sluggish economic activity, which has come to be known as "eurosclerosis". The Single Market scheme, which came into existence in 1992, was meant to be a response.

34 With Korea in favour of its inclusion in the discussion and Japan against it.

35 Japan and ASEAN also launched their first round of formal negotiations in Tokyo in April 2005 with the aim of completing the FTA talks within two years.

36 An agreement was indeed reached in December between Korea and ASEAN, with the exception of Thailand which insisted that rice should be taken out of Korea's list of sensitive products.

37 A Japan–Singapore FTA is already in existence, and a Korea–Singapore FTA has been signed in August 2005 with entry into force in March 2006. Yet because of their size these agreements cannot be compared to the other two arrangements.

38 In its initial form, it encompassed six member countries: the three Benelux countries, France, Germany and Italy, while the EFTA was made up of seven countries: Austria, the UK, Denmark, Ireland, Norway, Sweden and Switzerland.

39 In the context of WTO rules, FTAs must cover "substantially all trade", and zero duties should apply across the board to all sectors. In other words, there should be no *a priori* exclusion of any sector or sensitive product.

40 While the organization was initially aimed at addressing territorial and military issues, it has recently shifted to a wider range of issues, including regional trade.

41 There are indeed quite a few factors of risk such as the rise in unemployment, which may fuel social instability, the sorry state of the financial system, or the widening regional income disparities.

References

Abe Kazutomo (2003) "Economic Effects of a Possible FTA Among China, Japan and Korea", in Yangseon Kim and Chang Jae Lee (eds), *Northeast Asian Integration Prospects for a Northeast Asian FTA*, KIEP, 2003.

Ahearne, Alan, John Fernald, Prakash Loungani and John Schindler (2003) "China and Emerging Asia: Comrades or Competitors", *International Finance Discussion Papers*, Board of Governors of the Federal System, no. 789, December.

Ahn, Dukgeun (2004) "Modality of Korea–Japan FTA: From the Perspective of Korea", *mimeo*, January.

Ando, Mitsuyo and Fukunari Kimura (2003), "The Formation of International Production and Distribution Networks in East Asia", *NBER working paper*, no. 10167, December.

Baldwin, Richard (2003) "Prospects and Problems with East Asian Regionalism: A Comparison with Europe", *mimeo*, RIETI, January.

Chantasasawat, Busakorn, K.C. Fung, Hitomi Iizaka and Alan Siu (2003) "International Competition for Foreign Direct Investment: The Case of China", *unpublished mimeo*, December.

Chen Tain-Jy (2004) "Living under the Roof of WTO: Cross-Strait Economic Relations since WTO Accession", in KIEP, *Rising China and the East Asian Economy*, Conference papers, March.

Chia, Siow Yue (2004) "ASEAN–China Free Trade Area", *unpublished mimeo*, April, 24.

Cho Hyun-jun (2004) "China's Political Economic Approach toward FTAs with East Asian Nations and its Implications for Korea", *Journal of International Economic Studies*, vol. 8, no. 1, 2004.

Dubé, François-Philippe (2001) "Le régionalisme et le redéploiement industriel sud-coréen", *mimeo*, December.

Eichengreen, Barry, Yeongsop Rhee and Hui Tong (2004) "The Impact of China on the Exports of Other Asian Countries", *unpublished mimeo*, August.

Fung, K.C. *et al.* (2004) "Korean, Japanese and Taiwanese Direct Investment in China", in KIEP, *Rising China and the East Asian Economy*, Conference papers, March.

Gaulier, Guillaume, Francoise Lemoine and Deniz Unal-Kesenci (2004) "China's Integration in Asian Production Networks and Its Implications", *unpublished mimeo*, June.

Gilboy, George J. (2004) "The Myth Behind China's Miracle", *Foreign Affairs*, vol. 83, no. 4, July–August.

Ha, Byungki (2004) "Deindustrialization or hollowing out in the Korean Economy", *KIET Industrial Economic Review*, vol. 9, no. 2.

Hale, David and Lyric Hugh Hale (2003) "China Takes Off", *Foreign Affairs*, vol. 82, no. 6, November–December.

Ianchovichina, Elena and Terrie Walmsley (2003) "Impact of China's WTO Accession on East Asia", *World Bank Policy Research Working Paper*, no. 3109, August.

Kim Yangseon and Chung H. Lee (2003) "Intra-Regional Trade in Northeast Asia: Trends and Characteristics", in Yangseon Kim and Chang Jae Lee (eds), *Northeast Asian Integration Prospects for a Northeast Asian FTA*, KIEP, 2003.

Kwan, Chi Hung (2004a) "FTA not FDI", *Look Japan*, February, www.lookja pan.com/Lbecobiz/04FebEF.htm

Kwan, Chi Hung (2004b) "The Rise of China – Challenges and Opportunities for Japan", *mimeo*, August.

Kwan, Chi Hung (2002) "The Rise of China and Asia's Flying Geese Pattern of Economic Development: An Empirical Analysis Based on US Import Statistics", *NRI Papers*, no. 52, 1 August.

Lall, Sanjaya and Manuel Albaladejo (2004) "China's Competitive Performance: A Threat to East Asian Manufactured Exports?", *World Development*, vol. 32, no. 9, 1441–66.

Lardy, Nicholas (2003) "The Economic Rise of China: Threat or Opportunity?", *Research paper*, Federal reserve Bank of Cleveland, 1 August 2003.

Lee Chang Jae (2003) "Towards a Northeast Asian Economic Community: A Korean Perspective", in Yangseon Kim and Chang Jae Lee (eds), *Northeast Asian Integration Prospects for a Northeast Asian FTA*, KIEP, 2003.

Lee Chang-kyu (2004) "Economic Relations Between Korea and China", *External Issues*, The Korea Economic Institute.

Lee Keun and Mihsoo Kim (2004) "The Rise of China and the Korean Firms Looking for a New Division of Labour", in KIEP, *Rising China and the East Asian Economy*, Conference papers, March.

Lee Xinzhong and Seung Rok Park (2003) "The Effects of Foreign Direct Investment on China's International Trade", Korean Economic Research Institute, *Major research paper*, 2003–6.

Lemoine, Françoise and Deniz Ünal-Kesenci (2002) "Chine: Spécialisation internationale et rattrapage technologique", *Economie internationale*, no. 92, 11–40.

Munakata, Naoko (2003) "The Impact of the Rise of China and regional Economic Integration in Asia – A Japanese Perspective", *mimeo*.

Nam, Sang-yirl (2004) "Trade Structure and Trade Potential Between China, Japan and Korea", *mimeo*, KIEP, Seoul.

Nam, Young-Sook (2004) "Facing the Challenges of China's Industrial Rise: The Korean Case", in KIEP, *Rising China and the East Asian Economy*, Conference papers, March.

Ng, Francis and Alexander Yeats (2003) "Major Trade Trends in East Asia", *World Bank Policy Research Paper*, no. 3084, June.

Nicolas, Françoise (2004a) "L'irrésistible ascension de la Chine en Asie orientale", *Politique étrangère*, no. 2, Summer.

Nicolas, Françoise (2004b) "Revamping the Korean Financial System: Which Role for Foreign Investors?", *Asia Pacific Journal of Economics and Business*, vol. 8, no. 1, June.

Nicolas, Françoise (2003) "FDI as a Factor of Economic Restructuring: The Case of South Korea", in Bende-Nabende, Anthony (ed.), *International Trade, Capital Flows and Economic Development in East Asia: The Challenge in the 21st Century*, London: Ashgate.

Rumbaugh, Thomas and Nicolas Blancher (2004) "China: International Trade and WTO Accession", *IMF working paper* 04/36, March.

Sakakibara Eisuke and Sharon Yamakawa (2003) "Regional Integration in East Asia: Challenges and Opportunities", *World Bank Research Paper*, no. 3079.

Sheng Lijun (2003) "China-ASEAN Free Trade Area: origins, Developments and Strategic Motivations", *ISEAS working paper*, International Politics and Security Issues Series, no 1.

Shin Kwanho and Yunjong Wang (2003) "Trade Integration and Business Cycle Synchronization in East Asia", *KIEP working paper*, 03–01, February.

Shumei, Yao (2003) "Korea's FDI in China – Status and Perspectives", *CNAEC Research series*, 03–01, KIEP, Seoul.

Vatikiotis, Michael (2003) "Catching the Dragon's Tail: China and Southeast Asia in the 21st Century", *Contemporary Southeast Asia*, vol. 25, no. 1, April, 65–78.

Weiss, John and Gao Shanwen (2003) "People's Republic of China's Export Threat to ASEAN: Competition in the US and Japanese Markets", *ADB Institute Discussion Paper*, no. 2, January.

Wu, Friedrich *et al.* (2002) "Foreign Direct Investments to China and Southeast Asia: Has ASEAN Been Losing Out?", *Economic Survey of Singapore*, no. 3, 96–115.

Yongzheng Yang (2003) "China's Integration into the World Economy: Implications for Developing Countries", *IMF working paper*, December.

Zebregs, Harm, (2004) "Intraregional trade in Emerging Asia", *IMF Policy Discussion Paper*, April.

4 Financial integration in East Asia

Which role for Korea?

Heungchong Kim and Yunjong Wang

Introduction

Prior to the Asian financial crisis in 1997, few would have seriously argued for the creation of a system of regional financial cooperation in East Asia. Financial liberalization and market-led integration process were already taking place in the region. The financial crisis was a watershed that gave East Asians a strong impetus to search for a regional mechanism to prevent future crises. This search is now gathering momentum, opening the door to possibly significant policy-led integration in East Asia (Bergsten 2000; Henning 2002). Bergsten noted that East Asia might be on the brink of an historic evolution, as Europe was half a century ago.

Evidently, there is a movement toward Asian regionalism today. Although the proposal to create an Asian Monetary Fund (AMF) was scuttled, the leaders of ASEAN responded by inviting China, Korea and Japan to join in an effort to foster economic cooperation in the region. The ASEAN+3 summit in November 1999 released a "Joint Statement on East Asian Cooperation" covering a wide range of possible areas for regional cooperation. Recognizing the need to establish regional financial arrangements to supplement the existing international facilities, the finance ministers of ASEAN+3 at the meeting in Chiang Mai, Thailand in May 2000 agreed to strengthen the existing cooperative framework in the region through the "Chiang Mai Initiative (CMI)".

The major currency crises of the past decade have been regional in nature. Clearly, neighbouring countries have a strong incentive to engage in mutual surveillance and to extend financial assistance to one another in the face of potentially contagious threats to stability. Regardless of whether the sudden shifts in market confidence were the primary cause of the Asian financial crisis, foreign lenders were so alarmed by the Thai crisis that they abruptly pulled their investments out of other countries in the region, making the crisis contagious. The geographical proximity and economic similarities (or similar structural problems) of these Asian countries prompted the withdrawal of foreign bank lending and portfolio investment, whereas differences in economic fundamentals were often overlooked. If the channels of contagion cannot be blocked off through multilateral cooperation at the early stage of a crisis, countries without their own deep pockets of foreign reserves could not survive independently. Hence, neighbours have an interest in helping put out a fire (a financial crisis) before it spreads to them. As long as a crisis remained country-specific, there would be no urgent political need for unaffected countries to pay the significant costs associated with playing the role of a fire fighter.

The formation of a regional financial arrangement in East Asia also reflects frustration with the slow reform of the international financial system (Park and Wang 2002). The urgency of reform of the financial architecture in G7 countries has receded considerably, even if the current international architecture is perceived to be defective. The lack of global governance, including a global lender of last resort and international financial regulation, is not likely to be remedied anytime soon (Sakakibara 2003). As long as the structural problems on the supply side of international capital such as volatile capital movements and exchange rate gyrations of major currencies persist, the East Asian countries will remain vulnerable to future crises. It is therefore in the interest of East Asians to work together to create their own self-help arrangements. While the CMI is one such available option, it is equally important that East Asian countries continue to undertake financial sector restructuring and development. Without sound financial institutions and adequate regulatory regimes, Asian financial markets will remain vulnerable to external shocks. Regional policy dialogue should also contribute to strengthening the efforts to restructure and advance the financial markets in East Asia.

The three pillars of liquidity assistance – monitoring, surveillance and exchange rate coordination – are essential elements for regional financial and monetary cooperation, judging by the experience of the European Monetary System (EMS). At the same time, the history of European monetary integration suggests that the development of regional financial cooperation and its related institutions tends to be evolutionary. A shallow form of financial cooperation might comprise no more than a common foreign reserve pooling or mutual credit arrangement such as bilateral swaps. In other words, some kinds of shallow financial cooperation are conceivable without any strong commitment to exchange rate coordination under which exchange rates of the participating countries are pegged to each other or vanish through the adoption of a common currency. East Asian countries presently appear to pursue this form of financial cooperation (Henning 2002). Although fully fledged monetary integration is not viable at this stage, East Asia might begin to examine the feasibility and desirability of cooperation and coordination in exchange rate policies.

In the course of developing a regional financial cooperation system, the activities of the players, not only each government of the member states, but also international financial agencies, private financial organizations and other major countries, are particularly important. Japan, Hong Kong and

Singapore have long been regional financial hubs, but China, with a weak financial industry and an over-regulated domestic financial market, will also have a role to play.

The purpose of this chapter is to provide a view on the current status and future prospects for regional financial cooperation in East Asia and to discuss any roles of major players including Korea in the process of regional financial integration. The chapter is organized as follows: the first section reviews the current status of regional financial cooperation in East Asia and evaluates selected issues in regional financial cooperation; the following section addresses the positions of China and Japan and their views on financial cooperation in the region; and the final section concludes with a discussion of the future prospects for financial cooperation in East Asia and addresses the role of Korea in the course of the integration process.

Evaluation of the financial cooperation issues in ASEAN+3

Chiang Mai Initiative

The CMI has been a key initiative for Asian financial cooperation. It grew out of the realization that financial instability is unlikely to remain within national borders. Cooperative efforts at both regional and global levels are therefore required to counter the negative spillovers.

Some progress has been made in implementing the CMI since it started in 2000, with sixteen bilateral agreements concluded so far under the CMI. Japan has been playing a leading role in terms of both the number and amount, with seven agreements concluded with Korea, China, Indonesia, Malaysia, the Philippines, Thailand and Singapore. China has concluded six agreements with Japan, Korea, Indonesia, Malaysia, the Philippines and Thailand. Similarly, Korea has concluded six agreements with China, Japan, Indonesia, Malaysia, the Philippines and Thailand (see Table 4.1).

At the 8th ASEAN+3 Finance Ministers' Meeting held in May 2005, further commitments were undertaken to strengthen the mechanism of the CMI. First of all, to improve surveillance of the ASEAN+3 economies, early detection of irregularities and swift remedial policy actions were integrated under the CMI framework. Second, to strengthen the collective decision-making mechanism in the CMI, ministers agreed that countries having bilateral swap arrangements (BSAs) with a certain country in trouble should make a collective decision to provide liquidity, as a first step in the multilateralization of the CMI. Deputies of member countries have been tasked to explore further possible routes towards multilateralizing the CMI. Third, the size of swaps increased. The ASEAN Swap Arrangement (ASA), which increased to US$ 1 billion in 2000, has since been doubled to US$ 2 billion. Furthermore, subject to the approval of each member country, any BSA can be increased by up to 100 per cent. This implies that the current level of the BSAs of a total of US$39.5 billion could be expanded to US$79

Table 4.1 Progress on the Chiang Mai Initiative (as of 31 December 2003)

BSA	Currencies	Conclusion dates	Amount
Japan–Korea	USD/Won	4 July 2001	US$ 7 billion (a)
Japan–Thailand	USD/Baht	30 July 2001	US$ 3 billion
Japan–Philippines	USD/Peso	27 August 2001	US$ 3 billion
Japan–Malaysia	USD/Ringgit	5 October 2001	US$ 3.5 billion (a)
PRC–Thailand	USD/Baht	6 December 2001	US$ 2 billion
Japan–PRC	Yen/RMB	28 March 2002	US$ 3 billion equivalent
PRC–Korea	Won/MB	24 June 2002	US$ 2 billion
Korea–Thailand	USD/Baht	25 June 2002	US$ 1 billion
Korea–Malaysia	USD/Ringgit	26 July 2002	US$ 1 billion
Korea–Philippines	USD/Peso	9 August 2002	US$ 1 billion
PRC–Malaysia	USD/Ringgit	9 October 2002	US$ 2 billion
Japan–Indonesia	USD/Rupiah	17 February 2003	US$ 3 billion
PRC–Philippines	RMB/Peso	29 August 2003	US$ 1 billion
Japan–Singapore	USD/S$	10 November 2003	US$ 1 billion
Korea–Indonesia	USD/Rupiah	24 December 2003	US$ 1 billion
PRC–Indonesia	USD/Rupiah	30 December 2003	US$ 1 billion

Note: (a) The US dollar amounts include the amounts committed under the New Miyazawa Initiative: US$5 billion for Korea and US$2.5 billion for Malaysia.

billion if it is accepted in each bilateral case. The size of the BSAs also increased by transforming one-way BSAs into two-way BSAs. Fourth, the autonomy of the CMI is strengthened in that the swaps without the IMF-supported programme are increased from the current 10 per cent to 20 per cent in order to cope better with sudden market irregularities.[1]

In spite of these developments, the CMI has several limitations as current practices under the ASEAN+3 process cannot effectively capture emerging problems. Even East Asian policymakers who conceived the idea of the CMI would easily concede that the BSA system as it is currently structured has a long way to go before it can be accepted as an effective mechanism of defence against financial crises.

First, the CMI needs to expand its role to include exchange rate coordination. Under the current ASEAN+3 policy dialogue framework, the purpose of the CMI and mutual surveillance system is to prevent the occurrence of financial crises and contagion in the region rather than exchange rate coordination. It is true that the CMI starts from a different motivation from that in Europe, as the European facilities were created with the purpose of limiting bilateral exchange rate fluctuations among regional currencies. On the other hand, the CMI started with high capital mobility and flexible exchange rates. So far, the ASEAN+3 countries have not presumed any manifest exchange rate coordination. In the absence of such coordination, incentives for mutual surveillance will be limited because a member country facing a speculative currency attack is free to float its currency vis-à-vis those of neighbouring countries (Wang and Woo 2004).

The absence of exchange rate coordination in the CMI framework raises the further problem of the lack of credibility in the system. The CMI will work in the unusual case of a member country facing a severe liquidity crisis. Because exchange rate coordination requires more frequent intervention of the fund, member countries could accumulate ample experience in implementing the instrument if the CMI were to include the goal of enhancing exchange rate stability. This in turn would give countries more confidence and credibility in implementing BSAs.

If the region reaches a stage at which coordination of exchange rates becomes feasible, then the CMI should expand to assume this role. There are, however, many obstacles to such coordination, including big differences in levels of GDP and growth and inflation rates within the region, mainly between Japan and other developing economies including China. The Chinese capital market is also still highly protected and the exchange rate system pegged to the US dollar is another obstacle in establishing any regional monetary policies. Chai and Rhee (2005) argue that the degree of financial market integration in East Asia is much less advanced than in the EU, and the East Asian financial market is much more exposed to outside shocks, especially those from the US, than the European financial market. This kind of environment makes it difficult to create an exchange rate coordination system. Nevertheless, in order to enhance the effectiveness of the CMI scheme, it is now time to consider widening the coverage of the CMI.

Second, the CMI needs to establish its own surveillance mechanism. More than five years have passed since the system was established in May 2000, and leaders of the CMI group have yet to produce an operational structure for BSAs, in particular a monitoring and surveillance mechanism. Under the improved CMI framework, 20 per cent of the swap arrangements can be disbursed without IMF involvement. But the swap-providing countries need to formulate their own assessments about the swap-requesting country, because the swap can be disbursed only with the consent of swap-providing countries. Most participating countries agree in principle that the CMI needs to be supported by an independent monitoring and surveillance system to monitor economic developments in the region, serve as an institutional framework for policy dialogue and coordination among the members, and impose structural and policy reform on the countries drawing from the BSAs.

If bilateral swap arrangements are activated collectively and supported by a surveillance system, then they constitute a *de facto* regional monetary fund. The CMI could then be used as the base on which to build an elaborate system of financial cooperation and policy coordination by following in the footsteps of European monetary integration.[2] At this stage of development, many countries in East Asia do not share a common goal concerning the restructuring of the CMI into a forerunner of the AMF. The thirteen countries have failed to articulate the ultimate objectives of the CMI arrangement.

All the above measures can be regarded as gradual improvements rather than fundamental reforms under the architecture of the CMI. In the long run, however, the participating countries are likely to wean themselves from their reliance on the IMF. If the CMI develops into more or less an independent financial arrangement from the IMF, then the regional financial arrangement should be designed to discipline the borrowers to adhere to sound macroeconomic and financial policies by imposing conditionalities. However, the ASEAN+3 countries at the current stage do not seem well prepared for establishing a policy coordination mechanism in the surveillance process.

Third, there seems to be mismatch between the coverage of the CMI and the needs of regional economic integration. Regional integration in terms of trade needs to support the future development of the CMI and further regional financial integration, which has not been the case so far. A region-wide East Asian FTA covering ASEAN+3 countries has been slow to materialize because China and Japan are seeking bilateral trade agreements rather than multilateral ones, resulting in a bewildering pattern of regional trade agreements in East Asia (Scollay and Gilbert 2001). It essentially consists of a web of bilateral arrangements, many of which are still on the drawing board. There has apparently been no formal attempt to build a regional multilateral agreement like the Common Market agreement. Bilateral agreements are unlikely to foster a collective framework (Wyplosz 2004).

ABMI (Asian Bond Markets Initiative)

The aim of the ABMI is to create and develop efficient and liquid bond markets in Asia, which would contribute to better utilize the aggregate savings in the region for Asian investments. Korea was one of the initiators. The initiative is also expected to contribute to minimize the risk of maturity and currency mismatches that were the main causes of the financial crisis. At the informal ASEAN+3 Finance and Central Bank Deputies' Meeting held in Tokyo on 13 November 2002, Korea made a proposal to discuss regional bond market development under the ASEAN+3. Japan subsequently presented a comprehensive approach to foster bond markets in Asia, the "Asian Bond Markets Initiative" at an ASEAN+3 informal session held in Chiang Mai on December 2002.

Since 2002 when the idea of the ABMI was launched, the ASEAN+3 group has shown great interest in developing regional bond markets in East Asia so that local borrowers can issue bonds denominated in local currencies. However, member countries already recognized that the current Asian bond markets is not yet able to play this role. This issue should be studied further and a favourable environment for the Asian bond market should be created. On February 2003, some member countries proposed to engage in further study on a voluntary basis in order to achieve tangible results. The member countries agreed at the Tokyo meeting to organize six working groups under the Asian Bond Initiative to conduct detailed studies on various aspects of bond market development.³

The issues related to the Asian bond markets are composed of two parts: one is to facilitate access to the market for a wider variety of issuers, and the other is to create an environment conducive to fostering bond markets in East Asia. Considering underdeveloped bond markets in Asia, small market size and consequently low liquidity have seriously hindered both issuers and investors from active participation. To address those impediments, it is necessary to facilitate the market participation of as many issuers and investors as possible. It is also important to promote the issuance of as many kinds of bonds including currencies and maturities as possible. To do these, the development of government bond markets is of utmost importance in order to establish benchmarks for domestic bond markets. Following governments' initiatives, government financial institutions, multilateral financial institutions and government agencies in the region are encouraged to issue bonds to raise funds for financing domestic private enterprises. Another important issue related to the first part is to decide the proper currency of denomination when issuing bonds. Bonds denominated in local currencies would help both local issuers and investors avoid exchange risks.

As of 2004, some progress had been reported in the first issue.⁴ Outstanding local currency government bonds grew by 32 per cent for East Asia excluding Japan in US dollar terms, and the outstanding corporate bonds also grew by 10 per cent on average in US dollar terms in Indonesia, Korea, Malaysia, Singapore and Thailand. More specifically, ringgit-denominated bonds were issued by the ADB and IFC in Malaysia in November and December of 2004, and Korea and Japan issued cross-country primary collateralized bonds obligations in December 2004. Malaysia issued a 15-year bond and Korea began a policy of issuing longer-dated securities beyond the 3–5 year maturities traditionally preferred by local investors, which would contribute to extending government yield curves in both countries. Progress has been made in widening the issuer base, through asset-backed securities, Islamic bonds and bonds issued by multilateral development banks, which can be supported by growing investor demand in the region. In the long run, the creation of markets for bonds denominated in a currency basket would help reduce exchange risks and may possibly pave the way for markets for bonds denominated in Asian Currency Units, if market demand exists.

To create an environment conducive to fostering bond markets in the region, the provision of credit guarantees through existing guarantors such as ADB and IFC and possibly an Asian Regional Guarantee Facility would be important. Strengthening the rating system needs to go hand in hand with efficient guarantee agencies. This part has been extensively examined in the working group 2 on credit guarantees and investment mechanisms, and the working group 5 on local and regional rating agencies, and the study is still ongoing.

Given the low degree of regional financial integration in East Asia, the ABMI would be welcome as a means to facilitate financial market development in East Asia. Despite strong enthusiasm of the ASEAN+3 countries for constructing bond market infrastructure and increasing the supply of, as well as demand for, these bonds, the creation of deep and liquid bond markets in the region will take a long time. It will require more extensive domestic financial reform, institutional harmonization among the member states and substantial investment for building the infrastructure by the ASEAN+3 (Park and Park 2003). Furthermore, the continuing globalization of financial markets and advances in information technology allow financial companies in the international financial centres to dominate the international banking and investment business. We cannot observe any home bias at the regional level, unlike at the country level. For example, a regional portfolio is not necessarily easy to hedge. Having better information at the *regional* level does not seem to be enormously more advantageous than at the *global* level (Lee *et al.* 2004).

To develop bond markets in East Asia, more areas of market development should be considered: the first is to supply high quality financial personnel to serve the Asian financial markets. It is related to invigorating the role of the existing Asian financial institutions in cross-border transactions or businesses within the Asian market. In the long run, establishing a regional finance institute to train and develop financial personnel for the Asian market would be important. The second is to harmonize and streamline the existing rules and regulations. The third issue related to the ABMI is the choice of currency denomination of bonds. It was originally agreed that the bonds issued under the ABMI should be local currency denominated. It would be an interesting point to note which currency among the member countries would dominate the regional bond market.[5]

Other issues related to fostering financial cooperation in East Asia involve the creation of a research group to promote further regional financial cooperation under the ASEAN+3 framework, the enhancement of the effectiveness of economic review and policy dialogue, monitoring capital flows, and creating an early warning system. These areas are also under examination at the ASEAN+3 level.

The countries

Rethinking East Asia

Over the past decade, a number of East Asian countries have liberalized their financial markets by reducing restrictions on inward and outward capital flows. As a result, net private capital inflows to East Asia were conspicuous in the mid-1990s. The inflows to East Asia were driven by a mixture of push and pull factors, including the pursuit of perceived large profit opportunities, the diversification of Japanese overseas direct investment, the expansion of institutional investors and country funds, the improvement of regional ratings, and the easing of capital account restrictions (de Brouwer 1999). However, significant changes to the patterns of capital flows to East Asia have occurred since the financial crisis. Most East Asian countries have become net providers of international capital due to their current account surpluses. While receiving inflows of FDI and portfolio investments on a net basis, these countries have repaid large amounts of bank loans for the past several years.

In the course of these changes in the patterns of international capital flows, there has been no sign of the development of an integrated regional financial market. East Asian countries have developed stronger financial ties with Western Europe and the United States than with one another. This situation contrasts with developments in Europe, for reasons which are explained by Eichengreen and Park (2003). According to their analysis, Europe has gone further than East Asia in the integration of product and factor markets. While the EU has a true single market in goods and services, progress towards the creation of an Asian free trade area remains incomplete. While Europe has removed essentially all barriers to the free movement of capital and most barriers to the movement of labour, substantial limitations on factor mobility remain pervasive in East Asia. In Europe, regionalism is motivated in no little part by a desire for political integration that has no counterpart in East Asia. While Europe has built institutions of supranational governance (e.g. the European Commission, the European Parliament, the European Court of Justice and now the European Central Bank), East Asian integration is "weakly institutionalized". That is, it is predicated not on supranational institutions but on intergovernmental agreements that defer to the sovereignty of the participating states. Nor is integration in East Asia driven by an alliance of key nations like France and Germany or by a single hegemonic power (the role played by the United States in the Western Hemisphere); it is a more multipolar process.

Evidently, East Asia is less financially integrated than Europe. But, it does not mean that further financial integration in the region is naturally desirable. The degree of financial integration endogenously and positively responds to the correlation of shocks. Countries with integrated international financial markets can ensure against country-specific shocks through portfolio diversification. Thus, countries in East Asia are likely to have much larger welfare gains from global, rather than regional, financial integration, assuming that global financial integration ensures a better risk sharing arrangement than regional financial integration. Furthermore, as output shocks become less correlated, potential welfare gains from portfolio diversification increase, as does the degree of financial market integration (Heathcote and Perri 2002; Imbs 2003). In this regard, East Asian countries may find more opportunities to smooth consumption through global financial integration with Western Europe or the United States, when they find their output shocks are less correlated with countries outside the region than within the region.

China and Japan

It would require substantial leadership for the thirteen ASEAN+3 countries to form any Asian equivalent to the ERM or EMU over the next few decades. As a first step, they will have to increase the number and amount of the BSAs under the Chiang Mai framework. Such an extension also requires leadership that can foster coherence among the thirteen countries by mediating between the divergent interests of the members. China and Japan could be natural candidates expected to provide leadership in forging a regional consensus for expanding and consolidating the BSAs as a regional institution, but they have not yet been able to agree on a number of operational issues, including the surveillance mechanism.

China and Japan have different interests and hence different strategies for economic integration in East Asia. As far as China is concerned, economic integration with the ASEAN ten members, South Asian and central Asian countries may be more important both economically and geo-politically than financial cooperation or free trade with either Japan or South Korea. While China is a military superpower, it is still a developing economy with a huge gap to narrow in terms of technological and industrial sophistication vis-à-vis Japan, in spite of China's rapid growth. These differences in the economic and military status of the two countries suggest that, even if they manage to reconcile their troubled memories of the past, China and Japan may find it difficult to work together as equal partners for regional integration in East Asia.

China has become an active player in both the international and regional arena. Since the mid-1990s, China has expanded the number and depth of its bilateral relationships, joined various trade and security accords, deepened its participation in key multilateral organizations and helped address global security issues. Bilaterally and multilaterally, Beijing's diplomacy has been remarkably adept and nuanced, earning praise around the region (Shambaugh 2005). The pinnacle of this process was the Treaty of Good-Neighbourliness and Friendly Cooperation that China signed with Russia in 2001 (Medeiros and Fravel 2003).

China's regional rise and changing perceptions about China have prompted countries along China's border to readjust their relations with Beijing, as well as with one another. As China's influence continues to grow, many of these neighbouring countries are looking to Beijing for regional leadership or, at a minimum, are increasingly taking into account China's interests and concerns (Shambaugh 2005). At the same time, China also seeks an expansion and deepening of its trade and financial relations with those neighbouring countries.

Over the past few years, China and ASEAN have broadened and strengthened their relationship. At their landmark summit in 2002, China and

ASEAN signed four key agreements: the Declaration on Conduct in the South China Sea; the Joint Declaration on Cooperation in the Field of Nontraditional Security Issues; the Framework Agreement on Comprehensive Economic Cooperation (CEC); and the Memorandum of Understanding on Agricultural Cooperation. At their 2003 summit, China formally acceded to ASEAN's Treaty of Amity and Cooperation, becoming the first non-ASEAN state to do so (India subsequently followed suit). Based on the Framework Agreement, negotiations on parts of an ASEAN–China FTA have been completed, with the signing of the Agreement on Trade in Goods and Agreement on Dispute Settlement Mechanism at their 2004 summit.

The ASEAN–China FTA represents an interesting exercise of China's regional leadership. When Chinese Premier Zhu Rongji initiated the proposal at the ASEAN–China summit in 2000, the ASEAN countries widely shared a sense of threat that China could flood the market with a growing range of manufactures. They were also worried about competition with China for foreign direct investment. Despite these concerns, ASEAN governments welcomed China's initiative for a number of reasons (Chia 2005). First, the ASEAN governments accepted the reality of China's emerging economic role in the region and viewed China's growing demand for ASEAN goods and services as a potential new engine of growth. Second, China's offer of special treatment and development assistance for Cambodia, Laos, Myanmar and Vietnam as well as the extension of WTO most-favoured-nation benefits to non-WTO members have helped these countries to accept the China's proposal more readily. Third, China and ASEAN could go further than the WTO in liberalizing agricultural trade. An early harvest programme covers a large group of agricultural products under HS1 to HS8, representing over 600 tariff lines to be liberalized. In part, this favourable offer to ASEAN demonstrates that agriculture is not a sensitive sector to China, unlike with Japan and South Korea.

In contrast, Japan has not been able to articulate its strategic interests in East Asia. While Japan has been at the forefront in supporting greater economic cooperation among the East Asian countries, its perspective on the geographical contiguity of East Asia has not been altogether clear, together with its shrinking trade importance in East Asia (Kim, 2002). Japan has been promoting integration among the "ASEAN+5", but it is not always clear which additional two countries should be included. At times, they are Australia, and New Zealand but at other times Taiwan and Hong Kong.

There is also the suspicion that Japan's interest in free trade and financial arrangements in East Asia is not for purely economic motives. Many analysts believe that Japan's active involvement in regional economic integration is motivated by its desire to maintain its traditional pole position on the one hand, and its anxiety over China's rising regional role on the other (Lincoln 2004).

Japan is also perceived to be a country insensitive to and unwilling to resolve wartime legacies and disputes on historical and territorial claims.

East Asian countries, especially China and Korea have not placed full confidence in the peacekeeping role of Japan, as Japan is considered not to have shown its will to de-link its past expansionary militarism. This matter undermines any kind of regional integration, such that East Asians regard Japan's expanded economic influence in the region as another economic invasion.

Future prospects and the role of Korea

Regionalism in East Asia is taking two forms: free trade arrangements (FTAs) and financial arrangements. These arrangements imply that geographically proximate countries hang together to foster trade on the one hand and to promote financial and exchange rate stability on the other. The two processes must reinforce each other. The euro area pursued trade integration first, but from a theoretical point of view there is no clear reason for this. Trade integration slowed down in Europe whenever there were concerns about exchange rate stability among member countries. In this regard, some form of monetary integration is an important condition for trade integration (Shin and Wang 2004). Furthermore, there are many good reasons for forming a monetary union before an FTA. A monetary union can quite significantly increase trade among member countries by serving as a device to avoid the bottlenecks that can be encountered during the process of negotiating and implementing a FTA. This increased trade is likely to occur mostly within similar industries, so weakening asymmetric shocks across member countries will also decrease the costs of maintaining a monetary union. A monetary union can also accelerate financial integration in the region, which might not be accomplished otherwise. Hence, a monetary union is a self-validating process.

A major hindrance to a monetary union in East Asia is the area's lack of historical experience in regionalism. Whatever economic benefits a monetary union may bring, they are unlikely to be realized in the near future if each country is unwilling to cooperate in the political arena. East Asian leaders should build a common framework where decisions are based on what is best for East Asia as such. At present, they do not show the same ambition as European leaders did fifty years ago. East Asia needs to develop ways of interacting that promote collaboration rather than competition between countries.

How would regional financial integration proceed in East Asia? One possible scenario is that China and Japan will come to realize that despite the differences in their strategies, they are together the key to developing a common political will in East Asia. Sakakibara (2003) and Murase (2004) argue that the role of China and Japan in East Asia's integration is synonymous with that of France and Germany in European integration. The Kobe Research Project report submitted to the fourth gathering of the finance ministers of the Asia–Europe Meeting (ASEM Finance Ministers'

Meeting) held in Copenhagen in July 2002 states that "It is essential for the Japan–China cooperation, as a core in East Asia, to lead the process of economic and financial integration, as the France–German alliance played a central role in the integration and cooperation process in Europe."[6]

This realization could soften their positions and encourage China and Japan to compromise on an institutional setting and augmentation of the existing financial architecture of East Asia. For instance, China may accept Japan's demand for *de facto* control over monitoring and surveillance in return for Japan's pledge for a substantial increase in financial assistance in the form of one-way swaps and ODA to ASEAN members. China could agree to this scheme, if it is confident about concluding a free trade agreement with the ASEAN members in the near future. China's free trade pact with ASEAN could circumscribe Japan's influence on ASEAN affairs even if Japan is a major provider of financial resources to the region.

Another scenario focuses on the possibility of China assuming a more assertive leadership role in regional integration. In view of the uncertain prospects for the Japanese economy, China could emerge as the region's engine of growth over the longer term if it sustains its own growth. Given the envisaged leadership role, China may choose to negotiate both the expansion of the BSAs and a free trade pact with ASEAN. In this case, the original CMI would become "ASEAN+1", with Japan playing the second fiddle. Realizing that financial integration is an integral part of a successful free trade area, China may indeed seriously consider this option. However, without Japan, ASEAN+1 will not be a viable arrangement for a regional financing scheme simply because China is hardly in a position to commit itself to financing the balance of payments deficits of all ASEAN member states. It is also questionable whether ASEAN will join any regional financial arrangement in which China is the dominant member, considering the weak position of financial developments in China.

A third scenario is the enlargement of the CMI to include Australia and New Zealand and possibly India. This is the route favoured by Japan which would find it easier to deal with China when there are more countries supporting its strategy. However, many members of ASEAN+3 believe that at this stage forming a critical mass of the CMI should precede any enlargement discussion. Since the enlargement is not likely to increase substantially the availability of short-term financing, most members of ASEAN+3 would not take the third scenario seriously.

Perhaps the most realistic scenario is that the countries participating in the CMI will muddle through, discussing at length the modalities of policy dialogue, the types of the surveillance system the CMI needs, and also an augmentation of swap amounts without making any substantial progress.

In the possible processes mentioned above, Korea and ASEAN would serve, as a mediator in the cultivation of a common political will between China and Japan. In particular, the role of Korea in East Asian financial integration can be examined. Murase (2004) pointed out the role of Korea by saying that "as East Asian monetary and financial cooperation move ahead, Korea can be expected to fulfil a similar role to that played by the Benelux countries in Europe. In the regional monetary system formation process, therefore, it could play a constructive role as a medium-sized industrialized economy supplementing Sino-Japanese leadership while representing the interests of smaller countries in the region. When it comes to setting up regional institutions sometime in the future, Korea could well rank alongside the key members of ASEAN as a possible location for the secretariat and other organizations."

His argument on the role of Korea raises an interesting aspect of regional cooperation in East Asia, but there remain issues concerning Korea's potential role in the process. First, in the EMU negotiation process, it is difficult to sort out the common view of the Benelux countries, especially in the early stages of negotiation. France's view and strategy on the EMU negotiation were duplicated more or less by Belgium's, and the Netherlands stood firmly by Germany throughout the negotiations. Only in the last stage of the EMU was a common Benelux view produced which was not so different from the agreed views of France and Germany. Second, Korea can take a strategic position between China and Japan. As China is still considered to be an inward-looking country that lacks policy harmonization with its neighbours and Japan has not shown leadership on regional issues, Korea can be a kind of "honest broker" in dealing with cooperation and integration issues. Third, it is important to note that, unlike China or Japan, Korea has a strong will to promote regional integration, including a kind of moral obligation to push for regional integration. Korea is one of the major countries concerned by North Korea's nuclear crisis and would be mostly devastated if a war in the Korean peninsula occurs. Recalling that one of the strongest motives for economic integration in Europe after World War II was to institutionalize a permanent peace in the region, Korea's geopolitical status encourages it to lead any kind of regional cooperation in East Asia for keeping peace in the region. Fourth, despite Korea's strong will to be an honest broker in the financial integration of East Asia, its capacity to perform this role is another matter. It is questionable whether Korea can be a mediator to foster the idea of financial integration, considering its low profile in regional financial initiatives. Fifth, if Korea's capacity to lead regional financial integration is quite limited, then it could develop regional financial integration with Japan and Singapore, the two leading countries who have comparatively advanced financial industries. As China is still too backward to be a key partner of financial integration in East Asia, a multi-speed process is the most realistic option.

Notes

1 The Joint Ministerial Statement of the 8th ASEAN+3 Finance Ministers' Meeting, 4 May 2005.

2 From the theoretical point of the neo-functionalists, initial steps towards integration trigger self-sustaining economic and political dynamics leading to further cooperation. Economic interactions create spillovers or externalities that need to be coordinated by governments involved. Such economic policy coordination at the regional level can be seen as an inevitable response to the increased economic interactions within the region. Once the integration process starts, spillovers deepen and widen integration by working through interest group pressures, public opinion, elite socialization or other domestic actors and processes (George, 1985).

3 Two working groups were established at first: a working group on creating new securitized debt instruments (chaired by Thailand), and a working group on credit guarantee mechanisms (chaired by Korea and China which joined later). Subsequently, four more working groups including a technical assistance coordination group were formed to study other issues related to fostering bond markets in Asia These are a working group on foreign exchange transactions and settlement system (chaired by Malaysia), a working group on issuance of bonds denominated in local currency by government agencies and Asian multinational corporations (chaired by China), a working group on local and regional rating agencies (chaired by Singapore and Japan), and a technical assistance coordination group (chaired by Indonesia with the Philippines and Malaysia acting as co-chairs).

4 ADB (2005).

5 The creation of US dollar denominated or euro denominated bonds was considered, with diminishing enthusiasm for the latter.

6 France and Germany also had a wartime legacy. Although de Gaulle's nationalism was generally popular within the country, he also appreciated that membership of the common market would benefit France economically. However, de Gaulle remained implacably opposed to any increase in the powers of the European Commission, or to any other increase in supra-nationalism. He showed just how opposed in 1965, when he precipitated the most dramatic crisis in the history of the European Community (George, 1985). It was German Chancellor Helmut Schmidt and French President Giscard d'Estaing who accelerated stalled integration process at the end of the 1970s. The joint initiative of Chancellor Helmut Kohl and President François Mitterand resulted in a great leap towards EMU in the beginning of the 1990s. The Franco-German alliance formed the core for the integration process in Europe, as it was the political will of these two countries that motivated further integration. See Kim and Park (2004).

References

ADB. (2005) "Progress Report of the Asian Bond Markets Initiative (ABMI)." in Asian Bond Online Website (http://asianbondsonline.adb.org).

Bergsten, C. Fred. (2000) "Toward a Tripartite World", *The Economist*, 15 July.

Chai, Heeyul and Youngseop Rhe (2005) *"Financial Integration and Financial Efficiency in East Asia"*, presented at the second Italian–Korean Economic Workshop, "Economic Policy, Growth and Economic Integration: East Asia and Europe in Perspective," Fondazione "Luigi Einaudi", 20 June.

Council on Foreign Relations (1999) *"Safeguarding Prosperity in a Global Financial System: The Future International Financial Architecture"*, Carla Hills and Peter Peterson, co-chairs, Morris Goldstein, project director, Washington, DC: Institute for International Economics.

de Brouwer, Gordon J. (1999) *Financial Integration in East Asia* , Cambridge: Cambridge University Press.

Eichengreen, Barry and Yung Chul Park (2003) "Why Has There Been Less Regional Integration in East Asia Than in Europe", forthcoming in *A New Financial Market Structure for East Asia*, edited by Takatoshi Ito, Yung Chul Park and Yunjong Wang, Edward Elgar.

George, Stephen (1985) *Politics and Policy in the European Community*, Oxford: Clarendon Press.

Heathcote, Jonathan and Fabrizio Perri (2002) "Financial Autarky and International Business Cycles", *Journal of Monetary Economics*, vol. 49, 601–27.

Henning, Randall C. (2002) *East Asian Financial Cooperation, Policy Analyses in International Economics*, Institute for International Economics, September.

Imbs, Jean (2003) "Trade, Finance, Specialization and Synchronization", *CEPR Discussion Paper* No. 3779, Center for Economic Policy Research, April.

Kim, Heungchong (2002) "Has Trade Intensity among ASEAN+3 really Increased?", *KIEP Working Paper*.

Kim, Heungchong, and Sung-Hoon Park (2004) "The Political Economy of the EMU Negotiation and its Implications to East Asian Monetary Integration", *Policy Analysis* 04–10, KIEP.

Kim, Heungchong and Yunjong Wang (2005) "Financial Cooperation and Financial Integration in East Asia", presented at the IFRI seminar held in Paris on 4 February.

Kim, Tae-Joon, Jai-Won Ryou, and Yunjong Wang (2000) *Regional Arrangements to Borrow: A Scheme for Preventing Future Asian Liquidity Crises*, Korea Institute for International Economic Policy.

Kuroda, Haruhiko and Masahiro Kawai (2002) "Strengthening Regional Financial Cooperation", *Pacific Economic Papers*, no. 332, 1–35.

Lee, Jong-wha, Yung Chul Park and Kwanho Shin (2004) "A Currency Union for East Asia", Chapter 4 in *Monetary and Financial Integration in East Asia: The Way Ahead*, Volume 2, edited by Asian Development Bank, Palgrave Macmillan.

Lincoln, Edward J. (2004) *East Asian Economic Regionalism*, The Brookings Institution, Washington DC.

Medeiros, Evan S., and M. Taylor Fravel (2003) "China's New Diplomacy", *Foreign Affairs* 82:6, 22–35.

Murase, Tetsuji (2004) "The East Asian Monetary Zone and the Roles of Japan, China and Korea", *mimeo*, Kyoto University.

Park, Yung Chul and Yunjong Wang (2002) "What Kind of International Financial Architecture for an Integrated World Economy", *Asian Economic Papers* 1(1), 91–128.

Park, Yung Chul and Yunjong Wang (2005) "The Chiang Mai Initiative and Beyond", *The World Economy*, vol. 28, no. 1, 91–101.

Park, Yung Chul and Daekeun Park (2003) "Creating Regional Bond Markets in East Asia: Rationale and Strategy", presented in the Second Annual Conference of PECC Finance Forum, Hua Hin, Thailand, July.

Pereira da Silva, Luiz A. and Masaru Yoshitomi (2001) "Can Moral Hazard Explain the Asian Crises?", *ADBI Research Paper*, no. 29, Asian Development Bank Institute, Japan.

Prasad, E., K. Rogoff, S. Wei and A. Kos (2003) "Effects of Financial Globalization on Developing Countries: Some Empirical Evidence", *mimeo*, IMF.

Sakakibara, Eisuke (2003) "Asian Cooperation and the End of Pax Americana", in *Financial Stability and Growth in Emerging Economies: The Role of the Financial Sector*, edited by Jan Joost Teunissen and Mark Teunissen, FONDAD, The Hague.

Scollay, R., and J. Gilbert (2001) *New Regional Trading Arrangements in the Asia Pacific*, Washington, DC: Institute for International Economics.

Shambaugh, David (2005) "China Engages Asia: Reshaping the Regional Order", *International Security*, vol. 29, no. 3, 64–99.

Shin, Kwanho and Yunjong Wang (2004) "Sequencing Monetary and Trade Integration", Chapter 17 in *Exchange Rate Regimes in East Asia*, edited by Gordon de Brouwer and Masahiro Kawai, London: RoutledgeCurzon.

Wang, Yunjong (2000) "The Asian Financial Crisis and Its Aftermath: Do We Need a Regional Financial Arrangement?", *ASEAN Economic Bulletin*, vol. 17, no. 2, 205–17.

Wang, Yunjong (2004) "Instruments and Techniques for Financial Cooperation", Chapter 9 in *Financial Governance in East Asia*, edited by Gordon de Brouwer and Yunjong Wang, London: RoutledgeCurzon.

Wang, Yunjong (2004) "Financial Cooperation and Integration in East Asia", *Journal of Asian Economics*, vol. 15, 939–55.

Wang, Yunjong and Wing Thye Woo (2004) "A Timely Information Exchange Mechanism, an Effective Surveillance System, and an Improved Financial Architecture for East Asia", Chapter 11 in *Monetary and Financial Integration in East Asia: The Way Ahead*, Volume 2, edited by Asian Development Bank, Palgrave Macmillan.

Wyplosz, Charles (2001) "Regional Arrangements: Some Lessons from Postwar Europe", presented at the conference on *The Role of Regional Financial Arrangements in Crisis Prevention and Management: The Experience of Europe, Asia, Africa, and Latin America*, organized by the Forum on Debt and Development (FONDAD) in Prague on 21–22 June.

Wyplosz, Charles (2004) "Regional Exchange Rate Arrangements: Lessons from Europe for East Asia", Chapter 7 in *Monetary and Financial Integration in East Asia: The Way Ahead*, Volume 2, edited by Asian Development Bank, Palgrave Macmillan.

5 Integration? What Integration?

Monetary co-operation in East Asia, the rise of China, and implications for Korea

Ulrich Volz

Introduction

Since the Asian crisis hit, financial integration has been looming high on the agenda of East Asian policy-makers. Many ideas have been developed and discarded, various initiatives have been called into action, and numerous task forces have been set up. Over the past few years, a multitude of declarations and initiatives concerning financial integration have been announced by the Association of Southeast Asian Nations (ASEAN) and ASEAN+3 (ASEAN plus China, Japan, and Korea) groupings. This has been complemented by initiatives from various other regional fora, such as the Executives' Meeting of East-Asia and Pacific Central Banks (EMEAP) or Asia-Pacific Economic Cooperation (APEC). And yet there is a lack of clarity and consensus about what is to be achieved, and in which direction financial and monetary integration in East Asia are heading. East Asian countries seem to have different interpretations of "financial integration" and even more diverse ambitions. While ASEAN already constitutes a highly heterogeneous group, this is even more true for the ASEAN+3. The countries involved appear to be driven by differing strategic interests. This is particularly the case for China and Japan, who both seem to regard Southeast Asia as their own backyard. Both countries are eager to maintain or increase their influence in the region, and eye each other conspicuously. Squeezed in-between the two giants is Korea, trying to secure its economic position. The ASEAN countries too, fearing competition from China's masses of under-employed, try to position themselves as attractive destinations of foreign investment and seek to maintain their status as thriving export nations.

In this context, this chapter addresses two central questions that arise when discussing financial integration in East Asia: First, what form of integration is to be achieved? And second, who are the players and who assumes the leadership role(s) in the integration process? Should integration focus on the ten ASEAN countries or should it also include China, Japan, Korea, and possibly even other candidates?

The increasing participation of China in regional production networks has created a complex web of economic linkages and given rise to tighter interdependence within the region. This new state of play provides a strong incentive to push for the deepening of economic policy cooperation and for exchange rate coordination. This chapter develops the arguments for monetary integration in East Asia and explores possible scenarios regarding the membership and leadership of such an integration effort.

The first section starts off with a discussion of different forms of cooperation in the field of money and finance. The next section contains a discussion of the potential candidates for integration in East Asia. This is followed by a section that develops the arguments for coordinated exchange rate stabilization in East Asia and argues that regional monetary cooperation and integration would reap the highest benefits if all countries in the region, including Japan, were to be included. The concluding section delineates implications for Korea's role in this process.

What form of integration is to be achieved?

In the early 1960s, Bela Balassa (1961) developed a five-step approach for regional integration, in which countries start integration with a free-trade area and succinctly move on to a customs union, a common market, economic and monetary union, and finally to political union. Europe has more or less followed this route up to monetary union, but there is no obvious reason why East Asian countries should follow the same path. Dieter and Higgot (2003) have pointed out that this typology was developed in a different historical context and argue that East Asia might be better suited to some kind of "monetary regionalism", concentrating more on the financial side of integration. In any case, there is no predetermined sequencing of regional integration, nor is it a priori clear what degree of integration (if any) is to be achieved in East Asia.

Table 5.1 lists different forms of cooperation in the field of money and finance. Cooperation is understood in a broad sense and seen as a means to achieve integration. The classification, which is by no means exhaustive, distinguishes five levels of cooperation, starting with relatively low-key forms.

First, countries may agree to cooperate in an informal or institutionalized exchange of information and decide to hold regular meetings and consultations between governments and financial authorities. One step further would be the launch of a regional regulation and surveillance framework through which countries would foster the development and appliance of common standards for the financial sector and institutionalize the joint monitoring of monetary and fiscal policies. Each country's commitment would be rather limited in these areas of cooperation, making it relatively easy to reach an agreement. Nevertheless, each of these measures can bring great benefits by fostering the stability of regional financial markets. East Asian countries have been quite active in these forms of cooperation since the crisis. They have, for instance, established regular meetings of finance ministers and central bank governors within the ASEAN and ASEAN+3 frameworks, and have set up the ASEAN surveillance process.

A third form of regional cooperation relates to the development of regional financial markets. Since the crisis, East Asian countries have indeed demonstrated concerted efforts to foster regional financial markets, particularly bond markets. Schemes such as the Asian Bond Market Initiative and the Asian Bond Funds I and II aim at providing regional liquidity and investment opportunities. The underdevelopment (or lack) of regional capital markets has been identified as one of the underlying causes of the crisis. This awareness has certainly contributed to the relatively quick progress of current bond market initiatives.

Fourthly, the creation of regional support mechanisms or the pooling of official reserves is a way to complement international facilities (particularly those of the IMF) in order to help out countries with temporary balance of payment problems. Already during the crisis, Japan suggested the creation of an Asian Monetary Fund to complement IMF lending. This move had been opposed by the US, and instead ASEAN+3 countries have engaged in bilateral lending arrangements under the Chiang Mai Initiative (CMI). The CMI initiative, however, already shows the hardships of cooperation, demanding true commitment and involving financial resources. While cooperation in regulation and surveillance is relatively cost-free and painless, common reserve pooling is much more sensitive, as no country wants to risk losing money because of the hazardous behaviour of its partners.

Finally, the fifth area of cooperation relates to exchange rate policies. Again, different degrees of cooperation are conceivable, ranging from rather loose cooperation in the form of common inflation targeting, more severe forms such as common exchange rate pegs or baskets, and highly demanding forms of exchange rate coordination such as a regional monetary system, or even a monetary union. To any such forms of coordinated exchange rate stabilization this chapter also refers to as monetary integration.

Table 5.1 Forms of regional cooperation in the field of money and finance

Information exchange	Regular meetings/consultations
Regulation and surveillance	Common standards
	Joint monitoring of monetary and fiscal policy

Development of regional
    financial markets
	Initiatives to foster the development
	    of the banking sector, bond or equity markets

Regional support mechanisms/reserve pooling	Bilateral or multilateral lending arrangements Regional monetary fund
Exchange rate coordination	Common inflation targeting
	Common exchange rate pegs/baskets
	Regional monetary system
	Monetary union

While low-key forms of cooperation such as the (informal) exchange of information, regular consultations between national authorities, and initiatives to improve the quality of financial sector supervision, for instance, are almost unanimously desirable, this is not necessarily the case for higher forms of cooperation, for example cooperation in the field of exchange rates. The degree of cooperation needed in the more complex and sensitive fields listed in Table 5.1 depends on two aspects: (1) the degree of real integration which is to be achieved, and (2) the political ability and willingness to cooperate, including an agreement on a common set of policy objectives and how to achieve them.

The degree of real integration that is to be achieved

The more markets are intertwined, the greater is the necessity of cooperation between national authorities. Spillover effects can transmit shocks from one country to another. For instance, Glick and Rose (1999) have shown that financial contagion is related to real integration and that currency crises follow the patterns of international trade. The necessity of macroeconomic policy cooperation and harmonization in general, and in the field of money and finance in particular, depends on what kind of integrated regional market is envisaged (Eichengreen 1998). A customs union, for instance, can be sustained with a moderate level of policy cooperation, without the need for exchange rate cooperation. But deeper integration implies even more open domestic markets and more intense cross-border competition, making changes in national policies or exchange rates more disruptive.

As will be discussed later, East Asia has already reached a relatively high degree of real integration. Because of the importance of intraregional trade, but also because East Asian countries compete against one another in third markets, exchange rate spillover effects from one country to another are of great importance. Because of neighbourhood effects, national decisions to fix or float should not be made independently. This need not imply a fully fledged regional monetary system or even a monetary union. If East Asian countries are only striving for a fully operating free trade area, this could in principle work with a regime of more or less flexible exchange rates that avoids sharp disruptions, just as is the case in the North American Free Trade Area (NAFTA). If, instead, East Asian leaders want to foster deeper integration and aim for a single market in goods and services, they will need to contemplate explicit exchange rate cooperation or even monetary union, as the Europeans did. Section 4 will come back to this point and argue that not only the complex web of economic linkages that has developed in East Asia provides a strong argument for regional exchange rate stabilization, but that there are also other reasons in favour of East Asian monetary integration.

The political ability and willingness to cooperate

The form of cooperation also depends on its feasibility. Each country participating in a joint cooperation effort needs to be willing and able to compromise on policy issues with its counterparts. Countries must be able to find an agreement on a common set of policy objectives and how to achieve them, and must be able to sell the results to their constituencies at home.

The requirements for successful regional exchange rate cooperation, for instance, are set very high, especially if the countries involved have reached the stage of economic and financial development where it is conventional to remove capital controls. A very strong commitment is required from all parties willing to engage in a regional exchange rate system, and the willingness to subordinate internal economic objectives under the objective of exchange rate stability is essential. A crucial prerequisite for any regional monetary arrangement to be successful is a far-reaching consensus on policy preferences (Volz 2006a). If the requirements are not fulfilled, exchange rate arrangements are destined to fail, potentially causing a crisis.

Who are the players and who assumes the leadership role(s)?

The question of what form of integration is to be achieved is directly linked to the question of who takes part in the integration effort and who assumes the leading role(s) in the integration process. The decision of how far integration should go and the political and economic ability to transfer these decisions into reality depends very much on the integration partners. Different groups of countries will have different motivations and ambitions with respect to regional integration. In the case of East Asia, it is as yet not clear which set of countries might eventually team up for integration. There are at least five scenarios:[1]

1 *ASEAN+ with China and Japan as leaders.* In this scenario, China and Japan would become some kind of East Asian "Franco-German engine of integration", which would lead a strong ASEAN+3 (or ASEAN+4 if Hong Kong is counted separately[2]). While this would create a true East Asian powerhouse, it is questionable whether these two countries will be able to overcome their animosities and develop a common political will. As the recent turmoil about Japan's war legacies and the Japanese prime minister's visits to the Yasukuni shrine have shown once more, the rivalry and the suspicion of one another run deep. Nevertheless, as will be argued below, the economic incentives for cooperation within ASEAN+3 are strong and they are reinforced by security considerations.

2 *ASEAN+3 muddle through.* This scenario would potentially fail to produce far-reaching policy results. It would, however, provide a platform for regional exchange with sporadic cooperation in single fields.

3 *ASEAN+3+Australia+New Zealand+India+ ...* While covering the tensions between China and Japan, this scenario could be regarded as a

"watering down" of integration efforts, as this grouping would be far too large to find consensus in sensitive policy areas. It would be similar to the rather loose economic cooperation that characterizes APEC, which was originally conceived by the US as a way of preventing the region from forming a closed economic bloc that would exclude the US.

4 *China becomes the undisputed leader of an ASEAN+*. China would win the competition for East Asian leadership against Japan and would emerge as the centre country of regional integration. This would perhaps allow Korea to play a role, but Japan would be left out in the cold. As will be discussed below, this would be a potentially dangerous constellation.

5 *ASEAN alone.* In this scenario, the ASEAN countries will continue integration without the participation of China, Japan, Korea, or any other outsider. This might be the country grouping that would allow for the furthest reaching integration, maybe in the form of an ASEAN Economic Community, which is envisaged as a common market with a free flow of goods, services, and investment – and maybe also monetary integration. While quite a heterogeneous group, the ASEAN countries have their relative (economic) insignificance as compared to China and Japan, and even Korea, in common. Furthermore, ASEAN countries feel a common urge to position themselves in a way to save their economic competitiveness as well as their security needs, which increases their incentives to team up.

These different scenarios imply different forms of regional cooperation and integration. The remainder of the chapter will argue that there is a strong case for exchange rate cooperation in East Asia and that the best group of countries for this would be the ASEAN+3.

The case for monetary integration among ASEAN+3

The status quo of East Asian exchange rate systems is suboptimal. The current situation can be described as the "East Asian dollar standard" (McKinnon 2005), where all East Asian countries, except Japan, orient their exchange rate policies, to differing degrees, to the US dollar. Table 5.2 presents the exchange rate classification countries report to the IMF as well as estimates for the weights of the currencies included in the hypothetical currency basket vis-à-vis which East Asian economies manage their domestic currencies.[3] It is evident that the exchange rate policies of virtually all East Asian countries have been very much, if not completely, oriented toward the US dollar. The estimated dollar weights in the hypothetical baskets of East Asian currencies range from around 65 per cent for Singapore and Brunei (the latter runs a currency board arrangement vis-à-vis the Singapore dollar), to 100 per cent for China, Hong Kong, Malaysia, and Vietnam.

The common de facto dollar (soft) pegs can be viewed as the outcome of a Nash non-cooperative equilibrium. While a common basket comprising the dollar, the yen, and the euro would have been superior for all countries (as it would have provided for more flexibility to adjust to fluctuations between those currencies), mutual trade relations as well as export competition on third markets made the dollar peg a logical choice for each individual country provided the others did the same (Montiel 2004).

Instead of continuing their (soft) pegs toward the dollar, which can be regarded as an implicit form of exchange rate cooperation, it would be beneficial for East Asian countries to let loose the dollar and instead engage in explicit, coordinated exchange rate stabilization within the region and maybe even work toward the long-term goal of creating a common currency.

There are several arguments in support of monetary integration in East Asia. We will discuss four of them: (1) the relationship between monetary integration and trade; (2) monetary integration as a way of overcoming the problems of "original sin" and "conflicted virtue"; (3) monetary integration as a strategy to (*re*)*gain* some degrees of monetary independence in the region,

Table 5.2 De jure and *de facto* exchange rate regimes in East Asia

	IMF Classification	Estimated weight of the USD in hypothetical basket (%)
Brunei dollar	Currency board arrangement (vis-à-vis the Singapore dollar)	65.28
Cambodian riel	Managed floating with no pre-announced path for the exchange rate	92.56
Chinese renminbi (yuan)	Conventional pegged arrangement (vis-à-vis the US dollar)	99.42
Hong Kong dollar	Currency board arrangement (vis-à-vis the US dollar)	99.37
Indonesian rupiah	Managed floating with no pre-announced path for the exchange rate	81.47
Japanese yen	Independently floating	42.74
Korean won	Independently floating	74.03
Lao kip	Managed floating with no pre-announced path for the exchange rate	89.15
Malaysian ringgit	Conventional pegged arrangement vis-à-vis the US dollar)	98.12
Myanmar kyat	Managed floating with no pre-announced path for the exchange rate	93.94
Philippine peso	Independently floating	91.04
Singapore dollar	Managed floating with no pre-announced path for the exchange rate	65.28
Thai baht	Managed floating with no pre-announced path for the exchange rate	69.23
Vietnamese dong	Managed floating with no pre-announced path for the exchange rate	100.40

Note: All dollar weight estimates are significant at the 1% level. The yen was regressed only on the dollar and the euro.
Source: Data are from Datastream (Reuters and Tenfore); classifications are from IMF (2005).

and, finally; (4) the role economic and monetary integration can play in avoiding political conflict in the region.[4]

Monetary integration and trade

First, and as was already briefly mentioned, real economic integration in East Asia has given rise to tighter interdependence within the region. Table 5.3 shows the direction of trade of East Asian countries. Intra-regional trade – defined as trade among ASEAN+4 as share of these countries' overall trade – on average accounted for almost 60 per cent of total trade in 2005. When taking absolute values for ASEAN+4 instead of an unweighted average, the ratio is still 48 per cent, almost the same as the 51 per cent of the euro area and the 55 per cent of NAFTA and considerably higher than for other regional groupings such as the Mercado Común del Sur (Mercosur, 12 per cent), the Economic Community of West African States (ECOWAS, 8 per cent), the Commonwealth of Independent States (CIS, 18 per cent), the Central American Common Market (CACM, 11 per cent), or the Andean Common Market (ANCOM, 7 per cent).

Korea is a bit below the regional average with a share of regional trade in total trade of 47 per cent. As for many other countries in the region (Cambodia, Lao, Malaysia, Myanmar, the Philippines, Singapore, and Vietnam), trade with greater China (China and Hong Kong) has now become more important for Korea than trade with Japan. With 13 and 12 per cent of total trade respectively, trade with the US and the EU are important for Korea, but the most important trading partners lie within the region, not outside. On average, trade with the US and the EU make about 12 and 11 per cent of the region's trade respectively. This rather moderate share of trade with the US is particularly interesting as it is commonly claimed that East Asian countries maintain their (soft) pegs vis-à-vis the US dollar because of strong trade ties with the US. This direction of trade analysis, however, clearly shows that intra-regional trade is much more important than trade with the US and hence, from a trade-perspective, it would be much more important for East Asian countries to maintain intra-regional exchange rate stability than maintaining stability toward the dollar. The solution is, of course, that through the common dollar pegging intra-regional exchange rate stability is indirectly achieved.[5] The question is whether intra-regional exchange rate stability could not be achieved directly, that is, without having an external anchor.

Trade within ASEAN as a share of total trade is much lower than for ASEAN+4, amounting to only 31 per cent on average.[6] But trade with the "+4" countries is of great importance for all ASEAN countries (except Lao), with an average of 31 per cent of ASEAN countries' trade being conducted with China, Hong Kong, Japan, and Korea – the same share as intra-ASEAN trade. For the ASEAN countries there is hence a strong incentive to maintain exchange rate stability not only within ASEAN but

Table 5.3 Trade of … with … as per cent of total trade, 2005

	USA	EU	ASEAN+4	ASEAN+3	ASEAN	Japan	Korea	China & Hong Kong	Hong Kong	China
Brunei	8.90	3.83	75.50	74.97	26.29	32.98	11.96	4.26	0.54	3.73
Cambodia	25.62	10.69	54.84	46.84	32.88	2.63	2.50	16.84	8.00	8.84
Indonesia	9.62	12.03	56.63	54.63	20.04	18.53	5.34	12.73	2.00	10.73
Lao	0.75	9.98	74.37	73.95	64.79	1.45	0.68	7.46	0.42	7.04
Malaysia	14.92	11.25	57.97	54.74	30.90	9.45	4.00	13.62	3.23	10.39
Myanmar	0.08	5.98	76.01	74.86	49.95	3.93	3.38	18.74	1.15	17.59
Philippines	15.14	11.22	59.31	52.73	18.70	15.66	4.10	20.85	6.58	14.27
Singapore	11.93	12.78	51.89	45.40	23.06	8.00	4.19	16.64	6.49	10.14
Thailand	11.28	11.22	52.88	49.54	19.97	18.00	2.68	12.22	3.34	8.88
Vietnam	11.11	12.77	55.31	52.67	22.15	11.40	7.07	14.68	2.64	12.04
China	14.93	15.28	39.63	30.02	9.17	12.97	7.87		9.61	
Hong Kong	10.51	11.00	65.86	65.86	9.35	8.19	3.30			45.02
Japan	18.15	13.12	40.16	36.77	13.39		6.40	20.36	3.39	16.98
Korea	12.98	12.02	46.97	43.55	10.65	13.29		23.03	3.41	19.61
Average ASEAN	10.93	10.18	61.47	58.03	30.87	12.20	4.59	13.80	3.44	10.36
Average ASEAN+3	11.95	10.94	57.04	53.13	26.30	12.36	5.01	15.12	3.91	11.69
Average ASEAN+4	11.85	10.94	57.67	54.04	25.09	12.04	4.88	15.12	3.91	14.25

Source: Author's own calculations with data from the IMF's Direction of Trade Statistics.

within ASEAN+4. From the perspective of China, Hong Kong, Japan, and Korea, trade with ASEAN is also important but on a considerably lower level, with 9, 9, 13, and 11 per cent respectively.

While trade patterns of East Asian countries are obviously different, in most cases they are not dramatically different. Overall, the relative similarity of the geographic distribution of trade of most East Asian countries would facilitate the adoption of a common exchange rate policy across the region and the fact that all countries have in common a high share of intra-regional trade would provide a strong incentive to do so. But not only because of the importance of intra-regional trade, also because East Asian countries compete against one another in third markets, exchange rate spillover effects from one country to another are of great importance.

There are numerous problems faced by countries that are close trading partners and competitors but that follow different exchange rate regimes.[7] First, a country that loses competitiveness as a result of a real exchange rate appreciation vis-à-vis its trading partners could be inclined to employ anti-dumping or other administrative measures (if tariffs are precluded through trade agreements) to protect domestic firms, which, in turn, could trigger a trade war as well as a round of beggar-thy-neighbour devaluations. Second, regional trade agreements may spark fierce competition for the location of investment, and swings in the bilateral exchange rates may have important consequences for the location of new investments and might even shift the location of existing investments. Third, and finally, a change of the exchange regime in one of the partner countries may cause an exchange rate crisis in the other because exchange rate depreciation in one country may reduce the credibility of the partner's commitment to a fixed parity and can generate speculative attacks on its currency. A country may thus be forced to abandon its preferred exchange rate policy due to the exchange rate disagreement.

Moreover, the recent literature on monetary integration has found a trade-creating effect of monetary union, reinforcing the trade argument for monetary integration. While there has been a lot of controversy about the actual magnitude of the trade-creating effect of monetary union, a broad agreement has emerged that a currency union has a significant positive effect on trade.[8] While it is impossible accurately to predict the trade creating-effect of a potential monetary union in East Asia, Volz (2006b) has estimated the effect that the similarity of currency regimes has on bilateral trade in East Asia, finding large and significant effects of exchange rate stability on trade.

In addition to trade linkages, intra-regional interdependence in foreign direct investment has also increased dramatically across East Asia (Kawai and Urata 2004). Declining transportation costs and decreasing trade barriers have brought about an internationalization of production processes, often referred to as production fragmentation or vertical specialization. In East Asia, this has led to the development of extensive regional production networks. In particular, multinational corporations have formed regional supply chains and production networks, taking advantage of intra-regional divisions of labour and promoting the specialization of production by breaking the production process down into different sub-processes within the same industry. Particularly China has grown into a manufacturing hub for East Asia, mainly serving as the last segment in the international production chain. The increasing participation of China in regional production networks has created a complex web of economic linkages and given rise to tighter inter-dependence within the region.[9] The region has thus reached a degree of real integration where macroeconomic policy and exchange rate coordination will become ever more important. While this need not imply a monetary union, policy coordination to achieve real exchange rate consistency is essential.

Monetary integration, original sin, and conflicted virtue

A second incentive for monetary integration is that it could help overcome the problems associated with a weak currency status and a lack of financial maturity. East Asian countries' (with the notable exception of Japan and to a lesser degree Korea and Singapore) lack of an international currency puts a number of constraints on their development prospects and increases financial fragility.

The international monetary system is characterized by currency competition and a hierarchy of currencies (Cohen 1998), where different currencies exhibit different qualities in their function as storage of wealth. Weak currency countries are confronted with what Eichengreen and Hausmann (1999) have termed "original sin", a situation in which the domestic currency cannot be used to borrow long term, even domestically. As a result, financial fragility is unavoidable because all domestic investment will have either a currency mismatch, where projects that generate domestic currency will be financed with an international currency, or a maturity mismatch, where long-term projects will be financed with short-term loans. Both currency and maturity mismatches increase the danger of financial crises. Original sin is widely viewed as a central cause for the Asian crisis.

Moreover, in a phenomenon McKinnon (2005) has named "conflicted virtue", weak currency countries are unable to lend in their own currencies, forcing creditor countries with weak currencies to cumulate currency mismatches. As most East Asian countries have turned into creditor countries after the Asian crisis, the excess build-up of foreign exchange assets has created a conflicted virtue problem for them. While Japan, Singapore, and Taiwan have had current account surpluses for more than two decades and China has had more modest current account surpluses since 1995, even the five former crisis economies (Indonesia, Korea, Malaysia, the Philippines, and Thailand), which had large current account deficits before 1997, have now accumulated large stocks of liquid dollar assets in both private and public portfolios. With mounting dollar claims, non-US holders of dollar assets have to worry more about domestic currency runs, which would cause a domestic currency appreciation and hence a decline of their net wealth. Countries are therefore inclined to avoid large-scale appreciation of their currencies, which might invoke protests from deficit countries about unfair competition through an undervalued currency.

A weak currency status therefore brings with it multiple problems, from retarding financial and real development and increasing the risk of financial crisis to triggering potential trade conflict. The only way to make a currency internationally accepted is by building an expectation that a government's liabilities will be perfect substitutes for other governments' liabilities. A number of conditions can be identified that contribute to building such expectations. First, the confidence in a currency's future value is dependent on the political stability of the country of origin (Cohen 2000). Second, countries need to develop sound and credible fiscal institutions. In conjunction with non-inflationary income policies, an austere fiscal framework lays the groundwork for a non-inflationary monetary environment with low nominal as well as real interest rates. Third, countries need to establish credible monetary regimes as an unpredictable monetary policy makes agents unsure about the future real value of their assets issued in domestic currency and may lead them to denominate them in international currency (Jeanne 2005). Fourth, not running into international debt but instead striving for a surplus in the trade and current account helps to create expectations of an appreciation of the national currency.

But developing sound fiscal and monetary institutions and generating export surpluses might not be enough. The literature on the determinants of key currency status points to another factor, namely, the size of the economy. Matsuyama *et al.* (1993) explain the international use of currencies and, succinctly, the determinants of key currency status as a function of relative country size and the degree of international economic integration. Because of network externalities and transaction costs, the global portfolio is concentrated in very few currencies. In some ways money is comparable to language, whose usefulness is also dependent on the number of people with whom one can communicate; similarly, a currency's utility rises with the number of other market participants using the same currency (Dowd and Greenaway 1993).[10] A currency's attractiveness increases with its transactional liquidity, which in turn is dependent on the existence of well-developed and broad financial markets that offer a wide range of short and long-term investment opportunities as well as fully operating secondary markets (Cohen 2000). Eichengreen *et al.* (2005) point out that larger countries offer significant diversification possibilities, while smaller countries add fewer diversification benefits relative to the additional costs they imply. As a consequence, the global portfolio is concentrated in a small number of currencies for reasons partly beyond the control of even the countries that follow sound domestic policies. Developing key currency status is hence a very difficult and maybe even impossible endeavour for small economies.[11]

In the face of these constraints, regional monetary integration could be employed by developing nations as a strategy for overcoming their weak currency status and the inability to enter into international contracts with domestic currency. While a hardening of the national currency could in principle also be achieved by each country alone through austere monetary and fiscal policies and through the generation of export surpluses, it might not suffice to develop an international currency. Monetary integration, however, could address both issues at the same time. One the one hand, it would place an external constraint on countries participating in the monetary integration process, facilitating the domestic policy adjustment necessary for a hardening of the currency.[12] At the same time, monetary integration would address the problems of original sin and conflicted virtue by creating a larger economic entity with vast investment opportunities which would be hard to ignore by international investors and which, if backed by austere monetary and fiscal policies, would increase chances of entering the club of international currencies. The underlying logic is that the whole would be equal to more than the sum of its parts.[13]

From this reasoning, a common currency across East Asia could potentially help all countries in the region to reap the benefits of having an international currency. For Japan, with the yen as the world's third most important currency after the US dollar and the euro, this argument is certainly less appealing than for the least developed countries in the region, which, on their own, will have little prospect of ever escaping their weak currency status.[14] Also, for China, the size argument does not apply; China's current lack of an international currency is a result of domestic policy shortcomings and particularly its financial sector weaknesses rather than the size of its currency area. One can assume that it will be only a matter of time until China will overcome these problems, but it might take decades rather than years. But for Korea, in contrast, the prospects of developing key currency status are much dimmer. While Korea has managed over the past decades to transform itself into a high-income economy, the international role of the Korean won is still nascent, even regionally, despite attempts by the Korean government to promote the international use of the won by granting export credits in won to other countries.

The region's current ambitions to develop a regional bond market are in fact nothing else but an attempt to fuse strengths in order to overcome the limitations faced by national financial markets. The Asian Bond Market Initiative and the Asian Bond Funds I and II are basically designed to create network effects and make it more attractive for regional and international investors to include East Asian bonds in their portfolios. This might be a step in the right direction for East Asia, and pursuing a similar cooperative path in monetary policy could help overcome the problems of original sin and conflicted virtue that are associated with a weak currency status. Individually, most East Asian nations will have little prospect of escaping this trap. Yet, united, the region is far too important to be ignored by currency traders. As a possible first move in this direction, in December 2005 the Asian Development Bank announced the launch of a currency unit comprised of a basket of regional currencies akin to the European Currency Unit. This virtual basket currency may give observers a taste of the kind of standing a regional East Asian currency could achieve in international financial markets.

The success of such a regional currency – be it a virtual basket currency or maybe even a "real" fiat currency later on–will be greater the larger the currency area it is used in. Also, the more affluent the countries included in it, the greater the potential for this (virtual) currency. This is a strong argument to include Japan, which would bring in deep and liquid financial markets, which, if partly denominated in a regional currency unit or the like, would significantly help to boost the acceptance of such a virtual currency. But it is not only Japan's potency in financial market development that would call for an inclusion of Japan, it is also China's impotence in the same field. While the Chinese authorities have been pushing for financial market reform, the Chinese financial markets are still in a very early stage of development and far from being able to absorb huge amounts of portfolio investment. Also, an East Asian "yuan bloc" is not in sight unless the yuan becomes fully convertible, which will require continued reform of China's foreign exchange market.[15] China, however, would contribute by its mere importance as the region's most important economy along with Japan as well as its status as the world's largest economy to be.

Monetary integration and policy influence

Third, regional monetary integration could be a way of (*re*)*gaining* some degrees of monetary independence in the region. This might seem paradoxical at first, as it is usually claimed that monetary integration means a *loss* of monetary independence. This, however, is true only if the participating countries enjoyed monetary autonomy before. In this context it is important to distinguish between sovereignty and policy autonomy: a country might well have the formal right to pursue a certain policy but find itself unable to do so because of policy choices of other nations (DeMartino and Grabel 2003).

In the European discourse, for instance, opponents of monetary union argued that giving up national currencies would mean the loss of a powerful policy instrument. By analysing the policy decisions of national central banks, Volz (2006b) shows that the monetary policy decisions of almost all Western European countries were driven to a large extent by the interest rate policy of the German Bundesbank[16] and that the member countries of the European Monetary System (except Germany) had already abandoned monetary and exchange rate autonomy long before entering the European Monetary Union (EMU). Germany has, in fact, been the only country that has actually lost autonomy through the EMU. Virtually all other EMU countries not only *did not lose* monetary autonomy but actually (*re*)*gained* a voice in monetary policy decisions through EMU membership. Instead of following the Bundesbank's policy stance, all EMU member countries are now represented through their national central bank governors in the European Central Bank's (ECB) Governing Council, the ECB's monetary policy-making body. Under current rules, the central bank governors of each euro area member, along with the six members of the ECB's Executive Board, have the right to vote at each council meeting, providing smaller countries such as Austria and Luxembourg with the same *de jure* influence on monetary policy as the larger members France, Germany, Italy, and Spain.[17] Among the central banks of the old EU member countries that did not join EMU, the monetary authorities of Denmark and Sweden have basically been forced to shadow ECB policy, without exerting any influence themselves on the policy they have to follow.[18]

Likewise, it can be argued that the current East Asian dollar standard has created a situation in which East Asian countries (except Japan and to a lesser degree maybe Korea[19]) have largely abandoned monetary policy autonomy. Although most East Asian countries maintain some form of capital controls that, in principle, should allow for monetary policy autonomy in the face of an exchange rate target, historical evidence suggests quite strongly that capital controls are porous and are easily circumvented (Edwards 1999). Furthermore, there is a growing amount of empirical literature that puts into doubt even the traditional argument that countries with flexible exchange rates are able to isolate their domestic interest rates from changes in international interest rates. Frankel *et al.* (2004), for instance, find that while floating regimes afford greater monetary independence than fixed regimes, floating regimes offer only temporary monetary independence.[20] Their findings suggest that besides the US, Germany (now the euro zone) and Japan appear to be the only countries that can independently choose their own interest rates in the long run.[21]

Moreover, the underdevelopment of domestic financial markets in East Asia (excluding Hong Kong, Japan, Korea, and Singapore) hampers the conduct of monetary policy, creating a situation wherein the vast majority of East Asian countries have not been able to effectively pursue independent monetary policy. The People's Bank of China (PBC), for instance, did not change interest rates for more than a decade until October 2004, and even this change was very modest and more symbolic than of practical import.[22] Similarly, Malaysia raised its rates in November 2005 for the first time since 1998. The most extreme case of a loss of monetary autonomy in East Asia is Hong Kong. To maintain its currency board vis-à-vis the US dollar, the Hong Kong Monetary Authority has to move in tandem with the Federal Reserve, even though local inflation development has been very different from US inflation over recent years.

If this argument is correct and the status quo level of East Asian monetary independence is limited, then the costs of monetary integration in East Asia, at least for the economically small and developing countries, are much lower than commonly assumed.[23] A common agency approach to monetary unification, as pursued in Europe, could theoretically pave the way for greater monetary policy flexibility in East Asia. Through the creation of a common currency, which could float freely against the dollar and the euro, East Asian countries could potentially gain some degrees of shared monetary independence. While they would still face an external constraint on domestic economic policies, the great difference between multilateral monetary union in East Asia and a continued (informal) dollar pegging under the East Asian dollar standard (or even full dollarization) is that the former would give members of the currency union a say in the common policy. Through a pooling of sovereignty, each member of the currency union would have a share in the central bank's policy-making. In contrast, continued dollar pegging (or dollarization), while basically requiring the same sacrifices in domestic policy autonomy as monetary union, would mean that all monetary policy influence is abandoned (permanently).[24] Already coordinated exchange rate stabilization or the creation of a regional exchange rate system would in principle increase the region's policy autonomy as compared to the present situation.

Admittedly, a delicate political problem would be the institutional design of a common central bank and the apportionment of power in an East Asian monetary union. A representational structure akin to that of the EMU, with equal rights between all members, would be unrealistic if either China or Japan were involved, making such an arrangement less attractive for the smaller Southeast Asian countries due to the potential dominance of the bigger member countries. Conversely, neither Japan nor China (nor Korea) would be likely to accept the disproportional representation of the economically smaller Southeast Asian member countries the way Germany did in Europe.[25]

Monetary integration and security considerations

Fourth, and finally, economic integration must not be solely analysed from an economic perspective. Hamada and Lee (2006) argue that there are other considerations and incentives that drive the political economy of monetary integration. They maintain that purely economic incentives may not exist for nations to join a monetary union and that, as was the case for the European Union and the creation of the euro, security reasons may turn out to be a critical motive for fostering monetary integration in East Asia. This is not to say that East Asian monetary integration is a "matter of war and peace" as the former German chancellor Helmut Kohl famously said about the EMU. It would, however, be negligent to completely ignore security considerations.

The close economic relationships that have developed within East Asia should not belie that the diplomatic relations between Japan and its neighbours, particularly with China and Korea, have been strained by various instances. For example, the Japanese prime minister's visits to the Yasukuni shrine, the Japanese threat to reduce foreign aid to China, and Japan's textbook description of wartime conducts have generated suspicion on the future course of Japan's diplomatic policy. Conversely, China's alleged operation of submarines within Japan's territorial sea near the Okinawa islands, its opposition to Japan's permanent membership in the United Nations Security Council, and the benign treatment of students' protest against the Japanese embassy in Beijing have courted resentment in Japan. Furthermore, China and Japan still continue their territorial dispute over the Senkaku/Diaoyutai islands north of Taiwan and south of the Ryukyu islands. And of course, Taiwan and North Korea remain unresolved issues that cast clouds on regional security. While there is no imminent risk of military confrontation, there is always a danger of (unintended) escalation that could have disastrous consequences for the whole region.

The problem, to paraphrase a Chinese saying, seemingly is that one mountain cannot accommodate two tigers. In this context it is important to recall that the main impetus for European integration did not come from an economic rationale but primarily from a desire to overcome centuries of war and the rivalry between France and Germany. The aim of the European Coal and Steel Community, which marked the beginning of European economic cooperation in 1951, was explicitly political in its aim of removing control of the two most important raw materials for the production of heavy weaponry from states that had just fought the bloodiest war in history (Duisenberg 2005). This drive for peace remained the key motivation behind further steps toward European economic integration.

While one shouldn't overstretch similarities between Europe and East Asia, the European integration process certainly has important lessons to offer for East Asian countries regarding how to overcome a legacy of wars and develop a peaceful and prosperous region. While economic integration – in which exchange rate and monetary cooperation has played an important role – has only been one pillar of European integration (besides cultural exchange, education, etc.), it has been an incredibly important one. For sure, security considerations alone should not be the only drive for monetary integration in East Asia, but given the arguments discussed earlier on, there already is a pretty strong economic case for regional monetary cooperation, and these security considerations can give an additional impetus. Moreover, they can guide the selection of what countries would be good candidates for regional monetary integration. While, for some, China might seem the natural choice for centre country in a regional exchange rate system due to its size and key role in the regional economy (particularly when anticipating China's continued growth in the medium or long run), such a selection might be counterproductive or even dangerous from a security perspective because regional integration built around China would inevitably exclude Japan, which could give ground to future political conflict and confrontation in the region. Instead of contributing to regional stability, integration could then lead to confrontation. The best framework for regional cooperation, when also including security considerations, would thus probably be ASEAN+3.

Concluding remarks and implications for Korea

This chapter has argued that there are several cases in support of monetary integration in East Asia. There are indeed hints that the current situation is about to change. China's announcement on 21 July 2005 to abandon the eleven-year old peg to the dollar and instead link the yuan to a basket of currencies might be the starting signal for a fundamental reconsideration of East Asian exchange rate relations, and thereby of the future shape of financial integration in the region.

Already before the Chinese decision to allow more flexibility through the introduction of a currency basket, Ho *et al.* (2005) detected a growing orientation of East Asian countries' exchange rate policy toward China. They argue that the rapid expansion of yuan turnover foreshadows a stronger influence of the Chinese currency in regional foreign exchange markets. Taking yuan non-deliverable forwards (NDFs)[26] as a proxy for the yuan spot rate (which at that time was still closely pegged to the dollar), Ho *et al.* find that expectations of the dollar/yuan rate exhibit significant co-movement with other regional currencies against the dollar. The co-movement with the yuan NDF should not be taken to imply that the Asian authorities have actually placed the yuan NDF in their implicit or explicit exchange rate basket, but it might indicate that East Asian currencies increasingly have an effective exchange rate orientation. In particular, the detected co-movement might actually reflect market participant's expectations that other Asian currencies would be allowed to strengthen too in the case of a Chinese revaluation, i.e. that they would follow the Chinese move.

And indeed, this is what happened. Following the Chinese announcement to drop its currency peg against the dollar, Malaysia instantaneously announced the end of its dollar peg and the ringgit's float against a trade-weighted basket of foreign currencies. While the new Malaysian arrangements differ in detail (the Malaysian central bank said it would rely on central bank intervention rather than on a currency trading band to maintain the stability of its managed float), the move epitomizes the role into which China has grown. China's new currency system is also close to that of Singapore, which has used a secret policy band to guide its managed float of the Singapore dollar against a foreign currency basket. As the Malaysian move demonstrates, it is not inconceivable that other East Asian countries may follow over time and that China gradually evolves as the centre of an (informal) East Asian yuan bloc. As China will not opt for a free float in the foreseeable future but will instead maintain relative stability vis-à-vis the dollar and perhaps the yen and euro, this would make it more acceptable for other countries in the region to follow the yuan. The realization of Williamson's (1999, 2005) proposal for a common basket peg of East Asian countries does not seem unlikely anymore, and neither does it seem improbable that such an (informal) arrangement would be centred around China.

China has not been shy of reminding its East Asian peers that it had played a stabilizing role during the Asian crisis by maintaining its dollar peg against criticism from Washington. Similarly, when describing the government's position on a yuan revaluation before it actually took place, Chinese officials did not become weary of reiterating that China would act in the interest of the whole region. For example, when China's premier Wen Jinbao set out conditions that needed to be met before China could move to greater exchange rate flexibility at the close of the National People's Congress, he added that, "When we decide on this, we must take into account not only our own companies' interests, but also the impact on the world and neighbouring countries" (FT 2005). This kind of courtship could indeed be regarded as an attempt to signal to other East Asian countries that China, unlike Japan, is willing to take an "altruistic" approach to regional integration and safeguard the interests of its Southeast Asian neighbours.

While China might seem a natural choice for country in a regional exchange rate system due to its size and central role in the regional economy, the chapter argues that the Chinese yuan will not be able to act as key or anchor currency for an East Asian "yuan bloc" unless China overcomes the deficiencies in its domestic financial system, develops deep and liquid financial markets, and unless the yuan becomes fully convertible. Instead of focusing solely on China, Japan should be welcome and encouraged to play an important role in regional monetary integration for two reasons. First, Japan remains the region's most affluent economy with highly developed financial markets and extensive trade and investment linkages with the rest of the region. Japan would add considerable economic weight to East Asian monetary cooperation and thus increase its chances of success. Second, a regional exchange rate system built around China would inevitably exclude Japan, which would certainly not be willing to subordinate to Chinese leadership. From a security perspective an isolation of Japan within the region could be problematic as such a situation could give ground to future political tensions and maybe even conflict in the region. As the best way forward, the chapter thus recommends monetary cooperation within the ASEAN+3 framework.

Korea, which has amicable relations with both China and Japan, should actively try to promote monetary cooperation and integration within ASEAN+3 and encourage China and Japan to overcome their animosities. In such a constellation, Korea could assume the role of a mediator helping to bridge the differences between China and Japan on the one hand, as well as between the (economically) smaller ASEAN countries and the two Northeast Asian giants, China and Japan, on the other hand. Korea would not only benefit economically from such cooperation, it could also help to increase the regions', and hence also Korea's, security situation by fostering exchange and understanding between East Asian governments and by helping develop a regional financial framework that could support stability and prosperity.

Because monetary cooperation is a sensitive area tat requires strong commitment from all participating parties, as well as the willingness and ability to subordinate internal economic objectives under the objective of exchange rate stability, a gradual approach to monetary integration would be preferable. This would allow East Asian countries to get to know their potential partners more closely and work out along the way what could be feasible and what not. A first move could be the coordinated adoption of currency baskets across the region, flanked by a strengthening of financing facilities under the CMI and a further enhancement of regional surveillance mechanisms. Such currency baskets would not need to be identical (the existing trade patterns would suggest relatively similar basket weights for most countries anyway) from the start. With time, the composition of the baskets could be harmonized among East Asian countries. If further monetary integration is desired, exchange rate bands could be introduced, developing a more formal regional exchange rate system and maybe at some point even a monetary union.

Notes

1 See also Kim and Wang in Chapter 4 of this volume.
2 For convenience, except for the direction of trade analysis in the section entitled "The case for monetary integration among ASEAN+3", the rest of the chapter will count Hong Kong as a part of China and refer to ASEAN+3.
3 Based on multivariate OLS estimations with first differences of logarithms in the exchange rate as suggested by Frankel and Wei (1994) with daily exchange rates from 21 July 2005 to 24 April 2006. On 21 July 2005, the Chinese central bank officially announced that it had abandoned the eleven-year-old peg to the dollar and instead linked the yuan to an undisclosed basket of currencies. Changing the sample period does not alter the results.
4 The first three arguments are outlined in greater detail in Volz (2006b).
5 And, of course, the motivation for stabilizing the dollar exchange rate not only comes from the trade side but also from the financial side as will be discussed later.
6 Obviously, the larger a group of countries, the greater the volume of trade between them, and hence the greater the benefits of exchange rate stability.
7 See Fernández-Arias *et al.* (2004).
8 See, for instance, Rose (2002, 2004), Frankel and Rose (2002), and Nitsch (2002, 2004).
9 For an analysis of business networks in East Asia see Tachiki (2005) and Hamilton-Hart (2005).
10 Which is also the reason why monetary unification is particularly attractive to small economies.
11 There is also empirical support for this view. See Eichengreen *et al.* (2005).
12 In the European context, Giavazzi and Pagano (1988) have termed this the "advantage of tying one's hands".
13 Size alone, obviously, is not sufficient to establish an international currency. Argentina, Brazil, and Russia are examples of large emerging economies that,

despite their size, have faced problems of original sin. (Russia is now turning into a creditor country thanks to oil and gas revenues, but it is now facing problems of conflicted virtue.) But, as explained before, good domestic policies are necessary as well, and these three countries have not been prime examples for prudent economic policy-making.

14 Japan, however, never managed to establish the yen as the regional key currency for East Asia, despite attempts in the 1980s and 1990s to create a "yen bloc".

15 See Zhang and Liang (2006).

16 Frankel *et al.* (2004) and Chinn *et al.* (1993) similarly find that interest rates in European countries had become completely insensitive to US interest rates but fully sensitive to German interest rates.

17 The current voting rules are soon to be replaced by a rotating system to ensure efficient decision-making in the face of an increase of the Council's current size of 18 members to 30 or more in the process of euro area expansion. The new voting scheme will give more weight to the larger euro area economies. But, irrespective of the distribution of voting rights, the ECB statutes stipulate that national central bank governors sit on the Governing Council in a personal and independent capacity, not as representatives of their own countries.

18 The situation is different for the UK, where the Bank of England has managed to continue its independent monetary policy tailored to the national economy's needs. This can be attributed to the size of the UK's economy as well as its financial sector, which give it a greater pull compared with smaller economies like Denmark and Sweden.

19 Korea is restrained in its monetary policy autonomy because it cannot simply ignore the exchange rate policy of the other countries in the region with the effect that it also has to watch the won's external value, which, without capital controls, automatically implies a restraint on the central bank's ability to conduct autonomous monetary policy.

20 This is not inconsistent with Kim and Lee's (2004) finding that the sensitivity of local interest rates to US rates has declined for Korea and Thailand since they moved toward less rigid exchange rate regimes after the Asian crisis.

21 See also Calvo and Reinhart (2001 and 2002) and Fratzscher (2002).

22 One must note, however, that China has managed to sterilize the large increase of foreign reserve holdings very well and has thus been able to control inflation. The PBC has also made use of other monetary policy instruments, such as reserve requirements for domestic banks and credit ceilings. Since the October 2004 raise of benchmark rates, the PBC raised rates two more times (in April and August 2006), indicating a more active use of the interest rate instrument. On China's struggles to implement an independent monetary policy see also Goodfriend and Prasad (2006).

23 This does not imply, however, that there are *no* costs involved with abandoning the national currency. First, monetary union brings about the loss of the exchange rate as an instrument for coping with idiosyncratic shocks to the national economy. Second, there would still be the political cost of giving up formal monetary independence, i.e. the loss of monetary policy autonomy *illusion*. Furthermore, giving up *de jure* independence could involve diplomatic costs in the form of political dependency on foreign nations. Thirdly, the exit costs of a monetary union can be assumed to be much higher than those of exiting a conventional exchange rate peg.

24 On the advantages of multilateral monetary union over dollarization see Alexander and von Furstenberg (2000).

25 On the power structure within the EMU see Berger and De Haan (2002).

26 A NDF is similar to a traditional forward foreign exchange contract in that an agreement is made to buy or sell a specific amount of one currency in exchange

for another currency for settlement on a predetermined future date at a pre-agreed rate. The key difference is that the NDF is settled at maturity for the difference in the spot rate and the NDF rate in the hard currency only – typically US dollars. For an overview of NDFs see Lipscomb (2005).

References

Alexander, Volbert and George M. von Furstenberg (2000) "Monetary Integration – A Superior Alternative to Full Dollarization in the Long Run", *The North American Journal of Economics and Finance*, Vol. 11 (2), 205–25.

Balassa, Bela (1961) *The Theory of Economic Integration*, Homewood, IL: Richard Irwin.

Berger, Helge and Jacob De Haan (2002) "Are Small Countries Too Powerful Within the ECB?", *Atlantic Economic Journal*, Vol. 30 (3), 263–80.

Calvo, Guillermo A. and Carmen M. Reinhart (2001) "Fixing for Your Life", in Susan Collins and Dani Rodrik (eds), *Brookings Trade Forum 2000*, Brookings Institution, Washington, DC, 1–39.

Calvo, Guillermo A. and Carmen M. Reinhart (2002) "Fear of Floating", *Quarterly Journal of Economics*, Vol. 117 (2), 379–408.

Chinn, Menzie D., Jeffrey A. Frankel and Steve Philips (1993) "Financial and Currency Integration in the European Monetary System, The Statistical Record", in Francisco Torres and Francesco Giavazzi (eds), *Adjustment and Growth in the European Monetary Union*, Cambridge: Cambridge University Press, 270–306.

Cohen, Benjamin J. (1998) *The Geography of Money*, Ithaca, NY and London: Cornell University Press.

Cohen, Benjamin J. (2000) "Life at the Top, International Currencies in the Twenty-First Century", *Essays in International Economics*, No. 221, Princeton, NJ: Princeton University.

DeMartino, George and Ilene Grabel (2003) "Globalization, Regionalism and State Capacity in Developing Countries: A Note", in Philip Arestis, Michelle Baddeley and John McCombie (eds), *Globalisation, Regionalism and Economic Activity*, Cheltenham: Edward Elgar, 266–73.

Dieter, Heribert and Richard Higgot (2003) "Exploring Alternative Theories of Economic Regionalism. From Trade to Finance in Asian Co-operation?", *Review of International Political Economy*, Vol. 10 (3), 430–55.

Dowd, Kevin and David Greenaway (1993) "Currency Competition, Network Externalities and Switching Costs: Towards an Alternative View of Optimum Currency Areas", *The Economic Journal*, Vol. 103 (420), 1180–89.

Duisenberg, Wim (2005) "Europe, an Engine of Peace", http://www.project-syndicate.org/commentary/duisenberg2/English.

Edwards, Sebastian (1999) "How Effective are Capital Controls?", *Journal of Economic Perspectives*, Vol. 13 (4), 65–84.

Eichengreen, Barry (1998) "Does Mercosur Need a Single Currency?", *NBER Working Paper*, No. 6821, Cambridge, MA: National Bureau of Economic Research.

Eichengreen, Barry and Ricardo Hausmann (1999) "Exchange Rates and Financial Fragility", Proceedings, Federal Reserve Bank of Kansas City, August, 329–68.

Eichengreen, Barry, Ricardo Hausmann and Ugo Panizza (2005) "The Mystery of Original Sin", in Barry Eichengreen and Ricardo Hausmann (eds), *Other People's Money: Debt Denomination and Financial Instability in Emerging Market Economies*, Chicago, IL and London: University of Chicago Press, 233–65.

FT (2005) "China Warns Against Renminbi Revaluation", *Financial Times*, 14 March.
Frankel, Jeffrey and Shang-Jin Wei (1994) "Yen Bloc or Dollar Bloc? Exchange Rate Policies of the East Asian Economies", in Takatoshi Ito and Anne Krueger (eds), *Macroeconomic Linkages: Savings, Exchange Rates, and Capital Flows,* NBER East Asia Seminar on Economics, Volume 3, Chicago, IL and London: University of Chicago Press, 295–329.
Fratzscher, Marcel (2002) "The Euro Bloc, the Dollar Bloc, and the Yen Bloc: How Much Monetary Policy Independence can Exchange Rate Flexibility Buy in an Interdependent World?", *ECB Working Paper* No. 154, Frankfurt am Main: European Central Bank.
Fernández-Arias, Eduardo, Ugo Panizza and Ernesto Stein (2004) "Trade Agreements, Exchange Rate Disagreements", in Volbert Alexander, Jacques Mélitz and George M. von Furstenberg (eds), *Monetary Union and Hard Pegs. Effects on Trade, Financial Development, and Stability*, Oxford and New York: Oxford University Press, 135–50.
Frankel, Jeffrey A. and Andrew K. Rose (2002) "An Estimate of the Effect of Common Currencies on Trade and Income", *The Quarterly Journal of Economics*, Vol. 117 (2), 437–66.
Frankel, Jeffrey A., Sergio L. Schmukler and Luis Servén (2004) "Global Transmission of Interest Rates: Monetary Independence and Currency Regime", *Journal of International Money and Finance*, Vol. 23 (5), 701–33.
Giavazzi, Francesco and Marco Pagano (1988) "The Advantage of Tying One's Hands: EMS Discipline and Central Bank Credibility", *European Economic Review*, Vol. 32 (5), 1055–82.
Glick, Reuven and Andrew K. Rose (1999) "Contagion and Trade: Why Are Currency Crises Regional?", *Journal of International Money and Finance*, 18 (4), 603–17.
Goodfriend, Marvin and Eswar Prasad (2006) "A Framework for Independent Monetary Policy in China", IMF Working Paper, No. 06/111, International Monetary Fund, Washington, DC.
Hamada, Koichi and Inpyo Lee (2006) "International Political Conflicts and Economic Integration", *mimeo*, Yale University.
Hamilton-Hart, Natasha (2005) "The Regionalization of Southeast Asian Business: Transnational Networks in National Contexts", in T.J. Pempel (ed.), *Remapping East Asia. The Construction of a Region*, Ithaca, NY and London: Cornell University Press, 170–91.
Ho, Corinne, Guonan Ma and Robert N. McCauley (2005) "Trading Asian Currencies", *BIS Quarterly Review*, March, 49–58.
IMF (2005) *Annual Report on Exchange Arrangements and Exchange Restrictions*, International Monetary Fund, Washington, DC.
Jeanne, Olivier (2005) "Why Do Emerging Economies Borrow in Foreign Currency?", in Barry Eichengreen and Ricardo Hausmann (eds), *Other People's Money: Debt Denomination and Financial Instability in Emerging Market Economies*, Chicago, IL and London: University of Chicago Press, 190–217.
Kawai, Masahiro and Shujiro Urata (2004) "Trade and Foreign Direct Investment in East Asia", in Gordon de Brouwer and Masahiro Kawai (eds), *Exchange Rate Regimes in East Asia*, London and New York: Routledge, 15–102.
Kim, Chang-Jin and Jong-Wha Lee (2004) "Exchange Rate Regimes and Monetary Independence in East Asia", in Gordon de Brouwer and Masahiro Kawai (eds), *Exchange Rate Regimes in East Asia*, London and New York: Routledge, 302–19.

Lipscomb, Laura (2005) "An Overview on Non-Deliverable Foreign Exchange Forward Markets", Federal Reserve Bank of New York, New York.

Matsuyama, Kiminori, Nobuhiro Kiyotaki and Akihiko Matsui (1993) "Toward a Theory of International Currency", *Review of Economic Studies*, Vol. 60 (2), 283–307.

McKinnon, Ronald (2005) *Exchange Rates Under the East Asian Dollar Standard. Living With Conflicted Virtue*, Cambridge, MA and London: MIT Press.

Montiel, Peter J. (2004) "An Overview of Monetary and Financial Integration in East Asia", in, Asian Development Bank (ed.), *Monetary and Financial Integration in East Asia. The Way Ahead: Volume 2*, Houndmills: Palgrave Macmillan, 1–52.

Nitsch, Volker (2002) "Honey, I Shrunk the Currency Union Effect on Trade", *The World Economy*, Vol. 25 (4), 457–74.

Nitsch, Volker (2004) "Comparing Apples and Oranges: The Effect of Multilateral Currency Unions on Trade", in Volbert Alexander, Jacques Mélitz and George M. von Furstenberg (eds) *Monetary Union and Hard Pegs. Effects on Trade, Financial Development, and Stability*, Oxford and New York: Oxford University Press, 89–100.

Rose, Andrew K. (2002) "Honey, the Currency Union Effect on Trade Hasn't Blown Up", *The World Economy*, Vol. 25 (4), 475–79.

Rose, Andrew (2004) "The Effect of Common Currencies on International Trade: A Meta-Analysis", in Volbert Alexander, Jacques Mélitz and George M. von Furstenberg (eds), *Monetary Union and Hard Pegs. Effects on Trade, Financial Development, and Stability*, Oxford and New York: Oxford University Press, 101–12.

Tachiki, Dennis (2005) "Between Foreign Direct Investment and Regionalism: The Role of Japanese Production Networks", in T.J. Pempel (ed.), *Remapping East Asia. The Construction of a Region*, Ithaca, NY and London: Cornell University Press, 149–69

Volz, Ulrich (2006a) "On the Feasibility of a Regional Exchange Rate System for East Asia: Lessons of the 1992/93 ERM Crisis", *MacMillan Center Working Paper FOX-03*, New Haven, CT: Yale University.

Volz, Ulrich (2006b) "Three Cases for Monetary Integration in East Asia", *MacMillan Center Working Paper FOX-04*, New Haven, CT: Yale University.

Williamson, John (1999) "The Case for a Common Basket Peg for East Asian Currencies", in: Stefan Collignon, Jean Pisani-Ferry and Yung Chul Park (eds), *Exchange Rate Policies in Emerging Asian Countries*, London: Routledge, 327–43.

Williamson, John (2005) "A Basket Numeraire for East Asia?", *Policy Briefs in International Economics*, No. 05–1, Institute of International Economics, Washington, DC.

Zhang Jikang and Liang Yuanyuan (2007) "Institutional and Structural Problems of China's Foreign Exchange Market and the Renminbi's Role in East Asia", forthcoming in Koichi Hamada, Beate Reszat and Ulrich Volz (eds) *Prospects for Monetary and Financial Integration in East Asia: Dreams and Dilemmas*, Cambridge, MA: MIT Press.

Part II
A new regional policy for Korea

6 Korea's contribution to the emerging regional architecture

An assessment

Jaewoo Choo[1] and Sophie Boisseau du Rocher

Introduction

South Korea's involvement in East Asian regionalism is a recent phenomenon, a trend that began some fifteen years ago. During the Cold War years, Seoul's diplomacy was marked by the "special relationship" it developed with Washington after the Korean War and the division of the country. These extensive and intense ties, based on an economic, political and strategic tripod, allowed South Korea to achieve unprecedented growth and to become an industrialized country by the late 1980s. This remarkable economic modernization process eventually generated some political consequences that are difficult to ignore in the contemporary studies of Asian democracy and therefore, affected its regional vision and contribution. Since its successful adoption of western democracy in 1987, Korea has become an appropriate model for the study of the links between economic development and political democratization. In addition, its case is widely adopted by those who want to emulate what Korea has achieved in its international socialization process based on economic and political success, including its membership of the United Nations (1991), the WTO (1994), and the OECD (1996).

Beginning in the mid-1990s, Korea's internationalization effort underwent a major shift in its orientation. In response to rising regionalization and growing interdependence within East Asia, Korea began to follow a two-pronged approach: First, to stabilize its own security environment and, second, to optimize economic opportunities in the surrounding region. At the time when there was a growing consensus within the international community that the new millennium would be the era of East Asia, Korea pro-actively promoted the idea of regionalization. Despite the past history of Japanese imperialism that is still regarded as a major impediment to regionalization, Korea once seemed to be capable of playing an intermediary role in bringing China and Japan together. While Korea, perhaps for the last time during the turn of the last century, enjoyed the highest leverage over China for its economic advantage, it also had a strong political relationship with Japan. Throughout the 1990s, it also developed a consistent partnership with ASEAN which highlights Korea's active search for closer regional cooperation.

In the twenty-first century, East Asia began to witness a substantial change in the existing power configuration, due to the fundamental changes in the international profiles of the respective East Asian states. The rise of China is certainly the most noticeable change of parameter that has profoundly affected the whole regional balance. Already a military and political powerhouse to begin with, astonishing economic achievements as a result of reforms and the open-door policy have allowed China to reach a position unattained by any of East Asia's other states. Managing (or even impacting) China is unthinkable, at least, by neighbouring states without external assistance, such as from the United States.

At the same time, because of its slow economic recovery and diplomatic awkwardness, Japan has further distanced itself from other regional players, as witnessed in its *de facto* loss of influence in building an East Asian community. Furthermore, tensions and conflicts between Japan and China seem to have intensified in recent times in many areas, such as Japan's quest for a permanent seat on the UN Security Council and its publication of purportedly distorted history textbooks, coupled with Prime Minister Junichiro Koizumi's repeated visits to the Yasukuni Shrine. By the same token, Chinese nuclear submarines' intrusion into Japanese waters and its unilateral drilling in the disputed territory of *Diaoyu-dao* (*Senkaku* island in Japanese) have alarmed a Japan fearful of China's rise. The paradoxical nature of the Sino-Japanese relationship (a dynamic economic relationship within a strained political one) and frequent recourse to nationalist resentment are capable of challenging and even threatening peace and stability in the region, as well as undermining the possibility of East Asian regional integration.

Nonetheless, hopes for community building in East Asia are not totally dead as new initiatives have recently been put forward, with the result that East Asian regionalism is purportedly moving beyond the economic sphere and is expanding both in terms of its geography and also its agenda. Growing interdependence and tightening financial links are not sufficient incentives to precipitate this regionalization effort. China has taken the initiative in this area, with Japan trying to react and follow.[2] Beijing is increasingly driving East Asia's agenda. In collaboration with the Malay government, China's suggestion to extend an invitation to India, New Zealand, and Australia while excluding the United States from the inaugural meeting of the East Asian Summit (EAS) held in November 2005 in Malaysia was overwhelmingly accepted by the member states of ASEAN+3 (APT), mirroring China's growing influence over East Asia's newly emerging regional architecture. The EAS is expected to replace APT in the coming years, thereby offering a new paradigm for East Asian regionalism. Being reckoned as the main architect of growing East Asian regionalism will only strengthen the international profile and influence of China as a regional, if not a global, power.

In this new paradigm, a few concerns naturally arise for Korea. China's growing influence, coupled with rising tension with Japan, is undermining Korea's role in the "new East Asian game". There are also claims by observers of East Asian affairs that, with China, Japan, Australia, and India on top, Korea may drop to second-tier status in this new game. In other words, Korea is at a critical juncture with respect to its regional position and strategy. This chapter attempts to examine the newly arising concept of East Asian regionalism in the context of the EAS and Korea's potential role in order to assess its possible contribution to the new paradigm. To substantiate the prospect of the EAS as a prelude to an East Asian Community and a substitute for APT or ASEAN+1, it will address the historical background behind the rise of this new concept. In this framework of analysis, the chapter will conclude by assessing potential challenges that new East Asian regionalism might pose to South Korea and by suggesting policy guidelines appropriate for the new paradigm.

South Korea's involvement in East Asia

What is ironic about South Korea's diplomatic initiatives in East Asia is that they took shape only after the country experienced fundamental changes in the domestic and foreign settings. From a domestic perspective, in 1987 Korea was finally able democratically to elect its own president after decades of authoritarian military rule starting in the early 1960s. Democratization in Korean politics had a profound effect, not only on Korea's domestic political structure and system, but also on its foreign policy. To some degree, it enabled the democratically elected leader Roh Tae Woo to pursue a much more independent policy based on national interests. In addition, in the midst of former President Roh's term (1988–92), the Berlin Wall tumbled and the Cold War came to an end. These developments led to the government's displacement of ideology as the judgmental yardstick in the decision-making process of foreign policy. The result was the adoption of the so-called "Northern diplomacy".

While the ultimate idea of Northern diplomacy was conceptualized on the hope that the normalization of relations with former socialist and communist states and their subsequent pressure on North Korea could enhance the prospects for peace and unification of the Korean Peninsula, the policy was broader. It strived to enhance national security, economic interests, and the nation's international status, as well as to seek other viable routes to unification. In other words, it was a policy with a focus on creating a much more favourable international environment for unification. Thus, it can safely be said to be the first Korean foreign policy with an outward looking vision and an autonomous orientation for national interests, thereby laying a solid foundation for successive governments to engage in regional and international diplomacy in a much more profound and autonomous way.

If the legacy of the Roh Tae Woo government's Northern policy was the enhancement of manoeuvrability for Korean foreign policy in the coming years as a result of improved ties with the surrounding states like China and Russia in particular, the aim of the foreign policy of Kim Yong Sam's government was to seize the opportunity created by such a legacy. Kim's government, adopting the so-called "New diplomacy", launched a foreign policy with a mission to enhance Korea's international profile and its leadership in Northeast Asia. The New diplomacy was based on the following five strategic pillars: (1) globalization; (2) diversification of relationships; (3) a pluralist approach to national interest; (4) regional cooperation; and (5) a forward-looking orientation. As such, it was the first time in Korean diplomatic history that its foreign policy was both regionally focussed and strategic in the sense of promoting regional cooperation. In other words, the New diplomacy was a response to the changing international structure and regional institutions in the aftermath of the Cold War.

The end of the Cold War was perceived by the Kim government as an opportunity to expand Korea's interests and attention in international relations. It shifted the focus of foreign policy away from security issues to such universal human values as democracy, liberty, freedom, welfare, human rights and the like. It also allowed the Korean Government to capitalize on the rise of pluralism in terms of international actors, such as individuals, NGOs, international and governmental organizations, reviving the importance of once forgotten civilian diplomacy. Furthermore, with a dramatic rise in the number of interregional and intraregional organizations, Kim's Government, convinced of their potential contribution to peace and stability on the peninsula, proactively participated in such organizations as APEC, ARF, Uruguay Round Negotiations and others. At the same time, it also sought ways to induce North Korea's participation.

These efforts at regional diplomacy failed to reach their goals as a result of the outbreak of the first North Korean nuclear crisis. The crisis impeded the government's efforts towards regionalism based on cooperation as it raised conflicts with the United States to the extent that it prevented the South from expanding the scope of its foreign policy beyond the peninsula. While the Kim government's intention behind the New diplomacy was to develop relations with Southeast Asia, then European Union, the Middle East, South America, and Africa, it ultimately did not go beyond the basic framework of Korea–US alliance relations. In other words, Korea's foreign policy objectives were polarized by the bilateral alliance, with the underlying implication that the security interests of the two nations came first.

Despite the constraints stemming from the military alliance with the United States, the Kim government was still able to achieve some landmarks in Korean foreign relations history, i.e. accession to membership in the OECD, the WTO, the UN Security Council, and the UN Economic and Social Council and Maritime Court, as well as the collaborative launching and subsequent hosting of the ASEM Conference. Korea's regional engagement efforts eventually proved to be very costly. After five years of globalization and regionalization initiatives, Korea's trade deficit reached $20 billion, doubling that of the previous year, and its foreign debt rose to $100 billion, exposing the country to the influence of the Asian financial crisis in 1997. Nonetheless, Korea, for the first time during Kim's era, elaborated its foreign policy interests in the context of regionalization and regional cooperation.

The 1997 Asian financial crisis proved the extent of Asian economies' interdependence, as opposed to – as most claim – the vulnerability exposed by lack of cooperative institutions and regional mechanisms. This growing regional interdependence underscored the rising importance of 'geographic proximity and the relationship between economic flows and policy choices'[3] within the region. In other words, Korea, like other victims of the crisis, had to adapt itself to the changing concept of regional economic interdependence, shifting from a deepening of regional economic flows to the necessity of political collaboration as an economic safety net.[4] Under the circumstances, on the occasion of the first meeting of the heads of ASEAN states and three Northeast Asian states in 1998, the crisis-stricken nations called for a regional arrangement that could possibly prevent the recurrence of a similar crisis. Many ideas such as the establishment of an Asian Monetary Fund, currency warning and swap systems, and others, all sprouted in the aftermath of the crisis. However, because of US disapproval, and to a certain extent opposition, some of these ideas ended in mere talks, and some were not even discussed.[5]

Instead, East Asian governments seemingly resigned themselves to what Mansfield and Milner (1999) called "commercial regionalism",[6] largely due to their rising resentment at Western responses to the crisis, by making steadfast efforts to promote political and economic arrangements at the regional level. They began to negotiate preferential trade agreements with each other, with a desire to discriminate against others who once opposed the region's blueprints for monetary and financial institutions. They have also undertaken sub-regional trade liberalization and various forms of cooperation in the monetary field as a result of their realization – born of the traumatic experience of the crisis – of their deepening economic interdependence.

The impact of the crisis on East Asian regionalism was twofold. While it strengthened the existing shared-identity that was first fostered by the end of the Cold War as to an "us vs. them" mentality,[7] it also induced East Asian governments to take a further interest in the idea of regionalism. Enlightened interest in regionalism also led governments to consider the importance of their domestic political and economic conditions. More transparent and systematic political and economic institutions became a highly demanded commodity. As a result in Korea, the preferences and political influence of domestic groups began to undergo a significant change. Beginning with Kim Dae Jung, consensus-based politics and the ensuing rise in the number of NGOs in Korean society have allowed heterogeneity to blossom fully in the nation's politics and economics.[8] Although this trend was not necessarily driven by a desire to undermine the authority of the National Assembly, it did prevent its unilateral way of making decisions. In other words, the rights of the people were much more established. Checks and balances began to operate in full fashion beginning in this period.

As the scale of Korea's export-oriented economy continues to expand in a pervasive fashion in the twenty-first century, Kenneth A. Oye argues that Korea has striven hard for regional liberalization in the face of strong domestic opposition. Although it is extremely difficult to quantify how much exporters preferred regional arrangements and PTAs as a way of discriminating against other international competitors, it certainly worked in favour of the interests of legislators and their supporting interest groups that regional arrangements offered greater gains than multilateral openness. After the humiliations of the 1997 financial crisis, which depleted the nation's foreign reserves, Korea immediately realized that the fate of its economy was beyond its own control and was already subject to regional developments. This realization had a great impact on societal actors with respect to trade policy and dictated Korean preferences, thus allowing the government to embark on regional trade initiatives.[9]

The dynamics of international politics have also generated a significant impact on Korea in terms of embracing regionalism and multilateral openness. Contrary to the old thinking on the need for a hegemon in order to maintain the stability of the international economy, the financial crisis exposed the incapability and sheer unwillingness by such a hegemonic power to adopt and implement sufficient measures at the outset of the crisis.[10] While the controversial debate on the lack of an immediate response from such a power continues inconclusively to date, the crisis-hit nations nevertheless share a general sense of untrustworthiness and disloyalty toward the United States.

Under the circumstances, the Kim Dae Jung government had to become proactive and vigorous in pursuit of regionalism as one of the viable measures to consolidate, if not create, peace and stability in East Asia. This vision was reinforced by the guidelines in the mission statement of the East Asian Vision Group (EAVG) in 1999. The Group made breathtaking progress with subsequent meetings in the next four years, during which the working group level meeting of East Asian Studies Group (EASG) was founded in 2000.[11] Complemented by the Studies Group's findings, the EAVG was able to put forward some action plans and feasible policy guidelines in an effort to lay the foundation for regionalism. As the two groups were generally regarded as being under the leadership and generous support of Kim Dae Jung's government, when the government fell in the trauma following the nuclear crisis, it literally became unable to carry out any of the action plans, not to mention its wishful thinking depicted in the mission statement.

China's rise and East Asian regionalism: ASEAN way vs. Chinese leadership

China's economic achievement continues to draw the world's attention. In addition to being the world's sixth largest economy (in terms of GDP), China surpassed Japan to become the third largest trading nation in the world in 2004. Backed by a large trade surplus and a continuing high economic growth rate, Chinese military spending is only second to that of the United States. Even if its military capability can still not be compared to that of the United States or even Japan, China plays on its potential influence and capacity to have an impact on regional stability and peace. Through a combination of economic dynamism, skilful diplomacy, and understated threat, China is shaping East Asia's future and is setting the pace of the proposed evolution: others have to adjust.[12]

These developments in Chinese multilateral diplomacy were possible for a couple of reasons. One can be attributed to its rising influence over the surrounding region due to its economic success. Growing interdependence with regional partners and the extension of its soft power are paying dividends. On these grounds, Asian economies are more dependent on Chinese dynamics and potential. With an average growth rate of 20 per cent since 1990, ASEAN–China trade totalled $105.8 billion in 2004, making ASEAN China's fourth largest trading partner. Replacing the United States, China in 2004 became Korea's largest trade partner. Beijing does not restrict its policy to "economics only" but plays very softly on its "soft power" capacity.

The second factor can be explained by China's successful exploitation of the US preoccupation with the war on terrorism and, therefore, on a growing regional scepticism over its strategic capacity to manage regional affairs. Ever since 9/11, the United States has not been able to spare its attention and efforts sufficiently to safeguard its national interests in East Asia as it did previously. Although there are some claims that the United States has successfully manipulated the international nature of the war on terrorism to permeate its influence and presence in China's neighbouring regions – further advancing its encirclement policy – its unilateral way of handling terrorism and managing Muslim issues has undermined its position in these regions and put a strain on its relations with local societies.

Amidst all this, East Asia is beginning to witness growing Chinese influence and ascending cultural assertiveness as a result of its burgeoning economy. The consequences of China's growing influence, whether intentional or not, are now mirrored in its active pursuit of regional diplomacy, or "good-neighbour policy" (*shanlin youhao zhengce*). Chinese emphasis on the importance of maintaining a friendly relationship with neighbouring states underlies its belief that international peace and stability will determine the fate of its economic modernization and socio-political stability. China can thus not afford any instability at its frontiers. Accordingly, it has been active in searching for peaceful solutions for any and all kinds of international conflicts of interest to facilitate its quest for development by continuously engaging itself in both bilateral and multilateral diplomacy.

From 1997, after it unveiled the "New Security Concept" (*xinanquanguan*) which emphasized the basic principles of its external policy, China has been trying to solidify its position by putting aside differences and building common grounds with its regional partners for common interest and mutual benefit. According to Robert Sutter, Beijing seeks "long-term gains" by: (1) securing its environment at a time when sustaining its economic development is the priority; (2) promoting partnerships that can assist its development; and (3) boosting its regional and international power and influence.[13]

Ever since its participation as an observer at the first ASEAN Regional Forum (ARF) in 1994, China's scepticism about multilateralism began gradually to dissolve. With the ARF, China has "engaged" to join the first regional Asia-Pacific multilateral security institution[14] and has become very active in either Track I or Track II. China has successfully transformed itself into a magnificent conductor of multilateralism and multilateral diplomacy. With the successful launch of the Shanghai-Five in 1996, which would later become the Shanghai Cooperation Organization (SCO) in 2001, China has been proactively pursuing multilateral diplomacy as a viable means of maintaining friendly relations with neighbouring regions and states. Cooperative multilateralism is now perceived by Beijing as one of the most effective diplomatic tools in preventing and managing international conflicts. China's perceptions and policies toward multilateral institutions continue to evolve significantly, from caution and suspicion to optimism and enthusiasm.[15]

Given Chinese acknowledgement of the effectiveness of multilateralism on the integration process and the importance ASEAN has gained through its thirty years of existence as the only regional institution in East Asia, China decided to employ a constructive diplomatic tactic in its approach to Southeast Asia by initiating the so-called "ASEAN+1 Free Trade Area (FTA)" as early as November 2000.[16] This tactic had the immediate advantage of positioning ASEAN as a long-term partner for China, thus illustrating China's goodwill towards ASEAN and its intention to convince ASEAN members that "a prosperous China is an opportunity rather than a challenge to ASEAN". Consequently, the first China–ASEAN Exposition was launched in 2004, an annual event to bring together enterprises from China and ASEAN. China's accession to the ASEAN Treaty of Amity and Cooperation (TAC) in 2004 completed this strategy to highlight the peaceful nature of its rise. Even, at the eleventh China-ASEAN Senior Officials Consultation, the implementation of a joint declaration for advancing a China/ASEAN Strategic Partnership was discussed and formalized in August 2003. China reiterated its willingness to join in the protocol of the Southeast Asia Nuclear Weapons-free Zone Treaty. Certain observers are dubious about such a rapprochement and assert that ASEAN will soon need other regional partners, such as Korea and Japan, to balance against the precarious ascent of China.

In Northeast Asia, in the wake of the second North Korean nuclear crisis in 2002, China played an intermediary role between the United States and North Korea, and succeeded in organizing the Six-party talks, a formula perceived by the international community as the best possible measure for a peaceful solution of the crisis. It has now made its desire to institutionalize the talks known to the world on a few occasions.[17] Beijing's rationale behind institutionalization draws on its previous success with the SCO and its current pursuit of ASEAN+1. It also has high expectations for the potential institutionalization of the talks based on the fact that they represent the first time when all six regional states congregated for security reasons. For the talks to be a success, it posits that any form of resolution would have to be legally effective, implying that commitments by the six parties be based on legal terms. Provided that all parties persevere in their efforts to uphold the talks, China's insistence on institutionalization is not unrealistic and may have to be realized.

China's economic and cultural resurgence, coupled with mitigated anti-American sentiments and the necessity to restructure regional ties to avoid the "contagion effect" of the 1997 crisis partly explain the search for a new regional setting.[18] In the current negotiations process, options are open. Old rules are challenged and previous modes of cooperation cannot be maintained. East Asia is undergoing a major evolution but without a clear direction. This push is currently generating a serious challenge to the fundamental ideology of regional integration in East Asia. Who and what country is going to put its footprint on the East Asian Community? Once acknowledged as a formidable principle,[19] the so-called "ASEAN way" could be on the verge of being replaced by what this chapter would label as "Chinese leadership" as Chinese power continues to ascend.[20]

The "ASEAN way" proved to be a vulnerable concept when exposed to international turbulence such as the 1997 financial crisis.[21] The incapacity of regional governments to counteract the crisis and organize common solutions forced them to seek external assistance, such as international help from the International Monetary Fund (IMF) and other groups (such as the Paris Club). In the end, national solutions prevailed. The crisis also compelled the Northeast Asian states to realize the degree of their economic interdependence with their counterparts in Southeast Asia, thereby forcing them to recognize that much closer financial and economic coordination was in serious demand.[22] Furthermore, it was an occasion for these states to recognize China's growing role in regional affairs, despite the previous Japanese *de facto* leadership.[23] The changing international structure and leadership in the wake of the crisis led regional states to realize the necessity to build a cooperative framework, namely APT.

What happened between 1997 and 2004 is very interesting and will be remembered as a period of "a great leap forward" for East Asian regionalism.

Four steps particularly stood out: (1) the emergence of China as a "responsible power" in the region after 1997; (2) the infamous relative neglect of its partners by the United States after the economic crisis; (3) the reorganization of economic (industrial, trade, and financial) networks fuelled by entrepreneurial energy and their loose orbit around the Chinese potential; (4) the diplomatic exploitation of these interdependencies by Beijing. As a result, eight years later, East Asia does not have the same appearance, the same balance of power, the same network of alliances to propel a new regional organization. South Korea, once a close ally of Washington, is now pondering the benefit of distancing itself somewhat from its old ally to move closer to its regional partners. ASEAN, once in turbulence, is now courted by its neighbours. India, once considered as an external partner, has been propelled into the regional game as a counterweight to China.

Changes are coming very fast. Seven years after the launching of the APT formula and without much success, negotiations convened in November 2004 at the eighth APT Summit meeting in Laos in an attempt to seek an alternative to APT. Although at the summit, regional states were able to generate a chairman's statement to strengthen APT, they simultaneously succeeded in reaching a consensus on inaugurating an "East Asian Summit" (EAS) in December 2005 in Kuala Lumpur. As the EAS was proposed by China (enriching an earlier proposal by Malaysian ex-Prime Minister Mohammad Mahathir), the intention and purposes of the EAS should be understood as a new "Asian approach" for the management of regional relations, inspired mostly by Chinese leadership. The purpose is to achieve a greater integration of ASEAN with China and India, Australia, and New Zealand. The inclusion of the Oceanic states in particular is of political significance since it could fend off discriminatory and antagonistic criticism of "racial issues" for the EAS' exclusive pursuit of the Asian way and the intended exclusion of the United States in its approach to regionalism.[24]

From the current membership perspective, the geographical range of East Asian regionalism seems to have naturally expanded to South Asia (India), Southeast Asia, Northeast Asia, and Oceania. Thus, the intention is easily perceived to have political, if not symbolic, implications against the current world trend of regionalization and the formation of regional blocs elsewhere: to strengthen the region's position against the deepening regionalization in other areas, such as America with its aspiration for Free Trade Area of the Americas (FTAA) taking root and the European Union with its enlargement. The scope of the agenda is not expected to be limited to economic issues such as trade and investment. As restated by Filipino president Gloria Macapagal-Arroyo, the EAS should be able "to hold its own agenda" following the declaration. It intends to include issues ranging from security to joint energy development in particular. It is expected to forge a longer-term Asian economic, social, cultural, and political community so as to "balance" the United States, Europe, and other groupings in the future.

According to Eric Teo Chu Cheow, optimism for the prospect of the EAS can be expected from the following developments in the region:

1 Beijing and New Delhi's growing importance to ASEAN was officially acknowledged at summit level for the first time at the 2004 APT Summit.[25]
2 A notable development is ASEAN's decision to speed up its own economic linkages in setting up an ASEAN Economic Community (EAC).
3 Although it was participating for the first time, India was officially inducted into the Asian economic integration process.
4 Sub-regional or pre-summit meetings were held by the poorest four ASEAN countries just before the main summit and participants pledged to work together to narrow their wealth gap with the six "older" members; they also pledged to move quickly to integrate their four economies so as better to attract foreign investment.
5 ASEAN invited for the first time Australia and New Zealand to the EAS, as it prepares to begin negotiating FTAs with both Canberra and Wellington in 2006.[26]

Based on these observations, China's leadership in the EAS is self-evident. A crucial decision taken was to organize an EAS in Kuala Lumpur in 2005, when Malaysia took over the chairmanship of ASEAN. It is already understood that the inaugural EAS in Malaysia will be followed by a second Summit to be held in China, thereby placing Beijing within the fundamental "core group" of the East Asian integration process. By hosting the second EAS in 2006, it could then affirm the group's agenda, scope, and goals in a more decisive way.[27]

Not everything is settled. First, there are differences of opinion among ASEAN members in fleshing out details of the EAS, notably the issue of membership. Second, the modalities of organization are still not defined. Japan has pressed for a system of co-chairmanship (with the chair rotating between an ASEAN and a non-ASEAN country); it has also proposed a "tiered" system consisting of an inner core of APT, a second tier of relations and cooperation with extra-regional players like India, Australia, and New-Zealand, and a third with the United States (Tokyo is suspected of doing all it can to keep Washington in the regional game, thus widening the gap with its partners). On this special proposal, ASEAN is divided, with some members refusing that non-regional members be allowed to join this club. Some participants suggest that everybody put some order in their own house, such as by consolidating ASEAN in Southeast Asia, and by slowing down Sino-Japanese rivalry in Northeast Asia. Third, because participants do not agree on the issues to be discussed, Japan and South Korea, supported by some countries like Thailand or the Philippines, are likely to raise issues related to democracy, human rights, good governance and the powers and duties of a regional institution while some others would prefer to focus on economic and trade issues which are apparently less controversial.

Nonetheless, China's aspiration to be the leader of the EAS will not go unnoticed in the near future. It will continue to rely on all diplomatic means to achieve this end. Its diplomatic tack on ASEAN, India, and others will continue. In other words, China intends to pursue a more active diplomacy around its southern periphery in Southeast Asia. A $400 million soft loan, for instance, was promised by China as a result of Hu Jintao's summit meeting with Filipino President Gloria Macapagal Arroyo in Manila in April 2005. It will be used to build a rail link between Manila and a former US airbase, Clark, prompting Manila to conclude a defence cooperation pact with China.[28]

In the following month when Hu Jintao paid a reciprocal visit to Manila, the two nations agreed to pursue joint energy cooperation around the Spratley islands, which drew fierce opposition from the Vietnamese government because of unsettled sovereignty rights over the area. However, Vietnam eventually decided in November to join the project with China and the Philippines. Chinese investments in Indonesian oil, gas, and power plants will certainly increase with the incoming Yudhoyono administration. Thailand and China are in pursuit of an "early harvest" agreement that was offered by China the year before on fruit and vegetables, a step that is regarded as critical towards realizing an FTA between ASEAN and China.

South Korea's possible contribution to the emerging regional architecture

There are many ways to achieve regionalism in East Asia. According to Donald K. Emmerson, there are five general approaches and featured themes that could be formulated based on existing schools of thought in the realm of international relations: realism (insecurity), culturalism (identity), rationalism (interests), liberalism (institutions) and constructivism (ideas).[29] These approaches are valid in the current setting of East Asian regionalism as highlighted in the previous section, but they leave aside the question of how a state as an individual actor can contribute to achieving regionalism. They rather explain how concerted efforts by these individual states to further regionalism play out as a result of evolving perceptions, calculations, and judgments of the circumstances in which states are forced, voluntarily or involuntarily, to accept the necessity to regionalize their political and economic interests. In other words, these approaches tend to go beyond explanations at the individual level.

States as individuals pursue regionalization and regionalism for the following reasons. First of all, from a purely economic perspective, there is a growing consensus on the need for regionalism, with a particular emphasis on the value of institutionalism as a result of ever-deepening interdependency. Thus, states are naturally drawn to the idea that regional institutions will foster economic openness and bolster the multilateral trade system, with positive economic effects.[30] Secondly, states decide to participate in regionalism largely as a result of domestic political developments. Whether states choose to enter regional trade arrangements and the economic effects of these arrangements depend on the preferences of national policy makers and interest groups, as well as on the nature and strength of domestic institutions. So domestic politics and systems do matter.[31] Thirdly, their decision is also subject to how they perceive the way power relations and multilateral institutions affect the formation of regional institutions, i.e. the particular states composing them and their welfare implications.[32]

To account for the role of individual states in shaping regionalism, some of the behavioural characteristics of the state as an international actor should be considered. One important characteristic is leadership, as seen within the integrative process of East Asian regionalism. Its long absence not only hindered the process but also prevented institution building, since leadership and institutional bargaining are two critical factors in the success of the process.[33] In addition, leadership is particularly important for a state like Korea, squeezed between a continental power (China) and a maritime one (Japan), with sufficient power to have a disruptive, if not changing, impact on the international system, and with a foreign policy tending to display a strong propensity towards "stabilizing and legitimizing the global order through multilateral and cooperative initiatives".[34]

Considering Korea's capabilities, it should be best regarded as a middle power not a small one. According to Mares' definition in the context of capabilities, "Middle powers have enough resources so that in an alliance with a small enough number of other states they are not merely 'price takers,' they can affect the system".[35] In contrast to the traditional definition, Korea shares the distinct characteristics of an emerging middle power as defined by Jordaan:

> [Korea is one of those] semi-peripheral, materially inegalitarian and recently democratized states that demonstrate much regional influence and self-association. Behaviourally, [it] opt[s] for reformist and not radical global change, exhibit[s] a strong regional orientation favouring regional integration but seek[s] also to construct identities distinct from those of the weak states in their region.[36]

Korea is therefore an emerging middle power, not a secondary power that can disrupt the international system via unilateral means or a small power whose influence is stipulated by the number of alliances.[37] In other words, theoretically speaking, Korea has fulfilled all the criteria of middle power status: economically successful, democratic, and with a highly respected foreign policy with a strong regional orientation. But it has yet to succeed in asserting itself as a middle power in the current regional process, especially since 1997. Thus, a critical question naturally arises with respect to

Korea's status as a middle power: What constrains Korea from fully prac-
tising middle-power diplomacy or displaying middle-power leadership? The
answer to this question may still have to be inferred from Korea's failure to
assume the so-called "middle-power leadership". Regardless of the size of
the state, successful international leadership can be judged by whether a
state succeeds in advancing the common interest of a group of states, since
international leadership is exercised in a different setting (anarchical space),
and by different means (persuasion), for different motivations (self-interest)
and on a different basis (moral justification).[38]

Korea's leadership as a middle power, therefore, would have to be
judged based on whether or not it has successfully advanced the common
interest of a group of states. In the context of pushing forward regional
integration, there are a few common interests that can be facilitated by
successful international leadership. These interests range from consensus
building to identity building, from confidence building to institutional
building, and from peace and stability to development and prosperity. To
advance these interests in the region, structural leadership based on
national power must come into full play, with an implication that such leadership must come from leading states. However, such leadership in East
Asia has been rare between two antagonistic and archrival states (China
and Japan), leaving Korea to seek other ways to overcome this crucial
factor.[39]

Korea has not been able to fulfil these expectations for several reasons.
First, rivalry between China and Japan is too overwhelming for Korea to
influence by itself. China and Japan are too powerful for Korea to handle
alone. In addition, recent attitudes and behaviour by both the Chinese
public and officials have not been helpful, in spite of their shared antagonism towards the Koizumi government. Second, distrust vis-à-vis Japan still
prevails to date. Japan's unwillingness fully to recognize its past wrongdoings, both in text form (as in history text book) and in behavioural form
(apology) as demanded by the victims of its imperialism and militarism only
dampens any prospects for confidence building.

Third, Korea's inability to match the capabilities and power of China
and Japan to facilitate cooperation between them fails to meet the fundamental precondition of international cooperation theory.[40] According to
this theory, in order for Korea to foster cooperation by amending the differences between the two regional powers, it must be more powerful. Such a
role has been, and is, only viable with the collaboration and cooperation
of the United States under the current power configuration. However,
South Korea's relations with the United States have gone sour in recent
years. Finally, Korea's preoccupation with national security concerns in
its foreign policy remains a major obstacle to the further pursuit of its
potential international leadership as demonstrated by the outbreak of the
two nuclear crises. As mentioned before, a sudden outbreak of international conflict in the Korean Peninsula has always had a detrimental impact

on South Korea's foreign policy pursuits. Two North Korean nuclear crises indeed have adversely affected its regionalization efforts.

Under these circumstances, it might be best for Korea to utilize its status as a middle power and the external structure of its international surroundings by seeking collaboration and cooperation from other possible middle power states in the region. In other words, Korea has actively to pursue a constructive approach in its relations with other regional players even if these were not previously highly respected by Korea. These states might include those in Southeast Asia, and to a certain extent, Oceania and South Asia as a result of their inclusion in the newly conceptualized East Asian regionalism. It will be a daunting challenge to the South Korean government, which has not realized the importance of relationships with them in the past. It would be certainly difficult to expect an immediate outcome from whatever initiatives South Korea undertakes in this area.

South Korea must first subscribe to many of the principles underlying ASEAN.[41] To a certain degree, it tends to share a similar identity since the launching of APT. It also seems to have adjusted to the idea of the benefits of cooperation based on multilateralism and regionalism since the 1997 financial crisis as reflected in its role in promoting the EAVG and EASG. Nonetheless, Korea was not very pragmatic and constructive in its approach, for instance, to the ASEAN states. Besides its participation in multilateral fora such as APT and ARF, it has not actively built relationships with them. In the economic realm, for instance, Korea's trade volume with ASEAN is rather marginal.[42] Moreover, in the political realm, high-level diplomacy including summit meetings is rarely conducted.

South Korea's potential contribution to the regional process in East Asia can only be maximized if and when it places greater value on relations with the Southeast Asian states. Stuck between two large giants like China and Japan, as long as their rivalry remains intact, other mediating forces need to come into play to harmonize them. The only viable precondition in this setting will be the determination and will of the other regional players. This is where Korea can make a positive contribution to East Asian regionalism. While the Southeast Asian states may feel they have a shared identity and vision on regionalism, they lack confidence and trust to convey their feeling to others. In this sense, Korea should team up with them not only as a middle power similar to their status, but also as an external assurance on the righteousness of their belief in regionalism. Korea's connection with ASEAN would also help it to acquire a greater sense of security and confidence in its pursuit of regionalism.

Another possible Korean contribution lies in democracy. Korea is regarded as one of the most democratic states in East Asia. For East Asian regionalism to become an effective organ, it would have to be institutionalized and based on democratic norms and values. While regional states have experience with other international institutions, it would be an immediate challenge as to how much of democratic values and norms they are willing to reflect in institutionalizing their own regionalism based on multi-lateralism and cooperation. Korea, with substantial experience in a gradual yet progressive democratization, could take the lead in promoting democracy within regional institutions and in achieving institutionalization in a democratic way.

Policy recommendations for Korea

The expansion of the concept of the region, of the number of states involved, and of the scope of agenda, coupled with the new EAS framework, will add a new dimension to the current definition of East Asian regionalism. In terms of actors, there will be an increasing number of regional powers. With participation by India, Australia, and New Zealand, East Asia will become one of the largest integrated markets in the world. By 2010, the combined ASEAN economy is expected to be worth \$1 trillion, and China \$1.4 trillion.[43] With the success of the China–ASEAN FTA, the combined trade volume would reach \$130 or \$140 billion per year. In comparison, annual ASEAN–US trade is \$120 billion and ASEAN–EU trade stands at \$110 billion.

In light of international structures, a number of sub-regions and tiers are expected to surface in accordance with the size of their market and economic power, not to mention leadership. It does not necessarily mean that East Asian regionalism will be divided into sub-regionalisms because the ultimate goal is to integrate the entire region on an equal basis. Sub-regionalism can nevertheless provide an impetus for wider regional integration. Those lagging behind or with relatively weaker economies can use sub-regionalism as a means of coordinating their needs to advance their process of integration.

In terms of the agenda, the EAS will involve significant political and strategic implications. With few exceptions, most East Asian nations share the same fate of heavy reliance on energy imports. They face a common challenge as to how to secure and diversify their energy sources as well as to how to safeguard the transportation routes for their imports. To achieve this end, regional states will be in great demand not only for policy coordination but also for military cooperation. Furthermore, in order to develop potential oil and gas fields in the South China Sea where territorial disputes are yet to be settled and act as a major hindrance, tense political negotiations will be necessary. Under the circumstances, some of the historic legacies, such as Japan's unremorseful and immature behaviour with respect to its past wrongdoings, will have to be solved before East Asian regionalism comes to fruition.

Against this background, there are some major challenges confronting Korea. Before it drops to a second-tier member state in the "new" East Asian regionalism, it must establish an East Asian policy. It needs to set a new framework for its vision for East Asia. It must also develop a set of goals and interests that it would like to pursue in its policy towards the region. Otherwise it might suffer another devastating loss of face like it did with the EAVG which now exists only in name. At the time when the Group was initiated, Korea was still one of the forces that states within the region could not simply overlook because of its economic strength and correlating political influence. However, not because Korea's economy regressed, but because of newly rising economies and Korea's failure to adapt, it failed to live up to its potential for playing a leading role in the regionalization process. Secondly, Korea must allocate more resources and support, at both governmental and academic levels, towards the constructive development of policies to facilitate closer cooperation with Southeast Asia, both collectively and individually. Few academic and policy-oriented studies on South Korea's relations with ASEAN have been published. Since 1979, for instance, according to the largest academic journal database in Korea, the Korean Studies Information Service System, there have been 159 research papers written on the subject of ASEAN. The most popular topic was on bilateral economic relations, with twelve publication records, most of them recently published and with a special emphasis on trade and investment. On the subject of APT, only eight works by Korean scholars appeared in leading Korean journals during the same period. What is astounding is that there are as many research papers (seven) on China's relations with ASEAN published in similar journals.

In addition, according to the same database records, only seven articles have been published on topics directly concerning ASEAN regionalism and intraregional cooperation. What needs to be particularly emphasized here is that most of these studies rarely extend their research focus beyond the geographic boundary of the regional concept, and tend to be very exclusive in connecting the subject to Korean policy or relations. In addition, lacklustre interest in ASEAN affairs by the Korean academic community is mirrored in Korea's governmental research institutions. For example, a leading Korean foreign policy think tank, the Institute of Foreign Affairs and National Security (IFANS), has published only ten working papers on ASEAN since 2000, all by a single author and in Korean.[44] Of the ten works, four have exclusively dealt with APT while the rest focused on intraregional development. Although this research may not appear to have direct relevance to Korea's bilateral relations with ASEAN, the topic is usually dealt in the conclusion or policy implications.

Korea needs to become more proactive in its study of ASEAN, if it is seriously to seek to assume a role in the development of East Asian regionalism. Given the narrow focus of much Korean research on such issues as trade, APT, ASEAN regionalism, and intraregional cooperation and development, there is an urgent need to expand the scope and range of research perspectives. Without a deeper understanding of ASEAN in relation to ever expanding regionalism, South Korea's position and role could only be severely undermined. To overcome this challenge, much more generous support and greater attention from the government must be provided to academic circles as well as related governmental sectors. Related governmental agencies, including leading governmental research institutions, will have to inspire and enlighten by presenting concrete policy goals with respect to ASEAN.

Last, but not least, Korea must work hard to find ways to develop and strengthen its relationship with ASEAN where it accords with its own goals and interests. At this critical juncture, ASEAN is the only viable middle power with which Korea can cooperate to advance the interests of small states and middle-power nations in the current regional integration process. The emerging reality for the newly developing architecture of East Asian regionalism has already warned us that it will be a forum for regional powers seeking predominance. To avoid becoming a victim of power politics, Korea must proactively look for constructive measures to build relations with those who have the political will and commitment to promote the interests of those weaker and smaller states.

Indeed, such efforts must be actively carried out at governmental level. Thus, Korea should devote greater efforts and resources in developing relations with the regional states, especially those who are relatively weak and small when alone but could have an incremental effect on the outcome of regional affairs when in conjunction with other similar actors. More specific and constructive measures to achieve this end must be sought by both the government and the academic community. Furthermore, much more concrete follow-up measures following summit meetings, the ARF and the APT must be implemented by government officials and related agencies. Korea has been quite sluggish in keeping up with these measures in the past.

Moreover, other than those occasions stemming from such regional meetings, Korea should make greater efforts to strengthen ties by initiating diplomatic contacts on its own. One of Roh Moo-hyun's official state visits to ASEAN states was Vietnam in September 2004 as part of his trip to an ASEM meeting held in the same country at the time. The last time Koreans remember their presidents visiting ASEAN states for the sole purpose of bilateral ties and goodwill is long forgotten.

Notes

1 Jaewoo Choo is grateful to the East Asian Institute (EAI), National University of Singapore for generous support for this study and for granting an opportunity to give a talk on 26 August 2005. He would also like to acknowledge valuable and insightful comments, which were critical to the completion of this chapter, from the research staff members including Wang Gungwu, John Wong, Lam Peng Er, Samuel Ku, Tang Shiping, and Lai Hongyi.
2 Calder defines Japan's such diplomatic behaviour as "reactive diplomacy". For more elaboration see Calder (1988).
3 Fishlow and Haggard (1992).

4 According to Fishlow and Haggard (1992), regionalization is referred to "the regional concentration of economic flows at an intraregional level", whereas regionalism can be defined as "a political process characterized by economic policy cooperation and coordination among countries".

5 For US opposition to these ideas and for the inefficient US response to the crisis, which is recognized and interpreted in the same vein, see Emmerson (2005) p. 9, and Webber (2003) pp. 358–59.

6 See Mansfield and Milner (1999), p. 589–90.

7 Ravenhill (2002), p. 175.

8 For a better understanding of Korean NGO's involvement in East Asian regionalism, see Ku-Hyun Jung (1999).

9 Mansfield and Milner (1999), p. 604.

10 For studies on the displeasing experience of APT nations with the lukewarm US response at the outset of the AFC, see Kurlantzick (2001) and Ravenhill (2002).

11 For a well-explained description on Korea's proposal on, and role in, leading the EAVG and EASG, see Stubbs (2002), pp. 443–44.

12 Detailed studies on the rising China, its influence on regionalism, and its interaction with other regional players are well-compiled by Unger (2002).

13 Sutter (2002), p. 13.

14 Johnston and Evans (1999), p. 256.

15 Kuik Cheng Chwee (2005), p. 102.

16 Tongzon (2005), p. 191.

17 "Spokesmen of MOFA: I hope the six-party talks are institutionalized", *Renmin Ribao*, 25 February 2004. For an academic point of view, please refer to Jiang Xiyuan, November 2003, Pang Zhongying, "Building Regional Security System", *China Daily*, 26 March 2004; "Building a Regional Security Mechanism", *PacNet* (Pacific Forum CSIS), No. 13A, 5 April 2004; Jaewoo Choo, "China's Plans for a Regional Security Forum", *Asia Times*, 17 October 2003; and "*Zhongguo nirang liufanghuitan zhiduhua* (China plans to institutionalize six-party talks)", *Fenghuangwang* (www.pheonixtv.com.cn), 20 November 2003.

18 Webber (2001), p. 339, and Terada (2003), pp. 257–59.

19 Amitav Acharya (1999).

20 For an insightful analysis on China's vision of East Asian regionalism, see Rozman (2004), pp. 228–31, and Baogang He (2004), pp. 114–17.

21 Haacke (1999), p. 581. Structural weakness of ASEAN, APT, and APEC exposed during the 1997 AFC is extensively analysed by Webber (2001).

22 Webber (2001), p. 339.

23 For an argument on Japan's de facto leadership or uncommitted leadership in the context of East Asian regionalism, read Terada (2003), pp. 257–59.

24 There are, however, more issues concerning the membership eligibility of non-East Asian states than racial and geographical ones. Three criteria were presented at the foreign ministerial meeting of the ten ASEAN member states in April 2005 as follows: substantive relations with ASEAN; dialogue-partner status with the group; and the signing of ASEAN's TAC. They still do not sufficiently address the exclusion of the United States, naturally raising debate and questions. Richardson (2005), p. 351.

25 Teo Chu Cheow (2005), p. 1.

26 There have been significant developments on the part of the Oceania nations with APT member states in recent times and they were crystallized by their decision to join the TAC and to identify themselves with Asia as Australian Prime Minister revealed publicly during his last visit to Beijing in 2005. "Australia likely to join E Asia Summit", 6 May 2005 (http://www.smh.com.au/news/World/Australia-likely-to-join-E-Asia-summits/2005/05/06/1115092683286.html) (dd: 23 August 2005).

27 Teo Chu Cheow (2005), p. 2.

28 "RP, China sign $1.5 B worth of deals", *Sun Star*, 28 April 2005 (http://www.sunstar.com.ph/static/net/2005/04/28/rp.china.sign.$1.5b.worth.of.deals.html) (dd: April 30, 2005).
29 Emmerson (2005).
30 Mansfield and Milner (1999), pp. 589–90.
31 In addition, according to Amitav (2004), domestic political factors are also critical to norm-building and identity-building behind regionalism. With a particular emphasis on the interaction of "local beliefs" and "foreign norms".
32 Mansfield and Milner (1999), p. 589–90.
33 Tang Shiping (2002), p. 71.
34 Jordaan (2003), p. 165.
35 Mares (1988), p. 456.
36 Jordaan (2003), p. 165.
37 Mares (1988), p. 456.
38 Tang Shiping (2002), p. 71.
39 For an in-depth study on the reason why Korea should assume a role in undertaking a "mission" to build a regional community of cooperation, see Jung-Suh Koo (1995).
40 This view is widely shared by Sang Woo Rhee (1996).
41 Chul-Jin Suk (2002).
42 However, Korean scholars like Chang-Jae Lee (2000) place a far greater value on the positive consequences of continuous discussion, as in the context of APT, on economic cooperation and major economic issues at regional level and boldly predict that it will have a positive influence on the regionalization process.
43 William Foreman, "China signs trade pact with ASEAN", *Associated Press*, 3 November 2004.
44 This Korean ASEAN specialist is Dr Bae Geung Chan. Please refer to IFANS' webpage for the list of publication at http://www.ifans.go.kr/ik_a003/ik_b011/ik_c007/search.jsp?rid=sik&orgcatid=sik_c007&wordtype=ARTSUBJECT&utfqry=ASEAN

References

Amitav Acharya (1999) "Culture, security, multilateralism: the 'ASEAN way' and regional order", *Contemporary Security Policy*, Vol. 19, No. 1, 55–89.
Amitav Acharya (2004) "How ideas spread: whose norms matter? Norm localization and institutional change in Asian regionalism", *International Organization*, No. 58, Spring, 239–75
Calder Kent (1988) "Japanese foreign economic policy formation: explaining the reactive state", *World Politics*, XL, No. 4, 517–41.
Chwee, Kuik Cheng (2005) "Multilateralism in China's ASEAN policy: its evolution, characteristics and aspiration", *Contemporary Southeast Asia*, Vol. 27, No. 1, 102–22.
Emmerson, Donald K. (2005) "What do the blind-sided see? Reapproaching regionalism in Southeast Asia", *The Pacific Review*, Vol. 18, No. 1, March, 1–21.
Fishlow Albert, and Stephen Haggard (1992) *The United States and the Regionalization of the World*, Paris, OECD Development Center, Research Project on Globalization and Regionalization.
Haacke, Jurgen (1999) "The concept of flexible engagement and the practice of enhanced interaction: intramural challenges to the ASEAN way", *Pacific Affairs*, Vol. 12, No. 4, 581–611.

He, Baogang (2004) "East Asian ideas of regionalism: a normative critique", *Australian Journal of International Affairs*, Vol. 58, No. 1, March, 105–25.

Johnston, Alastair Iain and Evans, Paul (1999) "China and multilateral security institutions", in Johnston, Alastair Iain and Robert Ross (eds), *Engaging China: the management of an emerging Power*, London: Routledge.

Jordaan, Eduard (2003) "The concept of a middle power in international relations: distinguishing between emerging and traditional middle powers", *Politikon*, Vol. 30, No. 2, 165–81.

Jung, Ku-Hyun (1999) "Nongovernmental initiatives in Korea for Northeast Asian cooperation", in Tsueno Akaha (ed.), *Politics and Economics in Northeast Asia: Nationalism and Regionalism in Contention*, New York: St. Martins Press, 347–65.

Koo, Jung-Suh (1995) "Pan-Asianisms for primacy of East Asia", *Korea Focus*, Vol. 3, No. 2, 34–41.

Kurlantzick, Joshua (2001) "Is East Asia integrating?", *The Washington Quarterly*, Autumn, 19–28.

Mansfield, Edward D, and Milner, Helen V. (1999) "The new wave of regionalism", *International Organization*, Vol. 53, No. 3, 589–627.

Lee, Chang-Jae (2000) "Northeast Asian economic cooperation: the need for a new approach", *NIRA Review*, Autumn, 5–10

Mares, David R (1998) "Middle powers under regional hegemony: to challenge or acquiesce in hegemonic enforcement", *International Studies Quarterly*, Vol. 32, 453–71.

Ravenhill, John (2002) "A three bloc world? The new East Asian regionalism", *International Relations of the Asia-Pacific*, Vol. 2, 167–95

Rhee, Sang Woo (1996) "Japan's role in New Asian order", *Korea Focus*, Vo. 4, No. 3, 22–36.

Richardson, Michael (2005) "Australia–Southeast Asia relations and the East Asian summit", *Australian Journal of International Affairs*, Vol. 59, No. 3, 351–65.

Rozman, Gilbert (2004) "Democratization in greater China: the Northeast Asian regionalism context", *Orbis*, Spring, 228–31.

Shiping, Tang (2002) "Institution building under 10+3: tackling the practical issues", *Global Economic Review*, Vol. 31, No. 4, December, 3–16.

Stubbs, Richard (2002), "ASEAN plus three: emerging East Asian regionalism?", *Asian Survey*, Vol. 42, No. 3, 434–50.

Suk, Chrul-Jin (2002) "Outlook for Asian regional cooperation: European experience", in Pai Guohua and Zhang Xizhen (eds), *Dongya diquhezuo yu hezuojuzhi* [Regional Cooperation and Mechanism in East Asia], Beijing: Central Compliance and Translation Press, 46–56.

Sutter, Robert (2002) "China's recent approach to Asia: seeking long-term gains", *NBR Analysis*, Vol. 13, No. 1, March, 20–21.

Teo Chu Cheow, Eric (2005) "New challenges for building an East Asian community", *China Brief*, Vol. 5, Issue 2, 18 January, The Jamestown Foundation, Washington, DC.

Terada, Takashi (2003) "Constructing an 'East Asian' concept and growing regional identity: from EAEC to ASEAN+3", *The Pacific Review*, Vol. 16, No. 2, 251–71.

Tongzon, Jose (2005) "ASEAN–China free trade area: a bane or boon for ASEAN Countries ?", *World Economy*, Vol. 28, No. 2, 191–210.

Unger, Danny (2002) "A regional economic order in East and Southeast Asia?", *Journal of Strategic Studies*, Vol. 12, No. 4, 179–89.

Webber, Douglas (2001) "Two funerals and a wedding? The ups and downs of regionalism in East Asian and Asia-Pacific after the Asian crisis", *The Pacific Review*, Vol. 14, No. 3, 339–72.

Xiyuan, Jiang (2003) "DPRK Nuke problem and new framework of multilateral security cooperation in Northeast Asia", *SIIS Journal*, Vol. 10, No. 4, November, 24–37.

7 China's ascendancy and the future of the Korean Peninsula

Taeho Kim

Introduction

On 24 August 2005, both China (People's Republic of China – PRC) and South Korea (Republic of Korea – ROK) celebrated the thirteenth anniversary of establishing diplomatic ties – with no great fanfare. It was no issue in the pages of South Korea's major newspapers. Beyond the stereotyped verbal rituals, neither government tried to seize it as a public relations event. Rather, an increasing number of policy analysts and university professors from both countries called for a more balanced and more sober-minded approach to the otherwise "mutually beneficial" relationship.[1]

For their part, South Koreans have long been familiar with the prosperous nature of their relations with China and with the latter's growing importance to the future of the Korean Peninsula. On the positive side of the ledger, for instance, China has emerged as South Korea's "three no. 1s": its largest trading partner, its largest export market, and its largest trade-surplus source. It is indeed music to the Korean economist's ears as the economy has remained stagnant, while its trade dependency rate reached 61.6 per cent in 2003. As a matter of fact, the ROK's $13.2 billion trade surplus with China in 2003 constituted a whopping 80 per cent of the country's total trade surplus![2] Other impressive statistics indicating these growing ties abound and will be introduced shortly.

On the other hand, there also exists a growing yet little discussed list of potential problems and issues underlying this otherwise prosperous relationship. These include: the well-publicized fate of the North Korean "refugees" in China; the PRC government's occasional condescending attitude towards visa application; the planned visit by the Dalai Lama to Seoul; Korean attendance at Chen Shui-bian's inauguration ceremony in Taiwan; and the various yet longer-term effects of the "rise of China". The most inflammatory of all, however, has been the Chinese attempt to incorporate the history of Koguryo (or Goguryeo) – Korea's ancient kingdom that existed from 35 BC to AD 668 – as part of its own. When the Chinese foreign ministry deleted all reference to Koguryo from its website on 22 April 2004, it infuriated the South Korean public and government alike. To rub salt into the Koreans' wounds, it then removed from the website the entire history of Korea up to 1948, thus opening a Pandora's box with which neither side can win in the end.

This chapter attempts to shed some light on this little discussed yet highly consequential aspects of the Sino-ROK relationship, not only by addressing their 13-year ties but also by subjecting the China factor in the ROK's regional and security policy to a careful, detailed, and impartial examination. After identifying principal trends and major developments in China's post-Cold War relationships with South Korea in particular and with the two Koreas in general, it examines actual and likely future differences between China and South Korea on a panoply of peninsular and regional issues. The chapter then addresses South Korea's emerging security challenges of balancing the American alliance and Chinese cooperation. Overall, it poses a critical question: How will the China factor play out in South Korea's future security environment and in the evolving US–South Korean relationship?

To telegraph the major arguments and findings of this chapter, the seeming "convergence" of interests between Beijing and Seoul in many aspects of their bilateral ties does not necessarily mean that the former is supportive of South Korea's major policy goals – especially when they come to concrete issues or longer-term questions on the Korean Peninsula. They share "common aversions", not "common interests", in a sense that both countries share a desire to avoid war on the peninsula and to prevent North Korea's nuclearization.[3] It is thus necessary to understand correctly that the ongoing trends and developments in South Korea's interactions with the US and China could be those of fundamental, sustaining, and impregnated nature to warrant educated guesses and reasoned speculations for the unfolding future strategic configuration on the Korean Peninsula and beyond. In short, the current state of Sino-South Korean relationship can be likened to standing right in the eye of the typhoon without knowing where the shelter is.

The China factor in the ROK's regional and security policy

Fundamental factors underlying the South Korean calculus of the China issue are China's geographical proximity to the Korean Peninsula, its continuing influence on North Korea, its growing bilateral ties with South Korea, and the implications of a "rising China." Furthermore, China is highly likely to remain a major actor in Korean affairs, including the unification process. These considerations underpin South Korea's views on its relations with China and on its regional policy.

Popular South Korean images of China are difficult to generalize – to say the least. Reflecting its chequered relationships with the outside world in general and China in particular throughout the twentieth century, South Korea eyes China in essentially three different images: a traditional great power – an image which had been built upon their largely unequal yet amicable pre-nineteenth century ties; a Cold-War adversary represented by their hostile experience during the Korean War (1950–53); and a new, pragmatic country with the so-called "good-neighbourly, friendly relationship", formed after the Sino-ROK normalization in 1992.

Besides, there exists a spectrum of opinions within Korean society regarding the most desirable state of bilateral ties between the ROK and China. A relatively small but growing number of human rights activists, together with religious and environmental groups, are most critical of China's policies in their respective issue areas. China's (mis)handling of North Korean refugees in China as well as its opposition to the visit by the Dalai Lama to Seoul are the most recent examples.[4] A score of recent bilateral agreements over fishery, trade, and investment, which would otherwise guide their growing economic interactions, may also generate displaced interests within South Korean society.

At the opposite end of the spectrum are a sizeable number of people who subscribe to the "comprehensive cooperative partnership" (*quanmian hezuo huoban guanxi*) between the two countries. Those with commercial, governmental, and other institutional ties with China tend to be in favour of a stable and prospering relationship with China. As elaborated below, rapid improvement in Sino-ROK ties throughout the 1990s have generated a thick web of individual and institutional interests within South Korean society, which remain sympathetic with Beijing.

The "China threat" argument, on the other hand, is distinctly a minority opinion aired by only a few groups of people scattered in the media, military, and ideological communities. Few foreign-policy analysts in Seoul, including both Chinese and non-Chinese academicians, institutional specialists, and journalists, are vocal about the possibility of a Chinese military threat to the Korean Peninsula or advocate policies to "deter", "contain" or "constrain" China, unlike their counterparts in Washington.

At the same time, it should be noted that while the above developments are largely externally driven, South Korea's changing domestic political dynamics – which date back to the February 2003 inauguration of the Roh Moo-hyun government or to the June 2000 North–South Korean Summit – have generated a new stream of peninsula-centred thinking, popularly known as the "policy for peace and prosperity", the "Northeast Asian hub", and the "Northeast Asian balancer".[5] It is this complex context, against which the ROK's overall interactions with China should be understood.

Barring any unforeseen developments in the near future, it is highly likely that a mixture of economic convergence, political convenience, and military indifference will define the ROK's overall interactions with China. Economically, there exists an essential consensus among the Korean business community that China is probably the last resort for their survival, at least for the time being. This sense of urgency on the part of the Korean business community will likely push for a higher level of industrial and technological cooperation between the two countries. While the government has recently instituted a system of protective mechanisms in response to the growing concern with technology leakage, its effectiveness is likely to be severely tested due to the growing interactions with China as well as to the technological nature of the problems.

On the military front, Sino-ROK "military exchanges and cooperation" are limited to exchanges in three areas: defence ministers and service chiefs; working-level policy and intelligence personnel; and short-term visits and academic contacts. While the frequency of their contacts throughout the 1990s was lopsided in favour of South Korea, it has become more or less balanced in the number and the level of visits in recent years. However, any discernible changes in South Korea's defence posture are deemed a remote possibility.

Any about-face in South Korea's interactions with China could well originate from none other than its own domestic political dynamics. It is well known that China's importance to, and its influence over, South Korea come from various sources: economic imperative, its relations with North Korea, and its presumed role in the Korean unification process. Moreover, there is a dawning reality that China has become a useful policy tool for the ruling party's peninsula-centred and populist ideology, which is often seen as opposed to that of an imposing and unilateral America. It is worthy of note, however, that the Korean public's favourable perception toward China plummeted after the Koguryo issue had erupted in 2004.[6] In the mid-to longer term, it is entirely possible that South Korea's political divergence with China on specific and concrete issues will affect the erstwhile discrete interactions with China in other dimensions. One cost-effective way of coping with this future uncertainty is to maintain exchanges and cooperation with China, while anticipating and preparing for the reversal of present courses.

China's post-Cold War relations with the two Koreas

Before analysing China's relationships with South Korea in particular and with both Koreas in general, it is necessary to understand the two major undercurrents that have buttressed China's Korea policy. One is the importance of the Korean Peninsula in the eyes of the Chinese for strategic and economic reasons, and the other its evolving policy goals toward the Korean Peninsula.

To begin with, the Korean Peninsula encapsulates China's continuing yet elusive quest to restore its past glory, to make a "rich country, strong army" (*fuguo qiangbing*), and to achieve great-power status. For one thing, not only was traditional Korea part of the Sino-centric world order up to the mid-nineteenth century, it was also there that the fledgling People's Republic confronted the mighty United States 50 years ago. For another, the 1992 Sino-South Korean normalization and their fast-growing economic and other ties testify to the vicissitude of Cold War politics and the validity of China's ongoing reform and open-door policy. For still another, as North Korea's newest nuclear gambit and a recent spate of anti-American sentiment in South Korea portend, China's potential to become a fully fledged major power will likely be tested again in the rapidly changing yet uncharted Korean Peninsula. This fundamental fact has taken on a new relevance in light of the global discourse over the "rise of China" – be that "China's peaceful rise" (*heping jueqi*),[7] "China's peaceful development" (*heping fazhan*)[8] or the "China threat theory" (*weixielun*).[9]

For this reason, throughout the 1990s and continuing to this day China has pursued a set of identifiable and consistent policy goals toward the Korean Peninsula. They include: a) stability and tension reduction; b) economic cooperation with South Korea and traditional ties with North Korea; c) its own role and influence, which often come at the expense of the ubiquitous United States; and d) harmonization of its peninsular interests with its global and regional ones – most notably its own unification agenda with that of Taiwan.

Notwithstanding a host of unforeseen developments and shocks throughout the 1990s on the peninsula and beyond – including the first nuclear crisis, the sudden death of Kim Il Sung, and America's regional hegemony, there is no doubt that China's policy toward the Korean Peninsula has achieved an overall success. Issues can be broadly grouped into three major areas: economic/trade, political/diplomatic, and military/security ones.

Economic/trade issue-areas

For the past 13 years since their diplomatic normalization in 1992 China and South Korea have remarkably improved their economic and trade relationships. Bilateral trade worth $6.4 billion trade in 1992 grew over 20 per cent annually to reach $23.7 billion in 1997, $31.3 billion in 2000, $57 billion in 2003, and $79.3 billion in 2004 – making each country a major trading partner of the other. In 2003, for instance, China for the first time emerged as South Korea's largest export market in history, and by the end of 2004 China became South Korea's largest trading partner as well.[10]

In 2004 a total of $3.6 billion South Korean investment was registered in China, which accounts for 46 per cent of the ROK's total overseas investment.[11] In 2003 alone, 2.96 million people travelled between the two countries. The frequency of contacts between the two sides is evidenced by over 20,000 Korean companies in operation throughout China, 380 passenger flights per week (i.e. about 54 flights per day), and by about 38,000 Korean students in China – which means that as there are over 85,000 foreign students in China two out of five foreign students in China come from South Korea![12] An array of other impressive statistics abounds as to tourism, educational, and cultural ties – most notably "Korean waves" (*Hanliu*) or "China fever" – between the two countries. This positive trend – which is likely to continue for the foreseeable future – will undoubtedly contribute to the ROK's economic development. At the same time, however, it should be remembered that Korea's increasing economic dependency on China is a double-edged sword which could restrain the ROK's diplomatic options by allowing China to enhance its position and influence on the peninsula.

In sharp contrast, Sino-North Korean economic relations have been severely constrained for many reasons including their different economic structures, North Korea's economic and financial problems and its self-imposed diplomatic isolation. Even if China remains North Korea's largest trade partner, accounting for an average 25 to 30 per cent of the latter's total trade, their two-way trade fell like a descending staircase from a peak of $900 million in 1993 to $656 million in 1997 to $488 million in 2000. Since then, it has gradually increased from $740 million in 2001 to $739 million in 2002 to $1,023 million (i.e. $1.023 billion) in 2003.[13]

A set of structural economic problems such as chronic fiscal and trade deficits, low competitiveness of its export goods and a lack of hard currency has long prohibited the improvement of North Korea's trade relationships with China. In fact, North Korea's principal export items to China such as non-ferrous metals are in short supply within North Korea as well, demonstrating again the gravity of its economic predicament. As long as the principles of a market economy reign in Beijing, prospects for an improved trade relationship with Pyongyang look bleak for the foreseeable future.

In fact, contrary to Chinese officials' wishful utterances on the resilience of its Communist neighbour, the depth of North Korea's economic problems is real and could become much worse in the years to come.[14] For the sake of its own interests including peninsular stability, China encourages the North Korean leadership to take reform measures aimed at more fundamental resolution of their economic problems. If the North Korean regime indeed takes a fundamental reform path, however, it will surely be the most perilous moment for its survival. Pyongyang's choice has been "deterrence through instability". This, in short, constitutes China's longer-term strategic dilemma as to the North Korean question.

Political/diplomatic issue-areas

Chinese attempts to strike a balance in its approach to both Koreas and to maintain traditional ties with North Korea have so far produced mixed results due to a combination of factors, including North Korea's closed nature, external hostility, and self-imposed isolation. While it is difficult to pinpoint the date, China for some time has wished to transform its traditional ties with Pyongyang based on ideological affinity and particularistic ties to a more mutually beneficial, state-to-state relationship. But the course of action North Korea followed in the 1990s reveals that its interests diverge from those of China.

As a matter of fact, a series of major developments on the peninsula throughout the last decade and beyond such as the simultaneous entry to the United Nations by both Koreas, South Korea's diplomatic normalization with the Soviet Union and China, its opposition to North Korea's attempt to replace the extant Armistice Agreement with a peace treaty with the United States, and the arrest of Yang Bin in spite of the apparent protestation by North Korea – to name but a few – further demonstrated the strained relationships between North Korea and China and the latter's overall "convergence" of interests with South Korea's.

On the other hand, aside from a vast improvement in their economic and other relationships, China and South Korea now regularly hold high-level meetings. On the Chinese side as well, the new line-up of the so-called "fourth-generation leadership" after the Sixteenth CCP Congress in November 2002, in which those with a substantial provincial or bureaucratic background were represented, strongly indicates China's continuing priority on economic development, which depends on regional and peninsular stability, among others.[15] In short, the generational turnover in the Chinese leadership, in tandem with its need to maintain political and social stability, will likely reinforce its current pragmatic policy orientation toward the Korean Peninsula. In a lychee nutshell, it can plausibly be argued that China's domestic economic reform, coupled with the end of the bipolar Cold War, has had the most far-reaching impact on the evolution of the relationship between China and the two Koreas and will continue to emphasize the importance of growing ties with Seoul.

Military/security issue-areas

In a similar vein, since the early 1990s and particularly after the death of Kim Il Sung in July 1994, security and military ties between China and North Korea have increasingly been subject to the rigidity of their political relations and China's national interest-based policy toward the Korean Peninsula. The lack of a mutually beneficial agenda, North Korea's domestic problems, and growing Sino-South Korean ties have also militated against the continued development of their bilateral relationship in this important issue area.

In fact, their political and military contacts have undergone several different phases. From April 1989 to August 1992, General Secretaries Kim Il Sung (three times), Zhao Ziyang, and Jiang Zemin and all their defence and foreign ministers had visited the other's capital. Even the period from Beijing–Seoul normalization in August 1992 to the death of Kim Il Sung in July 1994, ranking Chinese officials such as Hu Jintao, Qian Qichen, and Chi Haotian as well as North Korean military officers such as Choi Kwang, Ok Bong Lin, and Kim Il Chul made mutual visits. But there were no summit meetings.

In particular, since the death of Kim Il Sung till June 1999, when Chairman of the Supreme People's Assembly Kim Young Nam visited China, there had been an appreciable decline in the frequency and the rank of Chinese visitors. Since the death of Kim Il Sung in July 1994 the non-military, working-level contacts between the two sides were made mostly at the vice-ministerial level and among their respective international liaison, foreign affairs, economic and provincial-level units. Overall political and military contacts between Beijing and Pyongyang have also shown a gradual but unmistakable decline. Even the military-to-military contacts between their ranking officers are mostly goodwill visits and are symbolic and ceremonial in nature, not task-oriented meetings on salient military and security issues.[16]

North Korean leader Kim Jong Il's May 2000 visit to China – which was followed by his subsequent visits in January 2001 and April 2004 – as well as the feverish diplomatic activities that followed are undoubtedly intended to alleviate the growing pains of North Korea's deepening economic and diplomatic vulnerabilities as well as to arrest a further deterioration of its strained relationship with China. There are, however, no appreciable effects on their military-to-military contacts in particular and on their overall ties in general.

Recent visits by such top Chinese leaders as Jiang Zemin (September 2001), Jia Qinglin (May 2002), Wu Bangguo (October 2003), and Li Changchun (September 2004) helped to restore the level of Chinese visits, but their practical significance should not be exaggerated.[17] Finally, it is entirely possible that having maintained mutual contacts of little substance over a decade, both Chinese and North Korean militaries are now undergoing a serious yet little-publicized version of their own "alliance fatigue".[18]

Similarly, while China still maintains the July 1961 Treaty of Friendship, Cooperation, and Mutual Assistance with North Korea, the only country with whom China has a formal military alliance, the treaty has been widely interpreted in Beijing and elsewhere to be operative only when North Korea faces an *unprovoked* attack from an outside enemy – a highly unlikely event. It is ironic to note that many Asian security analysts and officials now believe that having a Chinese treaty obligation with a vulnerable North Korea almost certainly helps contribute to stability on the peninsula.

Between South Korea and China, on the other hand, there have been more frequent, more regular, and higher-level visits in recent years in the so-called "military exchanges and cooperation" field.[19] Divided into three areas – i.e. high-level visits (e.g. defence and service chiefs), working-level contacts (short-term visits and mutual consultation), and military academic and research exchanges (conferences and sports events), their militaries have gradually but steadily increased the scope of military-to-military exchanges and cooperation. It should be noted, however, that compared with the other non-military aspects of their bilateral ties the "military exchanges and cooperation" have yet to be balanced and institutionalized.

Some salient issues between South Korea and China

While the Beijing and the Seoul governments have long maintained that they see eye to eye on a host of peninsular issues – at least in their official proclamations and high rhetoric, there exist subtle but important differences between the two on the issues of Korean unification, the USFK (US Forces Korea), North Korean nuclear and missile programmes, and the US–Japan alliance ties – to name but a few.

For one thing, Article 5 of the 24 August 1992 Joint Declaration on the Establishment of Diplomatic Relations between the ROK and the PRC reads: "The PRC government respects the Korean people's desire to have the Korean Peninsula unified peacefully at an early date and support a *peaceful unification* of the Korean Peninsula *by the Korean people*" (italics added).[20] Since then, all ranking Chinese officials, when asked, have articulated their support for a peaceful, independent, and gradual unification of the Korean Peninsula. Then, a question naturally arises: What if the unification is not peaceful, not independent (devoid of US involvement?) or not gradual? To the best knowledge of this author, none of the numerous ranking Chinese officials have ever answered this question to the point. As noted at the beginning of this article, China's prime objective toward the Korean Peninsula is "stability" not unification – which is the ROK's national security objective. The fact remains that China's support for Korean unification is *not* unconditional.

For another, since the early 2000s and continuing to date the plight of the North Korean "refugees" (or "illegal economic migrants" by Chinese definition) has become a very salient bilateral issue between the two countries as well as for the international community.[21] While there are growing numbers of North Koreans entering into foreign embassies, international schools, and other sanctuaries in Beijing, the PRC government's position remains adamant: The issue touches upon China's sovereignty and ethnic issues and thus can be resolved only between the PRC and North Korea. Besides, it argues, the issues should be handled according to – in descending order of importance – Chinese domestic law, international law, and humanitarian concerns. There is a far cry between China's efforts to project an international image as an up-and-coming responsible power in the world and the often brutal handling of the North Korean refugees against their wishes.

For still another, the Chinese project – known as "Northeast Project" (*dongbei gongcheng*) – to incorporate the history of Koguryo into their own is the gravest of all potential problems between the two countries.[22] While the Chinese government averred that the project was an academic endeavour which began in 2002 by such provincial-level governments as Liaoning, Jilin, and Heilongjiang, it is anything but an academic one. In fact, the "Northeast Project" had begun much earlier – in 1996 – by the regional academies of social sciences located in the three northeastern provinces mentioned above and was ratified by none other than Hu Jintao – the current Party General Secretary and then a member of the Politburo Standing Committee – as a national-level project. It is for these reasons that the project was then led by the Chinese Academy of Social Sciences (CASS), the party's policy-development organ, and that three-trillion Korean won and manpower of about 1,500 were able to be devoted to it. In brief, it is a political – not an academic – project of the Chinese central government.

In light of the expected objections from both North and South Korea as well as from the world community, what prompted China to engineer the historical distortions? First, it stands to reason that the steady power shift in Northeast Asia – including China's rise, North Korea's nuclear crisis, readjustments in the US–ROK alliance, and Japan's elevated status in the East Asia strategy of the United States – must have a place in it. Second, North Korea's future and the two-million strong ethnic Koreans in the northeastern provinces must remain a serious concern for China's political leaders and strategists. Third, a unified Korea's possible claim over the Gando region well into the future can be nipped in the bud should any ancient histories of China's current northeastern region be incorporated as part of China's own proud and rich history.[23]

While the South Koreans have so far believed in China's position that an academic issue should be resolved in academic terms only, the dawning reality is that the "Northeast Project" is nothing but the Chinese government's official project, aided by the media, academic and policy units, and regional governments. The project and the lessons thereof should awaken the Korean people to the dangers of the self-fulfilling prophecy about China. Additionally, the recent "China bashing" in South Korea – largely triggered by the issue of historical distortion – should be harnessed into a new opportunity not only to rethink China's strategic intentions towards the Korean Peninsula but also to dispel the self-centred "China fantasy" many of us have held up to now.

While the above three issues remain most salient ones, there are many other potential problems that may surface one day. An overview of potential sources of differences between China and South Korea is provided below.

Balancing American alliance and Chinese cooperation: South Korea's emerging strategic challenge

The relationship between the United States and China is widely believed to be probably the most consequential bilateral tie in the contemporary world, whose impact reverberates throughout global and regional issues. It is thus encouraging to note that both the US and China have since 11 September 2001 worked together to improve their otherwise fragile relationship in such diverse areas as international terrorism, North Korea's nuclear moves, and their military-to-military contacts. On the other hand, it should also be acknowledged that despite their global pretensions and their derivative self-acclaimed role for peace and stability worldwide, the United States and China are countries with different attitudes, diverging perspectives, and conflicting world-views.[24] These differences are often brought to bear in their handling of regional and peninsular issues.

For instance, notwithstanding the long list of their outstanding disputes at both bilateral and regional levels, China and the United States have time and again argued – at the official and declaratory level, at least – that they share a set of common interests over the Korean Peninsula – namely peninsular stability, North–South Korean dialogue, and peaceful reunification. The question is, why?

In light of their vast differences in strategic visions, political systems, social values, and strategic objectives – notwithstanding their recent "normalizing" efforts – it is far more logical and (I would argue) more empirically valid to make a case that the United States and China will likely remain divergent over peninsular issues as well. Beneath the façade of the Bush administration's official China policy of a "constructive, cooperative, and candid relationship" the interests of the two countries could be significantly in conflict with each other when confronted with some concrete issues and longer-term agendas. Prominent examples include, but are not limited to, a North Korean contingency, future status of the USFK, and military capability and strategic orientation of a unified Korea.

It is also possible that a future political thaw on the peninsula, as was thought within reach months after the June 2000 North–South Korean summit, could also accentuate, and at a minimum has increased uncertainty over, a host of issues that involve the US, China, and the Koreas. Therefore, in light of the possibility for Sino-American competition, their likely diverging interests over the peninsula, and the "rise of China" (which is largely a fact of life, not an assumption, for most East Asian states including South Korea), South Korea needs continuously to prioritize its strategic relationships with the United States and with China. In practical terms as well as for the sake of its national interests, its means that the ROK should be able to reap the benefits of its alliance ties with the United States in addressing the growing importance of the "China factor".[25]

In a similar vein, future changes in inter-Korean relations could have a significant impact on the future course of the peninsula and the South Korean–US security relationship. Likewise, recent changes in both domestic and external dimensions in both South Korea and the United States have not only influenced the nature of the alliance, but have also raised new issues or old issues in a new form which are endogenous to the security alliance. While those substantive issues are largely subordinated to both countries' national interests so far, they could become sources of strain for the alliance if long unresolved.

As perhaps their divergent perceptions of, and policies towards, a series of ongoing North Korean nuclear crises (e.g. the "Six-Party Talks") best

Table 7.1 Chinese and South Korean positions on some salient peninsular and regional issues

Issues	Chinese positions	South Korean positions
History of Koguryo	Part of China's ancient history in its peripheral regions (Aware of South Koreans' sensitivity to the issue) want a "quiet" and academic approach	The issue touches upon Korea's national identity and historical continuity Call for both academic and diplomatic approach
Korean Unification	Support peaceful (and "independent") unification In fact, prefers stability to unification De facto support for the North Korean regime	Peacetime CBM necessary for a North Korean contingency Differences exist for specifics Call for discussions on post-unification relations
North Korean nuclear issue	Support a nuclear-free Korean Peninsula Maintain stability and peace on the Korean Peninsula Resolve the issue in a diplomatic and peaceful manner	North Korea's nuclear gambit is a threat to the peninsula and beyond Call for a diplomatic and multilateral solution, including China's "constructive" role
North Korean refugees in China	A sensitive issue that touches upon China's sovereignty, territories, and ethnic issues; "no refugees" in China A bilateral issue between China and North Korea, not South Korea	Forcible repatriation to North Korea unacceptable A humanitarian issue

US forces in Korea	Principled opposition to the stationing of foreign troops A historical issue to be discussed between South Korea and the US Remain wary of its possible role against China or a Taiwan contingency Every country's sovereign rights	A bigger issue in waiting when Korea is unified A stabilizing factor on the peninsula and in the region Never raise the issue with China Focus of the post-unification USFK is regional stability
North Korea missile (re-) launching	Opposes international pressure on North Korea Will do "what it can"	Major source of instability and MD
Strengthened U.S.-Japan alliance	"Asian edition of NATO" Will lead to Japan's rearmament Wary of its anti-China and Taiwan contingency role	Danger of missile proliferation Call for China's "constructive" role Contributes to peninsular and regional stability A bilateral issue between the US and Japan
Theater Missile Defence (TMD)	Opposes it for a number of reasons Welcomes South Korea's non-participation	North Korea as a primary rationale for its development South Korea's geographical, economic, technical reasons

illustrate,[26] the South Korean and the US governments need to coordinate their policy towards North Korea more tightly and more coherently than has been the case. Policy differences over North Korea do not augur well for the long-term development of the South Korean–US alliance, especially if they have to prepare for the day when they "run out of common enemies". It is these kinds of specific policy issues and longer-term questions that South Korea needs to take into consideration in formulating its strategic plan for its future security environment.

Looking ahead

In the closing pages of this chapter, it is appropriate to sum up the findings and arguments with respect to the questions raised at the outset. First, as long as China holds fast to its ongoing reform drive, continued stability on the Korean Peninsula is a key to its economic and other interests so that it will try to prevent a renewed conflict on the peninsula. For the same reason, China will continue to promote a friendly and beneficial relationship with Seoul and, at the same time, it will try to retain its lingering ties with North Korea, but it is highly likely that their economic ties will be increasingly subject to economic logic, structural trade problems, and the state of other issue areas. In the mid-to longer term, moreover, China will seek to transform its traditional "special" ties with Pyongyang based on ideological affinity and particularistic bonds to a more normal, state-to-state relationship based on hard-nosed national interests and mutual benefits.

Second, the seeming "convergence" of interests – common aversions in fact – between Beijing and Seoul in major aspects of their bilateral ties does not necessarily mean that the former is supportive of South Korea's major policy goals – especially when they come to concrete issues or longer-term questions on the Korean Peninsula. Under such circumstances and for the foreseeable future South Korea's "strategic prioritization" in its relations with the United States and with China will most likely be the most optimal strategic choice, even if South Korea should continuously and systematically pursue a specific set of confidence-building measures with China.

Third, in light of longer-term Sino-American competition, their likely diverging interests over the peninsula, and China's growing influence over the Korean Peninsula, it is entirely possible that China will become a source of *both* despair and hope in realizing South Korea's national objectives. While its growing economic and social interdependence with China is highly encouraging and should be continued, the ROK should also be aware of its attendant costs in other issue-areas – namely, diplomatic and security ones. In a similar vein, the intrinsic value of the "China factor" in South Korea's evolving security environment lies not in its supposed balancing role against a ubiquitous and unilateral America but in its potential and likely role in ensuring peace on the peninsula – with Korean unification included. In the long and often tortuous path to Korean security and unification, China will be no substitute for the United States for the foreseeable future.

Finally, it is this complex set of major external challenges that the ROK leadership will face for many years to come. How well and in what manner they handle the challenges could significantly affect not only the wealth and health of the Republic but also the future of the nation, including reunification. Furthermore, now that both the domestic and the international contexts upon which the ROK's foreign and security policies have been predicated are also undergoing extraordinary changes, it is necessary to understand correctly that the ongoing trends and developments in South Korea's interactions with the US and China could be those of fundamental, sustaining, and impregnated nature to warrant cooler thinking on the unfolding future strategic configuration on the Korean Peninsula and beyond.

Notes

1 One example of this reassessment effort was a two-day conference entitled "The Changing International Orders and Sino-ROK Relations in the 21st Century". The conference, co-organized by the Institute of Asia-Pacific Studies, Chinese Academic of Social Sciences (CASS) and by the Institute 21 for Peace Studies, *Dong-a Ilbo* and held in Beijing on 28–29 July 2005, included 16 experts on Sino-ROK relations from both sides.

2 Unless noted otherwise, all statistical data concerning China's relations with the two Koreas are based on the official publications of the ROK Ministry of Foreign Affairs and Trade (MOFAT). Occasionally, such primary sources as the data compiled by the Trade Research Institute (TRI) of the Korea International Trade Association (KITA) are employed; but they can be easily corroborated with those of the MOFAT. Trade volume between the ROK and the PRC in 2004 was $79.3 billion, and the ROK's trade surplus stood at $20.2 billion.

3 This is the term used by Brad Glosserman for describing the longer-term nature of the sino-rok relationship. See his "US–China: the next alliance?" *South China Morning Post*, 30 October 2003.

4 The Chinese government's position is that there are no North Korean "refugees", let alone defectors, in its territory. Its position has triggered strong protestations from various NGOs based in South Korea and elsewhere. See the editorial, *Chosun Ilbo*, 11 December 1999, p. 2. Another attempt by the Korean religious groups to invite the Dalai Lama was apparently foiled due to the ROK's concern over Chinese Premier Zhu Rongji's October 2000 visit to Seoul. See *Chosun Ilbo*, 19 October 2000, p. 3.

5 For a comprehensive exploration of the Roh Moo-hyun government's conception of the ROK's regional policy, see Geung Chan Bae (2005). The main body for the current ROK government's regional policy – especially its economic aspects – is the Presidential Commission on Northeast Asian Cooperation Initiative (NACI), but it has recently been marred by internal irregularities and has yet to come up with concrete policies – let alone positive responses from the neighbouring countries.

6 After the April 2004 election of General Assembly members, 63 per cent of the ruling party members (Woori Party) favoured closer ties with China compared to with the US. After the Koguryo case became a diplomatic row between the two

countries, the figure plummeted to 10 per cent or below. Similar results can be found in other opinion surveys. See, for example, Yonhap News, 10 August 2004 and Media Daum, 19 August 2004.

7 See, for example, Xia Liping and Jiang Xiyuan (2004); Zheng Bijian (2004).

8 For a difference between "peaceful rise" and "peaceful development", see Sukhee Han (2004). For an excellent analysis on the background and implications of China's "peaceful development" strategy, see Xiaoxiong Yi (2005).

9 There is simply too much literature on the "China threat". Most representative single volumes include Mosher 2000; Gertz 2000; Timperlake and Triplett 1999. For various reactions from the regional actors to a rising China, see Yee and Storey (2002); Pumphrey (2002).

10 According to the recent data released by the MOFAT, South Korea's trade with China in 2004 was $79.3 billion with a surplus of $20.2 billion. According to the Chinese statistics – which includes the ROK's trade portions with Hong Kong, it was $90.1 billion.

11 The ROK's accumulated amount of investment in China up to 2004 was $17.8 billion, which is close to its total investment in the U.S. ($17.1 billion).

12 The figures are drawn from an interview with the ROK's ambassador to the PRC. See Yonhap News (2004).

13 An increase in China's export to North Korea for the past few years should be interpreted as a form of Chinese assistance. The question of North Korea's dependency on Chinese oil and food has recently taken on new relevance in the discussion of possible international sanctions against North Korea. According to various official documents of the ROK, North Korea imported an average one million tons of oil from China in 1991–96 and it fell to a half million tons and below since 1997. Its grain imports from China are far more complicated to account for due in part to China's own harvest level and export policy, but approximately 300,000 tons of grain have been imported from China since 1997. For a series of recent but higher-level accounts of North Korea's oil and grain imports from China, see John J. Tkacik, Jr., "China Must Pressure Pyongyang (December 17, 2002)", available at www.heritage.org/Press/Commenrary/ed123102b.cfm; Phillip P. Pan, "China Treads Carefully Around North Korea". *Washington Post*, 10 January 2003, p. A14; Phillip C. Saunders and Jing-Dong Yuan, "Korea Crisis Will Test Chinese Diplomacy," *Asia Times*, 8 January 2003; Matthew Forney, "Family Feud: China vs. North Korea," *Time*, 23 December 2002; and Mark O'Neill, "Beijing Faces a Stern Test Over Nuclear Crisis in Its Back Yard," *South China Morning Post*, 3 January 2003.

14 For an excellent discussion on the depth and prospect of North Korea's economic problems and their various effects, see Eberstadt (2004), Chaiki Seong (2003), VanWagenen (2000).

15 See, for example, Dittmer 2003. For a recent discussion on the prospects for US–China relations under Hu Jintao, see Jaewoo Choo (2004).

16 For a detailed analysis on the military-to-military relationship between China and North Korea up to 1997, see Taeho Kim (1999, 2001).

17 For an analysis on the mutual visits between Beijing and Pyongyang, see Yonhap News, 24 September 2004.

18 Alliance fatigue, which is a natural symptom for any old alliance relationship, is particularly acute in the Sino-North Korea case as there is a growing divergence of interests between the two. See Sukhee Han (2004).

19 This does not mean, however, that their military-to-military ties are balanced or symmetrical in terms of frequency and the ranks of the visiting officers. For a comprehensive treatment of the PLA's military diplomacy in the 1990s in general and China's military relations with both Koreas, see Allen and McVadon (1999).

20 Unofficial translation by the author.
21 For the strategic context of the issues, see Jaeho Hwang (2004).
22 See a flurry of newspaper reports on the subject including B. J. Lee, "Historical Differences", *South China Morning Post*, 13 August 2004; Edward Cody, "China Gives No Ground in Spats over History", *Washington Post*, 22 September 2004, p. A25; Howard W. French, "China's Textbooks Twist and Omit History", *New York Times*, 6 December 2004; David Scofield, "China Ups and Downs in Ancient-Kingdom Feud with Korea", *Asia Times*, 16 August 2004; idem, "China Puts Korean Spat on the Map", *Asia Times*, 19 August 2004.
23 For this line of reasoning, see Jun-young Kang, "Hidden Motives behind China's Northeast Project", *Korea Herald*, 24 August 2004. The publication date, it should be noted, is the twelfth anniversary of the ROK–PRC diplomatic normalization.
24 See, for example, Bates Gill, "Contrasting Visions: United States, China and World Order", an unpublished mimeo presented at the US–China Security Review Commission Session on US–China Relationship and Strategic Perceptions, 3 August 2001. A dated yet still useful discussion on the impact of the diverging visions of the US and China on the Korea peninsula can be found in Olsen (1997).
25 In particular, see the conference proceedings on the First ROK–US–China Future Forum entitled "The Changing ROK–US–China Relationships and the Future of the Korean Peninsula", co-hosted by the Institute for Diplomacy and Security Studies (IDSS) and the Center for Contemporary China Studies (CCCS), Hallym University, Shilla Hotel, Seoul, 30 October 2004.
26 For a critical assessment on the North Korean nuclear crisis and on the participating nations' difference interests, see Mansourov (2003); O'Hanlon and Mochizuki (2003); Cha (2002); Quinones (2004).

References

Allen, Kenneth and McVadon, Eric A. (1999) *China's Foreign Military Relations*, Washington, DC, The Henry L. Stimson Center, October.
Bae, Geung Chan (2005) "'Northeast Asian Cooperation Initiative' and Korea's Diplomatic Tasks: A Strategy for Regional Cooperation", *Journal of East Asian Affairs*, Vol. 19, No. 1 (Spring/Summer), 1–26.
Cha, Victor D. (2002) "North Korea's Weapons of Mass Destruction: Badges, Shields, or Swords?", *Political Science Quarterly*, Vol. 117, No. 2 (Summer), 209–30.
Choo, Jaewoo (2004) "Hu Jintao's Foreign Policy and Sino-U.S. Relations: From A [sic] Korean Perspective", *New Asia*, Vol. 11, No. 3 (Autumn), 80–112
Dittmer, Lowell (2003) "Leadership Change and Chinese Political Development", *China Quarterly*, No. 176 (December), 903–25.
Eberstadt, Nicholas (2004) "The Persistence of North Korea", *Policy Review*, October/November, 23–48.
Gertz, Bill (2000) *The China Threat: How the People's Republic Targets America*, Washington, DC: Regnery.
Han, Sukhee (2004) "The Rise of China and East Asia's Changing Order" (in Korean), *New Asia*, Vol. 11, No. 3 (Autumn), 113–34.
Han, Sukhee (2004) "Alliance Fatigue amid Asymmetrical Interdependence", *Korean Journal of Defense Analysis*, Vol. 16, No. 1 (Spring), 155–79.
Hwang, Jaeho (2004) "Northeast Asia's Pandora's Box: North Korean Escapees", *Korean Journal of Defense Analysis*, Vol. 16, No. 1 (Spring), 49–72.

Kim, Taeho (1999) "Strategic Relations Between Beijing and Pyongyang: Growing Strains amid Lingering Ties", in Lilley, James R. and David Shambaugh (eds), *China's Military Faces the Future,* Armonk, NY: M. E. Sharpe, 295–321.

Kim, Taeho (2001) *Recent Changes in Sino-North Korea Relations and the ROK's Policy Options*, Seoul, KIDA (in Korean).

Mansourov, Alexandre Y. (2003) "North Korea Is Poised to Cross the Nuclear Rubicon: Will the Canary Die in the Mine?", *International Journal on World Peace*, Vol. 20, No. 3 (September), 17–28.

Mosher, Steven W. (2000) *Hegemon: China's Plan to Dominate Asia and the World*, San Francisco, CA: Encounter Books.

O'Hanlon, Michael and Mochizuki, Mike (2003) *Crisis on the Korean Peninsula: How to Deal With a Nuclear North Korea*, Washington, DC: The Brookings Institution.

Olsen, Edward A. (1997) "U.S. & China: Conflicting Korean Agenda", *Korea and World Affairs*, Vol. 21, No. 2 (Summer), 254–69.

Pumphrey, Carolyn W. (2002) (ed.) *The Rise of China in Asia: Security Implications*, Carlisle Barracks, PA: US Army War College Strategic Studies Institute.

Quinones, C. Kenneth (2004) "North Korea Nuclear Talks: The View from Pyongyang", *Arms Control Today*, Vol. 34, No. 7 (September), 6–12.

Seong, Chaiki (2003) "A Decade of Economic Crisis in North Korea: Impacts on the Military", *The KIDA Papers*, No. 3 (October), 1–9.

Timperlake, Edward and Triplett, William C. Jr. (1999) *Red Dragon Rising: Communist China's Military Threat to America*, Washington, DC: Regnery.

VanWagenen, Paul (2000) "U.S. Economic Sanctions – Non-traditional Success against North Korea", *Law and Policy in International Business*, Vol. 32, No. 1 (Fall), 239–61.

Xia Liping and Jiang Xiyuan, (2004) *Zhongguo Heping Jueqi* [China's Peaceful Rise], Beijing: Zhongguo Shehuikexueyuan Chubanshe.

Xiaoxiong Yi, (2005) "Chinese Foreign Policy in Transition: Understanding China's 'Peaceful Development'", *Journal of East Asian Affairs*, Vol. 19, No. 1 (Spring/ Summer), 74–112.

Yee, Herbert and Storey, Ian, (2002) (eds) *The China Threat: Perceptions, Myths, and Reality,* London: RoutledgeCurzon.

Zheng Bijian, (2004) "China's Peaceful Rise and Opportunities for the Asia Pacific Region", *China Strategy*, Vol. 3 (July 20), 2–4.

8 China and the United States

The new power configuration in East Asia and Korea's regional policy

Changsu Kim

Introduction

China's rise, US-Sino relations and US management of alliance relationships have become increasingly critical factors in shaping a new power configuration in East Asia, and they will continue to be the case in the first quarter of the twenty-first century. The United States wants to make clear that it maintains preponderance over the countries in the region, including China, Japan, the two Koreas and Taiwan. A re-emerging China may continue to challenge the *Pax Americana* in its backyard. And China's "peaceful rise" or, more recently, its "peaceful development" may pose a serious threat to the US national interest, or it may bring great benefits to the Americans as well as the Chinese.

There are two schools of thought, realists and liberals, who project different pictures of the future security complex of East Asia. As Joseph S. Nye Jr. aptly points out, it will be "important not to mistake analysts' theories for reality".[1] In other words, for various reasons that will be explained later, the United States and China may not need to "engage in an intense security competition with considerable potential for war", as realist strategists like to portend. Neither economic interdependence nor other socio-cultural networks in East Asia will automatically mitigate the instability inherent in the US–China rivalry, as liberal strategists like to envision. A more-or-less "straight line" projection of the future courses of the two hegemonic powers by these realists and liberals alike leaves little room for a middle-of-the-road projection that is characterized by an upward spiral of rising and falling tensions, heading towards an improved long-term relationship after a short-to mid-term confrontation.

China's astonishing economic growth and its concomitant military modernization *per se* do not give rise to an aggressive hegemon. Prudent policy in Washington and Beijing, in conjunction with occasional balancing roles of Japan and Korea, can make the seemingly confrontational bilateral relationship into a more cooperative and less confrontational one. Indeed, the two dominant powers can and will play the roles of strategic competitors and partners alternately in their long-term relations.

The core question apparently lies in "what kind of future US–China relationship do we want and what do we need to do now in order to achieve it?"[2] This chapter tends to side with those who believe that "belief in the inevitability of conflict can become one of its main causes",[3] and those who believe that "there is no inevitability in history except as men make it".[4] To be sure, the US–China relationship in the next twenty years will be shaped in a non-linear, complicated way by a variety of factors including bilateral and trilateral relations among the regional powers in East Asia and some salient issues of regional security concern.

This chapter starts with evaluations of the so-called rise of China and the threats China poses to the United States and to neighbouring countries in East Asia. It also covers how long the "reluctant empire" of the United States can be maintained with substantial security implications over East Asia.[5] Optimistic and pessimistic views of the future relations of the two great powers will be examined in some detail and a third view will be introduced and explained in greater detail. Perceptions and substance of the re-emerging China with potential hegemonic pursuits will be elaborated, along with how well America can, in concert with other allies and friends, "manage the rise of China" and maintain prolonged peace and prosperity in this increasingly important part of the world.

This chapter then proceeds to explore the dynamics of a new power configuration in East Asia for the next twenty years. A special emphasis will be given to reasons why the United States and China would rather develop their relations into amicable and cooperative ones as found among responsible democracies, freeing themselves from an inevitable clash of the two titans. Resurgent nationalism, rivalry between China and Japan, South Korea's hedging role between China and Japan, resurgent Russia and rising India, flash points in the Taiwan Strait and the Korean Peninsula, an expanded Asian-centric cultural identity among East Asian countries, the impact of globalization and advancement in science and technology, the spread of democracy and the information society and others would combine together to act as driving forces behind the long-term trend of productive, not destructive, competition and cooperation between the two largest economies in the world. History will not repeat itself, particularly in East Asia. Many tragic lessons of the past history of these regional powers will serve as a reminder that they should not explicitly treat each other as a prospective enemy, even if they may implicitly need to be ready for worst-scenario cases.

Finally, this chapter ends by proposing South Korea's regional policy alternatives toward neighbouring powers. Basic tenets of Seoul's security strategy and regional policy will be centred around the continued alliance with the United States, improving security cooperation with all other regional powers including Japan, China, and Russia, and building the foundation for multilateral security dialogue and cooperation in East Asia, so that South Korea can maintain peace and prosperity in and around the Korean Peninsula and achieve a timely, peaceful unification with North Korea.

US–China relations, 2005–2025

American pre-eminence, primacy, and global leadership

The world up to 2025 and, for that matter, the future of the United States in the years out to 2025 will be shaped largely by key drivers and trends such as demographics, natural resources and the environment, science and technology, the global economy and globalization, national and international governance, future conflict, and the role of the United States. It is obvious that no single driver or trend will dominate the global future to the year 2025; that key drivers will have varying impacts in different regions and countries; and that these drivers are not necessarily mutually reinforcing; in some cases, they will work at cross-purposes.[6]

It is widely shared among American strategists and futurologists that the United States will remain a superpower with unparalleled economic, technological, military and diplomatic influence. They believe that this unparalleled power will ensure America's pre-eminence as the most important actor in the international system. They also believe that the role of the United States as the leading proponent and beneficiary of globalization will have a major global impact.

Likewise, according to most futurologist reports published by US government agencies and institutions, America at 2025 will highly likely remain the single dominant power in the world arena.[7] Such preponderance will, however, be increasingly challenged by a number of important actors such as China, India and the European Union. These actors will seek to challenge and check the US leadership, or what they see as "American hegemony".

A nagging question for the United States in the next two decades centres on whether it can maintain a "benevolent empire", however misleading it may be, or hegemony despite challenges from potential peers, most notably China. Many American experts seem to predict a long life of their empire or, euphemistically, their "global leadership". Surely, for the next two decades America will remain an "informal empire", or a sort of "imperium" – a global influence that is disproportionate for a country that has less than 5 per cent of the world's population.[8] Moreover, according to Odom and Dujarric, The United States finds itself at the centre of an empire of a new type, wealth-generating and voluntary, not a traditional imperial system."[9] They contend that the major threat to this unique empire is ineffective US leadership, not a rising rival power centre like China. If the United States uses its own power constructively, they conclude, the American empire will flourish for a long time.

Indeed, the United States as a "liberal empire" has many advantages over other empires. It boasts the economics of a liberal empire, that is, "while membership pays, opposing the American empire does not pay". It also has various gaps with many aspiring hegemons in military power, demographics, economic performance, universities, science and technology, and the media

and mass culture. The United States can, therefore, maintain its status as a
"liberal empire", if it continues to guard, maintain, and sustain its liberal
institutions; maintain and steadily improve its military power; cultivate its
liberal institutions – political, economic, and military – as the organiza-
tional context and ideological standard for international relations; and
rethink the promotion of democracy in countries that have not yet achieved
liberal breakthroughs.[10]

As Joseph S. Nye, Jr. asserts, however, America as the only superpower
can't go it alone, unless it makes a more willing effort to make good
neighbours in a global information age.[11] America in the years leading up
to 2025 will have a national interest beyond its borders and its strategy will
focus on providing global public goods such as "maintaining regional balances of power and dampening local incentives to use force to change borders" as well as liberal democracy, human rights, etc.[12] In a similar vein,
American primacy will continue to exist as long as America's global strategy succeeds in managing the conflicts and relationships in the four critical
regions of Eurasia that includes East Asia.[13]

China's pursuit of hegemony

Has China already emerged as a hegemon in East Asia in 2005 or will it in
the next two decades? Will China be only an economic hegemon, or will it
become a hegemonic power in other areas as well, including the military?
Looking first at the Chinese economy with its tremendous potential, most
recent projections of the long-term Chinese economy have one thing in
common: the Chinese economy will be next only to that of the United
States or even surpass it by 2025.[14]

The Chinese government's goal to attain a "*xiaokang* society" by 2020
will be supported and substantiated by massive future projects. Under these
projects, China's GDP will increase from $1.17 trillion at 2002 to $4.1 trillion at 2020. This figure is too conservative, according to a recent report by
Goldman Sachs, which predicts China's 2020 GDP at $7.07 trillion. Also,
China aspires to become the world's leader in IT (Information Technology)
and even in BT (Bio-engineering Technology).

However, there is also a downside to it. China will conceivably fail to
sustain high economic growth due to difficulties for reforming its economy.
Growth will only slow down if economic reforms go off-track. Skyrocketing
energy consumption will probably dry up China's capital flows. An array of
political, social, and economic pressures will increasingly challenge the
Chinese government's legitimacy even to the point of survival.

To many US security experts who buy "China threat" theories, China has
emerged as a rival who resents its international pre-eminence. China has
acquired more than enough wealth to make remarkable investments in its
military, due largely to its continued high economic growth rate and awa-
kened sense of the impact of military forces in international affairs. In 2004,

for instance, China's defence expenditure registered 219,986 billion yuan, accounting for only 1.61 per cent of that year's GDP.[15] And a spokesperson for China's National People's Congress announced on 4 March 2005 that China's defence budget in 2005 has reached approximately $29.9 billion, a 12.6 per cent increase over the last year. However, China's real defence expenditures, including foreign weapons procurement (up to $3.0 billion annually from Russia alone), expenses for the paramilitary People's Armed Police, funding to support nuclear weapon stockpiles and the Second Artillery, subsidies to defence industries, defence-related research and development, etc. that are tucked into other budgets, can double or triple the officially published figures.[16]

It is in this light that many American China hands agree in viewing that PRC military modernization could alter the regional balance of power and raise stakes for the US forces stationed in the Asia-Pacific.[17] Even though China has not been successful in acquiring weapons systems that can change the cross-strait military equation or surrounding waters where US forces and Japanese Self-Defence forces are deployed, China has reportedly developed advanced cruise and anti-ship missiles and it will continue to enhance such military capabilities throughout the next twenty years.

China will continue to seek pre-eminence of its own in the next decades and probably re-emerge as a hegemon around 2020. With a robust economy and advanced military capabilities, China will search for strategic partnerships with nearly all of its neighbouring powers to boost its hegemonic status in East Asia. Not only will China improve ties with former rivals like Russia and India, but it will also carefully ameliorate relations with more imminent threats like the United States and Japan. Beijing will struggle for a "peaceful rise" or "peaceful development" to create a more favourable image in the eyes of the world. Regarding the Taiwan issue, Beijing will continue to press for its time-honoured "One China" policy and will probably seek to evade military confrontation with outside powers. Recent developments like the visits to Mainland China by Lien Zhan, the first Kuomintang leader to set foot on the mainland since the end of the civil war in 1949, and the People First Party's Chairman James Soong (Song Chuyu) laid the foundation for talks with the CCP, building historic landmarks for peace in the cross-strait history. China's Anti-Secession Law that mandates war and other "non-peaceful" means if Taiwan formally declares independence would remain unabated but would not be implemented either. Despite the existence of many factors that make things look negative, the Beijing government will probably reduce tensions across the Taiwan Strait as it restores confidence in its diplomatic power and adopts more pragmatic policies while Taiwan continues to make progress in democratization and bettering relations with the Mainland China.

On the North Korean nuclear and other weapons of mass destruction (WMD) issue, Beijing will continue to act as a broker and stabilizer to ensure North Korea as a buffer zone. Beijing's hosting and brokering at the

Six-Party Talks will likely continue as a responsible member of the international society and as a nation deeply concerned with crises along the borders. In addition to Pyongyang's nuclear programmes, Beijing might opt for serving as the venue for other regional arms control issues as well. China's special interest in preserving its stability and prosperity in East Asia for many years to come will certainly restrain its ambition to become an outright hegemon. Finally, with regard to Korean unification, Beijing will make sure there is no contingency in North Korea serious enough to invite American and South Korean military intervention.

Fluctuating Sino-American relations

Will China continue to challenge US hegemony in East Asia? Will the US posture as the only remaining superpower last for the next twenty years? Will the *Pax Americana* be replaced by the *Pax Concordia*, as some realist theories have suggested? Will the US continue to strengthen its security ties with Japan in its effort to contain and encircle China? In answering these questions, I argue that the American strategy toward Asia will alternate between containing and managing the rise of China to cooperatively engaging with a "Super China".

To be sure, the rapid economic growth of China and its threat will continue to alarm the American public and elite alike. Conservatives in the US government and think tanks will continue to raise their voice in support of a strengthened alliance with Japan. As America will continue to be deeply involved in the Middle East and other parts of the world in its global war on terror, China would probably go unchecked in its pursuit of regional expansionism. Thus, the United States would likely continue to push for containment of China with support from allies and friends. China, for its part, will continue to break through this US-led containment by expanding economic and security ties with many of its neighbouring countries in Southeast Asia, Northeast Asia, Central Asia and even in the Middle East. For instance, rapidly growing commercial ties between China and all other neighbouring countries including Japan, Korea, Russia, the United States, and even India will act "as a buffer against aggressive impulses and ultimately ease China's 'integration' into the international system without war".[18]

Sino-American relations in the coming decade, according to the prominent China expert Jonathan Pollack, are "unlikely to be characterized by an overt Chinese challenge to American strategic primacy". Rather, a more probable outcome is that "both states will continue manoeuvring for geopolitical advantage, and they will make intermittent tactical accommodation that obscures unresolved (and potentially unresolved) conflicts of interest, and they will prudently accumulate their military power over the longer term".[19]

With regard to the Taiwan and North Korean issues, the United States and China might opt for a protracted or gradual resolution without going to the extreme. As long as tensions remain high between Beijing and Taipei, the United States will continue to dispatch and deploy its military cap-abilities close to the Taiwan Strait, in close consultation with Japan. This shows a US intention to reinforce its initiative in military operations. The United States will not hesitate to show its will to contain and check China's potential military actions. The US willingness to obtain "strategic flex-ibility" of its forces stationed in South Korea and Japan undeniably stems from, among others, this strategic scheme to deter China's military attacks across the Taiwan Strait.

The reverse is tension reduction across the Taiwan Strait, which will work positively toward reducing tensions between Washington and Beijing, and will presumably have positive impact on US–Chinese cooperation in mana-ging the North Korean nuclear crisis. Also, such improved relations between the two powers will have consequences for South Korea's regional policy as well. In the near term, China's role in preserving peace and security in East Asia cannot but be anticipated and endured, while the United States is preoccupied with a more urgent crisis in the Middle East and its global war on terror. In fact, as former US Defense Secretary Donald Rumsfeld pro-fessed, two missions to achieve the US strategic goal of preserving the *Pax Americana* are "to transform the politics of the greater Middle East and to contain the growing military power of China".[20] Under these circumstances, the two powers would choose cooperation rather than confrontation in the near-to mid-term.

In predicting the future of US–China relations up to the year 2025, one has to consider advantages of a latecomer challenger. According to Robert Gilpin's theory of underlying dynamics of crisis in a shifting balance of power, China's costs as the rising state of changing the system decrease, while US costs as the traditionally dominant state of maintaining the international system increase. In other words, given China's expanding military, huge trade surpluses, and increasingly accepted regional dom-inance, the cost of changing the *status quo* will likely decline. Hence, China will be tempted to challenge the *status quo*, which is characterized by American pre-eminence.

In the United States, realists and liberals appear to line up according to their party affiliations and ideological constraints. Realists tend to predict future relations with China in a rather pessimistic fashion, while liberals in a rather optimistic fashion. The former includes Samuel P. Huntington, John J. Mearsheimer, Aaron L. Friedberg, and the so-called neo-cons such as Robert Kagan, Max Boot, and Thomas Donnelly, while the latter includes Zbigniew Brzezinki, Joseph S. Nye, Jr., David Shambaugh, and David Lampton.

A typical realist view of the prospects for Sino-American relations can be summarized as the following:

> integrating a resurgent China into regional and global balances of power in a peaceful and stable fashion poses the single greatest challenge

to the Asia-Pacific region … Those relations are likely to continue declining, or at least persist in an uneasy period of mutual hostility and suspicion, until such time as there is fundamental regime change in China.[21]

Another typical realist view is that "the stronger and more assertively nationalistic China becomes, the sharper the tensions will become".[22] One can also cite reasons for pessimism, including the lack of a strategic rationale for cooperation after the dissolution of the former Soviet Union, tensions generated by a rising power à la Gilpin, natural discord between dictatorships and democracies, cultural differences à la Huntington, China's resurging nationalism, and trade policy debates. To cite the now-famous Huntington's dictum, "the cultural and most dangerous dimensions of the emerging global politics would be conflict between groups from differing civilizations, that is, America and China".[23] These realists tend to suggest initial coercive engagement tailored to promote US interests and encourage the rise of democracy in China, to be followed by containment against China. Without exception, they prefer maintaining alliance relationships in East Asia and preserving a military capable of responding to Chinese aggression should it occur.

On the other hand, liberals tend to refute the realist view by arguing that power transition and strategic instability potentially inherent in the US–China rivalry would not be as traumatic as realists envision and that the economic interdependence and socio-cultural network in East Asia would work as mitigating factors. Meanwhile, "constructivists present a more cautious view that neither power nor norms and interests can determine the future dynamics of Northeast Asian security complex".[24]

Anyway, US–China relations for the next twenty years will probably unfold along the lines somewhere between the pessimistic realist views and the optimistic liberalist views. For roughly the first ten years or so, I would like to argue that US–China relations will be more confrontational than cooperative. The Chinese economy will likely grow at a steady pace and Chinese military capabilities will also increase, as the China threat theories suggest. Washington and Tokyo will continue to strengthen their security ties in deterring and containing Beijing's outward expansionism. However, after these confrontational years, the US–China relations will become more cooperative than confrontational for various reasons. They include changing American and Japanese perceptions of the China threat, Beijing's growing accountability as a responsible member in international affairs, common threats posed by a nuclear North Korea and possibly a unified Korea, a new power configuration in East Asia, which will be explained below.

After all, a fully fledged Sino-American Cold War is not inevitable. According to Aaron Friedberg, the two hegemonic powers will enter "a race between the accelerating dynamics of multipolarity, which could increase the chances of conflict, and the growth of mitigating factors that should tend to dampen them and to improve the prospects for a continuing peace".[25] One implication would be that the China threat would gradually yield to engagement with China over the next twenty years.

New power configuration in East Asia

Will the rough equilibrium of forces remain unchanged in the Asia-Pacific in the next ten to twenty years, or will the balance of power be altered by intervention of, for example, the United States? What will be the key drivers and trends that will help shape a new power configuration in East Asia out to the year 2025? Let us assume that the great strategic challenge of the future to the United States and the world alike will be no other than power relations in East Asia. North Korea, Taiwan, and China in the East Asian Community will continue to draw the keen interest of the world. Then, one can presumably recognize the significance of such key drivers and trends as resurgent nationalism, the impact of globalization, power plays of Japan and China, the balancing roles of South Korea, Russia, and India, proliferation of WMD and transnational threats, relatively peripheral and yet increasingly salient issues like Taiwan and North Korea including the collapse of the Kim Jong Il regime and reunification of the two Koreas, in projecting a new power configuration in East Asia.

The irony is that despite the primacy of US–China relations and their impact on regional security in predicting a new order in East Asia, some relatively peripheral issues may in fact turn out to be more determining factors in creating new power dynamics here in this part of the world. This appears roughly in line with the analogy of the B-list and C-list issues suggested by Nye.[26]

A salient A-list threat like a threatening China or the spread of nuclear materials may not turn out to be a dominant factor in assessing and predicting the Sino-American relations for the next two decades. Rather, it might be a B-list threat like situations on the Korean Peninsula and across the Taiwan Strait that would determine the direction of the bilateral relations of the two titans. Like C-list threats including "important contingencies that indirectly affect US security but do not directly threaten US interests", B-list threats will also "dominate media attention in the global information age".[27] The implication here is that many issues including Beijing's bilateral relations with Tokyo, Seoul, Pyongyang, and Taipei, along with those of Washington's, rather than Beijing–Washington relations *per se*, will count more for the new power configuration in East Asia. This is a significant diversion from the mainstream analysis and prediction about the new order in the Asia-Pacific era.

Take China and Japan as cases in point. As a rising economic and military power, China appears to be aspiring to become a hegemonic power in the Asia-Pacific. Not only has it asserted its traditional hegemonic status toward many nations in Southeast Asia, but it has also increasingly played a self-imposed dominant role in Northeast Asian security. This will continue to be the case in the years ahead. Japan's survival instinct has been stimulated by changing threat perceptions such as Pyongyang's nuclear and missile threats and China's outright attacks on its pride and reputation as the second economic power in the world. Due to a recurring, unresolved past history in their relations, North and South Korea and China have joined their hands in blocking Japan's bid for a permanent UN Security Council seat and in opposing Japan's claim on their territories. Meanwhile, many have come to view that a rebalancing of power is taking place throughout Asia, as "China ascends, Japan responds and India shrewdly reaps benefits from the clash of the two other Asian titans".[28]

In a similar manner, globalization will remain a powerful driver in East Asia as well. The likely role of science and technology will continue to expand as a driver of global developments. By 2015, compared with 2010, there will be even greater uncertainty over the direction of Beijing's regional policies. By 2020 or 2025, "globalization could be equated in the popular mind with a rising Asia, replacing its current association with Americanization".[29]

Now, let us turn to some key drivers in exploring the new power dynamics in East Asia through 2025. To save space and for clarity, they will include strengthening and weakening of the US–Japan alliance, Japan–China rivalry for regional hegemony, US–Korea–Japan trilateral security cooperation, the US–Japan–China strategic relations, responses to North Korea's nuclear weapons and other WMDs, and Korean unification.

Strengthening of the US–Japan alliance

A strengthening of the US–Japan alliance will last for a considerable period of time to fight the war on terror at the global level and to deter and counter regional threats primarily from North Korea and China. North Korea's nuclear weapons and other WMD and missiles will continue to pose a threat to the two close allies. And they will continue to boost their security cooperation in blocking the spread of terrorism and WMD in the form of international regimes and the Missile Defence.

As its influence expands rapidly and visibly in East Asia, China will likely confront head on with Japan, a long-time economic powerhouse and the leader in East Asia. In fact, Japan's assessment is that "North Korea's such military activities constitute a major destabilizing factor to the regional security and a serious challenge to the international efforts for non-proliferation".[30] China, on the other hand, "has a strong influence on the security in this region, has been modernizing its nuclear and missile capabilities as well as naval and air forces, and expanding its area of operation at sea. We have to remain attentive to its future course." These assessments will remain unchanged for the foreseeable future.

Indeed, America perceives China as a strategic competitor and Japan perceives China as a potential threat. These perceptions and decisions to bolster US–Japanese security arrangements well reflect common interests and values of the two largest economies. Japan has chosen, and will continue to choose, the United States to counter the threatening growth of China while giving the impression that it will never make the same mistake of becoming an aggressive military power.

This author would argue that such initial strengthening of the US–Japan alliance will gradually decline as the global war on terrorism loses its initial attraction and efficiency and as all major regional powers in East Asia adjust their strategies to deal with the rapidly growing China.

The Japan–China rivalry and balancer role of the US and ROK

After the end of the Cold War, power dynamics underwent a sea change in East Asia. This change has made Sino-Japanese competition even harsher. China's rise or re-emergence has driven a substantial increase in its defence budgets, causing alarm in Tokyo over how Beijing will employ its political and military might. At the same time, Tokyo's ever-strengthening alliance with Washington and its pursuit of a "normal country" with its expanding roles in the post-9/11 security environment have raised concerns on the part of Beijing. The driving force in the ostensibly clashing finger-pointing is power politics in East Asia. In addition, regional economic cooperation has provided Japan and China with a forum in which they compete for regional leadership.

For all their economic and cultural cooperation, China and Japan have recently shown growing antipathy toward each other, due largely to conflicting views on their past history and increasingly visible nationalist sentiments. Strong nationalistic sentiments in Japan and a sense of victimization in nationalistic China portend a new power configuration and strategic competition between the two Asian giants. Japanese Prime Minister Koizumi's recent visits to the Yasukuni Shrine have rekindled anti-Japanese sentiments in China and Korea. Also, Tokyo's reasserted claims over islands in the South China Sea, for example, have resulted in massive anti-Japanese demonstrations throughout China and Beijing's intention to boycott Tokyo's bid for permanent UN Security Council membership.

For the first time in 2004 China became the number one trading partner for Japan replacing the United States, but the leaders of the two Asian giants have not paid visits to each other's capital. Tokyo's embellishment of its history of war of aggression and Prime Minister Koizumi's paying tribute to the war dead including war criminals at the Yasukuni Shrine cannot be tolerated by Beijing. In the East China Sea, China is exploring oil fields in the seabed off the *Senkaku* islands (*Diaoyudao* for the Chinese), and as PLA submarines continued to infiltrate into the Japanese territorial waters, the JMSDF has been put a high alert. The 2005 issue of *Defence of Japan* defined China as a potential threat to Japan.

The rivalry between the two Asian giants will be greatly influenced by fluctuating US–Sino relations. Seeing China as a potential enemy, and in the face of the growing economic and military capabilities of China, Japan, and the United States have joined hands in containing China. However, this strategic competition between Tokyo and Beijing will not go unchecked. Put differently, Tokyo will probably choose to "balance" against the rising China in the foreseeable future, but at some point through 2025 Tokyo will probably choose to "bandwagon" with China. Japan will seek a *modus vivendi* with China as the region's rising power. Throughout, Japan and China will exert their respective influence over cross-Taiwan Strait tensions and North Korean contingencies and unification of the two Koreas. Overall, Japan and China, intertwined so deeply in many aspects of their relations, will seek a balance in the overall confrontational mode.

The US–Korea–Japan security cooperation

Trilateral security dialogue and cooperation among the United States, Japan and South Korea officially started during the first North Korean nuclear crisis of 1993–94. The US–Japan and the ROK–US alliances and ROK–Japan bilateral security cooperation have become increasingly active and strengthened. Security threats posed by North Korea and the prospects for North Korean collapse have been the driving force behind the new emerging bilateral security cooperation. It is noteworthy that the US–Japan Joint Declaration on Security of April 1996, the revised Guidelines for US–Japan Defence Cooperation of September 1997, and the passage of related laws and revision of ACSA were all done to effectively deal with possible contingencies in areas surrounding Japan. They have not only strengthened the existing cooperative systems regarding the North Korean problem and other security issues, but also they have successfully built a solid basis for implementing an engagement policy towards North Korea.

Japan has shown increasingly positive attitudes toward dismantling the Cold War structure on the Korean Peninsula and has continuously supported for mid-to long-term peaceful coexistence and unification of the two Koreas. Also, other concerns that had seized the minds of the Japanese leadership have apparently diminished, such as nuclear-free zone initiatives, the likelihood of unified Korea's leaning toward China, and regional arms races among unified Korea, Japan, and China.

The ROK and Japan have promoted other forms of security cooperation and defence exchange programmes, including exchange of high-level officials, Defence Staff Talks, the Security Policy Consultative Meeting, and the Intelligence Exchange Meeting, and port calls of navy ships and joint maritime exercises. At various such meetings, the two nations have often shared their views on Chinese participation in multilateral talks.

The three nations want to see some progress with the Trilateral Security Dialogue and the Trilateral Coordination and Oversight Group (TCOG) that have been lagging since April of 2002. Their security policies will place a special emphasis on creating a stable security environment, winning the war on terrorism, responding to rogue states that threaten the use of WMD, and strengthening their allied and friendly relations. Trilateral security cooperation will focus on how to "manage the rise of China". They want to improve broader government-to-government cooperation based on limited cooperation in the military field. The three nations will continue to consult and cooperate over the North Korean nuclear issue and coordinate their differences by a common denominator of peacefully and diplomatically putting an end to Pyongyang's nuclear ambition. However, the trilateral security cooperation might lose its initial fervour as new regional dynamics emerge in East Asia.

The US–Japan–China trilateral relations

In the years ahead these trilateral relations will probably replace the existing US–Korea–Japan trilateral relations as the most prominent form of trilateral relations in East Asia. The three key players will likely consult each other to deal with various regional security issues including the spread of WMD and other transnational threats. In particular, Washington will pay renewed emphasis to its traditional role of balancer, broker, and stabilizer between the two Asian powers. In other words, as the size of their economies and military capabilities become more comparable to each other, these three powers will look into what they can and cannot do in dealing with regional disputes and contingencies in East Asia. As an imperative for America's Eurasian geostrategy, to borrow Brzezinski's phrase, the United States will continue to engage itself in a Far Eastern anchor and maintain a close alliance with the maritime power of Japan while at the same time a cooperative relationship with the continental power of China.[31]

Responses to North Korea's nuclear and other WMDs

Issues pertaining to the Korean Peninsula will continue to draw keen attention from the neighbouring powers. The North Korean nuclear issue, for example, will continue to be internationalized and widely discussed. The ROK government will continue to welcome the efforts to bring forth a peaceful resolution to the North Korean nuclear issue on the part of all participating countries including the US and China. Indeed, South Korea will keep on placing special emphasis on reaching a basic understanding on how to handle North Korea, primarily on persuading and coercing Pyongyang to abandon its nuclear weapons programmes and, later, other WMDs.[32]

This was evident when ROK President Roh Moo-hyun revealed his government's intention to play a more active role in building an East Asian Community for peace and prosperity and in supporting the ASEAN integration process. He also stressed that a peaceful resolution of the North Korean nuclear issue and his "Policy for Peace and Prosperity" would contribute greatly to peace and prosperity in East Asia as an integral whole.

In the year 2005, Pyongyang's declaration of possession of a nuclear arsenal, and its renewed demand at the fourth round of the Beijing Six-Party Talks for a peaceful use of nuclear power and its subsequent agreement in principle to abandon its nuclear programmes in return for recognition and aid from the United States and its Asian allies, have altered the positions and negotiating strategies of the five other participating countries. Paradoxically, the nuclear ambition of the Pyongyang regime works to enhance cooperation among these otherwise conflicting and competing regional powers like the United States, China, and Japan.

In addition to curbing Pyongyang's nuclear and other WMD gamble, these regional powers would continue to press Pyongyang to implement gradual reforms, while making low-profile preparations for possible contingencies in North Korea, particularly the loss of control over Pyongyang's WMDs.

Korean unification

In a new era of North–South reconciliation and cooperation, the ROK–US alliance and the USFK can and should play an important role of facilitating the integration and unification of the two Koreas. Conventional as well as non-conventional arms control on the Korean Peninsula can make smooth progress, if the United States continues to play the role of a balancer and stabilizer. In addition, US technical assistance in Korean arms control, structural and operational, will have positive impact.

The timing and formula of Korean unification will fundamentally alter the relations among the regional powers in East Asia. If there is a sudden, unexpected collapse of the Kim Jong Il regime, South Korea and the United States, on the one hand, and China, on the other, will have great difficulty in managing such a contingency in North Korea. As a recent episode of conflicting positions of Seoul and Washington regarding North Korean contingencies and their respective measures suggests, the two allies may encounter many hurdles, including Beijing's possible occupation of some part of North Korea.

Obviously, the four surrounding powers that have long dealt with the two Koreas will enter a new phase of adjusting their relations with the two Koreas in preparation for a new unified Korea and with other regional powers. This may be viewed as a kind of "futures trading" in international relations. The primary concerns of these regional powers will be on the characteristics and intimacy of their relations with the unified Korea, prospects for unified Korea's force structure, and how to maximize their national interest. Here again, to gain support of the regional powers in its effort to achieve a peaceful unification, South Korea will need to maintain a regional security alliance with the United States and secure an environment favourable for continued US military presence.

China's rise and its impact on the future ROK–US alliance

China's rise has also some bearing on the future course of the ROK–US alliance. In the past, debates on the ROK–US alliance relationship were centred on shifting the alliance in accordance with major changes or "triggering events" in inter-Korean relations. However, the changing power dynamics surrounding the Korean Peninsula in general and China's growing influence and exercise of power in particular can add to the shaping of the alliance relationships in the years when Pyongyang's threat is likely to decline.

Surely, China's rise and the concomitant PLA modernization will have a growing impact on the end state of the ROK–US alliance and work as one of the major determinants of transition paths to Korean unification. Also, the rationale for continued alliance will rest on many common interests of the two nations, including prevention of the rise of a hostile hegemon in and around the Korean Peninsula.

Likewise, many nagging questions in the ROK–US alliance, such as the withdrawal of US forces and relocation of military bases and facilities, transfer of wartime operational control, changes in combined command relationships, i.e. the Combined Forces Command (CFC) and the United Nations Command (UNC), will be considered increasingly in conjunction with shifting US–China relations.

South Korea's regional policy

South Korea will continue to work hard to overcome the challenges and threats it will face in the years to come. First and foremost, it will seek to resolve the North Korean nuclear issue peacefully and diplomatically and to pave the way for a peace regime on the Korean Peninsula. As the United States continues to revise its military presence overseas, South Korea will develop a comprehensive and dynamic alliance with the United States to better fit the changing security environment and it will continue to implement a cooperative self-reliant defence posture. Based on such a comprehensive and dynamic alliance with the United States, South Korea will occasionally play a role in facilitating peace in Northeast Asia, primarily between China and Japan. Strengthening regional cooperation with all neighbouring powers will be on top of South Korea's agenda for the next twenty years.[33]

In the foreseeable future, South Korea's regional policy will be centred on implementing new strategic visions laid out by President Roh Moo-hyun, such as cooperative self-reliant defence posture, conditional strategic flexibility granted for American forces stationed in the Republic, an economic hub in Northeast Asia, and a balancing, harmonizing role in promoting peace in Northeast Asia. As President Roh recently proposed, South Korea will follow the strategic line of "playing a balancing role not only on the Korean Peninsula but also for the peace and prosperity of Northeast

Asia. ... The power equation in Northeast Asia will change depending on the choices we make."[34]

Towards a comprehensive and dynamic alliance with the US

The two allies will continue to search for common interests and values and accordingly for a formidable rationale for continued alliance. Even though the two traditional allies have shown diverging assessments of the North Korean military threat and in how to deal with a nuclear North Korea, they will manage to abridge those gaps and find the rationale for a comprehensive, dynamic and enduring alliance. South Korea will continue to ensure that improving inter-Korean ties will not be incompatible with its modified alliance with the United States, and will make its best effort to properly manage the relationship between the two. Also, it will continue to manage the delicate relationship between the US–Japan alliance and China's regional hegemony. The two allies will continue to consult and try to agree on some important elements of their alliance, such as strategic flexibility, changing command relationship, and defence burden-sharing.

South Korea will envision a future alliance with the United States that can best prepare for an uncertain future rather than specific threats. Some measures that will ensure a smooth path to a new security system include: adjusting the alliance to better fit the changing security environment of Northeast Asia; expanding the role of the USFK in maintaining stability and peace of the region while adjusting the level of its military presence; and expanding ROK contributions to regional security as its national power grows. Also, South Korea will continue to see the need to shape an environment favourable for a stable stationing of American forces in South Korea, for example by mitigating and effectively dealing with anti-American sentiments.

One of the goals of South Korea's future alliance with the United States will be to secure a peaceful coexistence and unification with North Korea. Peaceful coexistence and unification would be possible on the Korean Peninsula only if another war is deterred and prevented, if crises in the North are managed in a rapid and effective way, and if the blessing of neighbouring countries is secured. Absent any of these conditions, the Korean unification process would face many difficulties entailing tremendous sacrifice and opportunity cost. The three conditions will probably remain unchanged, but their combination will definitely change.

Therefore, South Korea will make sure that the major tasks of the future ROK–US security alliance will be centred on supporting and securing a peaceful unification of the two Koreas. The two allies will consult and prepare a mid-to-long-term blueprint for their restructured alliance and security system in general. Also, in close consultation with Washington, Seoul will seek to promote multilateral security and military cooperation in East Asia as a means to safeguard a peaceful unification on the two Koreas.

Despite lingering suspicions and misgivings on the part of Japan and China, alternatives to the current alliance with the United States appear to be unlikely, and the best alternative is the restructuring of the alliances as we now know them.[35] At this year's SPI (Security Policy Initiative) meetings, which is a follow-up to last two years' FOTA (Future of the ROK–US Alliance Policy Initiative) meetings, and other related security fora, Seoul will consult with Washington to overcome weaknesses in the alliance, which include a lack of a common long-term vision for Northeast Asia and different views of the regional security at present and in the future.

Towards a future-oriented relationship with Japan

South Korea will consistently pursue confidence-building measures with Japan. Increasing exchanges and cooperation in various fields including defence exchange and cooperation will feature the two nations' new era of cooperation, despite the perennial dispute over some issues such as history textbooks, territorial claims over *Dokdo* Island, and unremitting visits to the *Yasukuni Shrine* by some cabinet members. In particular, as North Korea continues to pose a serious threat to Japan, policy coordination towards North Korea will continue with zeal and consistency. Also, Seoul's concerns about the rise of right-wingers in Japanese society, Constitutional amendment and rearmament, and expanding JSDF roles overseas will restrain the extent of our bilateral cooperation but at the same time will provide the rationale for continued confidence building with Tokyo. Thus, maritime and naval cooperation will remain high on the agenda for frequent discussions between the military authorities. Potential dispute over the issue of *Dokdo* Island and the naming of the East Sea or the Sea of Japan will also require a peaceful and diplomatic resolution between Seoul and Tokyo.

With regard to Pyongyang's nuclear weapons and missiles that can hit strategic targets in Japan, Seoul and Tokyo will consistently consult and cooperate in intelligence sharing and interdicting the flow of these weapons, parts, and related technologies. Also, with regard to contingencies in North Korea, Japan will be required to consult fully in advance with South Korea and the United States, lest it cause unnecessary frictions with South Korea.

Containing vs. bandwagoning vs. hedging towards China

China has long been perceived to have certain influence over North Korea through its long ties and the provision of food and energy. But as it has turned out, Beijing's influence over Pyongyang's economic and political reform and nuclear weapons and other WMD is limited. If North Korea will be found to possess nuclear weapons, China's close ties with North Korean will be mitigated or even endangered, even though some China experts admit that they have no other option but to live with a nuclear North Korea and continue to provide food and oil.

And yet, China's economic interdependence with South Korea has become so high that a hostile policy towards each other is not a feasible option.[36] The two Asian countries have conflicting views on some salient peninsular and regional issues, and, therefore, South Korea will continue to hold in check the extent of its security cooperation with China. Put differently, balancing the ROK–US alliance with the ROK–PRC security cooperation will remain one of Seoul's emerging strategic challenges. Equally puzzling will be when and how long South Korea can and should join the United States in containing China or when it can make an independent decision to jump on the bandwagon of the *de facto* hegemon of China.

It is obvious that the "seeming 'convergence' of interests between Beijing and Seoul in many aspects of their bilateral ties does not necessarily mean that the former is supportive of South Korea's major policy goals – especially when they come to concrete issues or longer-term questions on the Korean peninsula".[37] In light of the longer-term Sino-American rivalry, there will be diverging interests over the Korean Peninsula. And given China's growing influence over, and interdependence, with the Peninsula, it is entirely possible that China will become a source of both despair and hope in achieving South Korea's national objectives.

For Seoul, a peaceful and diplomatic solution of the North Korean nuclear issue will remain a high priority to ensure peace and stability on the Peninsula and its vicinity. A strategy to maintain a friendly, stable relationship with China will thus remain a must over the long haul. Also, with regard to contingencies in North Korea, which Beijing does not seem very interested in discussing openly, Seoul has become increasingly suspicious of Beijing's pre-emptive takeover of some part of the North. The well-documented project of the Chinese government to claim the history of the ancient kingdom of *Goguryeo* (Koguryo) in northeast China as part of Chinese history infuriated the Koreans and the Korean government.[38] This new perception of Chinese hegemony among the Korean public and elite will have a lingering impact on South Korea's relations with China.

Conclusion

Unlike the realist strategists who buy the so-called China threat theory, liberal strategists in America prefer engagement to containment when it comes to the long-term US policy toward China. For the latter, viewing China as a menace is likely to become a self-fulfilling prophecy. They insist, "The United States must also avoid creating a self-fulfilling prophecy of strategic rivalry with China. ... But it is not inevitable; cooperation could still produce historic advancements."[39]

This chapter argues that, for various reasons explained above, the overall US–China relationship for the next 20 years will be more cooperative than confrontational. It also argues that, unlike many familiar projections, the US–Japan alliance will continue to strengthen but will eventually weaken with the rise of the Chinese empire. Therefore, South Korea or a unified Korea should adjust its strategy to benefit from, or bandwagon, the China–US strategic framework in its endeavour to strengthen its strategic stance in East Asia. In particular, even China apparently prefers cooperation and stability in its relations with the United States to confrontation and hostility.

Anyway, US–China relations will have profound implications for world politics as a whole – whether it returns to a hostile balance-of-power arrangement or moves in the direction of a peaceful and stable concert of powers. These outcomes, both at the regional and the global level, will in turn have important consequences for the developments on the Korean Peninsula.

At present and in the near future, the Korean Peninsula will likely find itself in a vortex of power politics among the United States and China, on the one hand, and China and Japan, on the other. In the next twenty years, South Korea will likely undergo major changes in its alliance relationship with the United States, while China's influence will continue to grow in East Asia. In the near future the main pillar of East Asian security will move to the US–Japan alliance. If the ROK–US alliance were to break apart, South Korea would lose a lot, because geopolitically its strategic choices are far too limited. For its relative weaknesses, therefore, South Korea, along with the United States, can and will play a balancing role in promoting peace especially between China and Japan. The security of South Korea, whatever goals it may present to achieve in the future, should be based on continued alliance with the United States.

It will be far from beneficial if South Korea opts to weaken or even abandon its alliance with the United States and to strengthen its security cooperation with China instead, under the assumption that the United States and China will remain confrontational. It will be also desirable if South Korea can maintain and expand the existing security cooperation with Japan. Put in a nutshell, the best strategy for South Korea will be to strengthen its alliance with the United States, maintain security cooperation with Japan, and gradually expand security cooperation with China. Resolving regional security issues without excluding any particular regional players would be the best policy for South Korea in its endeavour to promote peace and prosperity in East Asia.

Notes

1 Joseph S. Nye, Jr., "China's 'peaceful' rise a threat to U.S.?," *The Korea Herald*, 19 March 2005, p. 6.
2 Lampton (2004).
3 Nye (2005).
4 Lampton (2004).
5 Kennedy *et al.* (2003).
6 The National Intelligence Council, *Global Trends 2015: A Dialogue about the Future with Nongovernment Experts*, December 2000.

7 See The National Intelligence Council, *Global Trends 2010*, 1997; The National Intelligence Council, *Global Trends 2015*, December 2000; The National Intelligence Council, *Mapping the Global Future*, December 2004.
8 Kennedy *et al.* (2003), p. 17.
9 Odom and Dujarric (2004).
10 Odom and Dujarric (2004), pp. 216–17.
11 Nye (2002).
12 Nye (2002), p. 144.
13 Brzezinski (1997).
14 See, for example, Goldman Sachs report on major economics at 2050, entitled *Dreaming with the BRICS*, October 2004, and National Intelligence Council, *Mapping the Global Future*, December 2004.
15 China's Information Office of the State Council, *China's Endeavors for Arms Control, Disarmament and Non-Proliferation*, 1 September 2005.
16 Office of the Secretary of Defense, *The Military Power of the People's Republic of China 2005*, pp. 21–22.
17 For a recent account, see Edward Cody, "China Builds a Smaller, Stronger Military", *The Washington Post*, 12 April 2005, A01.
18 Robert Kagan, "The Illusion of 'managing' China", *The Washington Post*, 16 May 2005.
19 Jonathan D. Pollack, "American Perceptions of Chinese Military Power". Available at http://www.nwc.navy.mil/srd/Reports/Chinese%Military%20Power2.htm, accessed on 8 March 2005.
20 Thomas Donnelly, "Allies and Allies: It's Worth Remembering that American Has Important Friends outside of Europe", *Daily Standard*, 23 February 2005.
21 Mazarr (1995), p. 7.
22 David Shambaugh, cited in Steven Mufson, "Sino-U.S. Relations 'Pushed Into a Danger Zone'", *The Washington Post*, 21 June 1995, A17.
23 Huntington (1996), p. 13.
24 For detailed discussions, see Jong-Yun Bae and Chung-in Moon (2005).
25 Aaron Friedberg, *Ripe for Rivalry*, as cited by Mazarr (1995), p. 39.
26 Nye (2002), p. 149.
27 Nye (2002), p. 149.
28 Jim Hoagland, "Power Plays in Asia", *The Washington Post*, 21 April 2005, A23.
29 *Mapping the Global Future* (2004), p. 12.
30 See *National Defense Programme Guidelines, FY 2005*, December 2004; *The Council on Security and Defense Capabilities Report: Japan's Vision for Future Security and Defense Capabilities*, 2004.
31 Brzezinski (1997), p. 151.
32 For discussion on such an approach, see Alan D. Romberg and Michael D. Swaine, "The North Korea Nuclear Crisis: A Strategy for Negotiations", *Arms Control Today*, May 2003.
33 ROK National Security Council, *Peace, Prosperity and National Security: National Security Strategy of the Republic of Korea*, May 2004.
34 Address at the 40th Commencement and Commissioning Ceremony of the Korea Third Military Academy, 22 March 2005.
35 Bruce E. Bechtol, Jr., "The ROK–US Alliance: Perspectives, Perceptions, and Implications of a Changing Strategic Environment," paper delivered at the 2005 KAIS International Conference, Hotel Capital, Seoul, 25 March, p. 91.
36 Changsu Kim (2004).
37 Taeho Kim (2005), p. 148.
38 For a detailed account of how the history of the "Northeast" has become the history of "China", see Park Sun-young (2004).

39 James F. Hoge, Jr., "A Global Power Shifting in the Making", *The New York Times*, 24 June 2004.

References

Bae, Jong-Yun and Moon, Chung-in (2005) "Unraveling the Northeast Asian Regional Security Complex: Old Patterns and New Insights", *The Korean Journal of Defense Analysis,* Vol. XVII, No. 2 (Fall), 7–34.

Brzezinski Zbigniew (1997) *The Grand Chessboard: American Primacy and Its Geostrategic Imperatives*, New York: Basic Books.

Huntington, Samuel P. (1996) *The Clash of Civilizations: Remaking of World Order*, New York: Simon & Schuster.

Kennedy Paul, Perle Richard, and Nye, Joseph S. Jr. (2003) "The Reluctant Empire: A Time of Great Consequence", *The Brown Journal of World Affairs*, Vol. X, Issue I (Summer/Fall), 11–31.

Kim, Changsu (2004) "Security Relations among Major Powers in Northeast Asia: Views from Seoul", in Yan Xuetong and Zhou Fangyin (eds), *Security Cooperation in East Asia*, Peking: Peking University Press, 166–86.

Kim, Taeho (2005) "Sino-ROK Relations at a Crossroads: Looming Tensions amid Growing Interdependence", *The Korean Journal of Defense Analysis*, Vol. XVII, No. 1 (Spring).

Lampton, David M. (2004) "The United States and China: Competitors, Partners, or Both?", a paper delivered at US Foreign Policy Colloquium, George Washington University, Washington, DC, 4 June.

Mazarr, Michael J. (1995) "The Problem of a Rising Power: Sino-American Relations in the 21st Century", *The Korean Journal of Defense Analysis*, Vol. VII, No. 2 (Winter).

Nye Jr., Joseph S. (2002) *The Paradox of American Power: Why the World's Only Superpower Can't Go It Alone*, New York: Oxford University Press.

Odom William E, and Dujarric, Robert (2004) *America's Inadvertent Empire*, New Haven, CT and London: Yale University Press.

Park Sun-young (2004) "China's 'Northeast Asia Project': Launch of a 'History War'?", *Korea Focus*, Vol. 12, No. 5 (September–October), 125–44.

9 China and South Korea's future strategy

Robert Dujarric

Introduction

For almost all of Korea's history, China has been either its only significant neighbour or at least the most influential one. In many ways, the twentieth century, which saw Japan and then the United States (for the South) achieve pre-eminence in Korean affairs, is an abnormal interruption of the Sino-centric life of the peninsula.

The nearly twenty years since the fall of communism, and even more the past half-decade since the election of President Roh in 2002 and America's invasion of Afghanistan in the wake of 9/11 and the attack on Iraq, have seen a transformation of the Republic of Korea's (ROK) strategic environment. With the exception of infrequent contacts, such as the Red Cross Talks of the 1970s, North Korea (DPRK) was only present in the South Korean environment as a threat. In many ways, the ROK in its early years stopped being an Asian nation. Its only solid political relationship was with the United States. Ties with Japan were only established in 1965 and remained largely confined to commerce. The DMZ was a wide trench cutting off the ROK not only from the North but also from the rest of Asia. Thus the ROK was a *de facto* island state floating off Asia.

Today, however, South Korea is being re-Asianized. The DPRK has emerged as a political interlocutor and, though the amount of commerce remains small, as a trade and investment partner as well. China has gained an important strategic foothold in South Korea, thanks to its growing economic weight and its influence – perceived or real – over developments in North Korea. Japan's relations with South Korea may be bad but they are of more consequence to the ROK than twenty years ago. The abduction issue (Japanese nationals kidnapped by North Korea), Japan's concern over the DPRK nuclear and missile programmes, Japanese sanctions against North Korea, and the evolution of the Japan–US Security Treaty into a regionally focused alliance have given Tokyo a greater role in Korean strategic affairs. Russia is marginal, but it does have relations with the ROK, whereas until the waning days of the Soviet Union, South Korea had no ties with the USSR. Mongolia, where North Korean seek refuge, Southeast

Asian countries, where Korean investors built factories and some North Korean exiles end up on their way to the South, are other nations which have emerged as elements of the ROK's strategic equation (the ROK did send troops to Indochina during the Vietnam War but this was a component of the ROK–US relationship which happened to be located in South Vietnam). South Korea has also shown an interest in playing a role in defining the international regime in Asia. Its government hopes that though the ROK is weaker than Japan, it can take advantage of its better ties with Beijing to be more influential in designing the new Asia than Japan.

Although the United States remains South Korea's key strategic partner, its influence has diminished. First, as noted in the foregoing paragraph, other countries carry more weight in South Korean's political-military developments. Thus, the relative position of the United States has, by definition, declined. Second, the Clinton administration's slow response to the Asian financial crisis of 1997–98 hurt American credibility in Korea and Asia. Third, American plans to cut down the size of the US Army in Korea, which have already been partly implemented, weaken the United States in Korea, as does the ROK–US plan to abolish the Combined Command. Fourth, the Bush-43 (by opposition to the 41st president, the current president's father) administration's emphasis, which many would call an obsession, with Southwest Asia has drawn US political and military resources, as well as the attention of top policy-makers, away from Northeast Asia. The war in Iraq has also been a drain on US military assets, with some army and Marine Corps units relocated from East Asia to Iraq. Fifth, major policy disagreements over the management of the North Korean nuclear and missile crises have exposed a deep rift between Seoul and Washington. Sixth, President Roh, unlike his predecessors, has never been sure whether the United States is Korea's welcomed ally and protector or a nefarious occupier.

These developments have given China a rare opportunity to assert its influence on Korean affairs. With America otherwise engaged – and defeated – in Iraq, ROK–US relations under strain, Japan hurt by its ineffective management of the history issue, Russia weakened by its internal problems (its GDP is smaller than the ROK's), China may think that it can reverse the disastrous consequences of the twentieth century on its position in Korea. Some Koreans would welcome such a development. For Koreans who dislike American imperialism, hate Japanese neo-nationalism, think of North Korea as a lost brother, there are good reasons to seek a closer partnership with Beijing. China's ability to achieve these goals will depend on several factors. There are, however, several factors to analyse before passing judgement on the ROK's China strategy.

Factors influencing Korea's China policy

South Korea's domestic politics

The first one is the evolution of South Korean politics. Taeho Kim's contribution to this volume in Chapter 7 lists several issues which divide South Korea from China (see his Table 7.1 for a summary of these questions). But on only one is there a South Korean consensus. All South Koreans, or at least all those who have commented on the issue, disagree with China's Northeast Project contention that the ancient kingdom of Koguryo was within the Chinese cultural and political sphere. But even on this issue, the intensity of opposition to the Chinese position on Koguryo varies. Conservatives have been more vociferous than progressives (as the left is called in Korea). They point to the Koguryo dispute as an additional reason to maintain close ties with America and avoid conflict with Japan.

On all the other major questions which might hamper Sino-Korean co-operation, there is a deep division of views within South Korea. South Korean conservatives see the military alliance with the United States as the cornerstone of their nation's security. Despite misgivings about Japan, they favour a strengthened security relationship with Tokyo. The idea of a tri-lateral alliance between Seoul, Washington, and Tokyo appeals to them. For the South Korean left, however, the American presence is better than Japanese colonization but nevertheless represents an undesirable infringement on the rights of the Korean people. As for Japan, rather than seek to defuse the tensions with Tokyo (admittedly caused by Prime Minister Koizumi's pilgrimages to the Yasukuni Shrine, continued Japanese claims on Tokdo, and other Japanese actions), President Roh seemed to relish "declaring diplomatic war" on Japan. He saw it as a tool in his campaign against the Grand National Party which he attempted to tar with the brush of collaboration with the colonial regime. The divergent reactions of the South Korean right and President Roh to the campaign by leftwing activists to remove General MacArthur's statue in Incheon was telling. Conservative groups rallied to defend the monument. President Roh, however, explained that it was better to keep the statue so as not to displease the American government but offered no defence of the American commander's role in the liberation of South Korea. Conservatives lament the planned dismantlement of the Combined Forces Command whereas the left welcomes the removal of "US wartime control" over the ROK armed forces. Therefore, for the conservatives, the relationship with China must not be allowed to displace America as the cornerstone of Korea's security strategy. For the left, however, a rebalancing of Korean policy in favour of Beijing that would minimize American influence is a welcome change to the Asian balance of power.

North Korea is another divisive factor in South Korea. On one end of the spectrum, there are South Koreans who consider the Kim dynasty to be the number one enemy of the Korean nation. On the other side, there are North

Korean sympathizers who see the DPRK as a victim of American imperialism (conservatives label the left-wing Democratic Labour Party the "Dear Leader Party"). For those who are thoroughly opposed to North Korea, China may be at best a partner that can help manage the nuclear and missile crisis, but it is surely not an ally. For the left-wing elements sympathetic to North Korea, however, China is to be thanked for its economic aid to the North, while the United States and Japan are to be condemned for the sanctions they impose on the DPRK.

Unification is another area where there is no consensus in Korea, though the divergences are more complex than the opposition between the right and the left regarding attitudes towards the United States, Japan, and South Korea. Nearly all South Koreans believe in the goal of unification. But the reality is that very few ROK citizens, regardless of their political orientation, wish for an immediate merger between the South and the North. They know that the Republic of Korea lacks the capacity to successfully absorb the North. Therefore, though there are significant differences regarding the modalities of assistance to the DPRK, most South Koreans favour some sort of aid to the North to prevent its collapse. Conservative South Koreans, who tend to be more suspicious of China than their left-wing compatriots, however, are particularly concerned by the impact of China on the unification process. They are worried that, as a result of the growing economic interaction between China and the DPRK, China is increasingly establishing itself as the leading, perhaps one day hegemonic, power in the North. These conservatives fear that China may detach the North from the Korean nation, making it impossible to ever realize the dream of a unified sovereign Korean state.

Finally, there is a divide between those South Koreans who emphasize the Asian mainland and those who look to the Pacific. For some South Koreans, the future of the country lies with China, closer co-operation with DPRK, and a greater role for their country as an actor in the creation of a new Asian order. But others, mostly conservatives, put much more importance on Seoul's relationship with the United States and Japan. They do not ignore Asia but believe that to avoid falling into the Chinese orbit and to face the DPRK the ROK must be solidly anchored to the US-led alliance systems in the Asia-Pacific region.

The United States

The second issue is American policy. Despite China's rise, the United States remains vastly more powerful than the People's Republic. Not only does its military rank no. 1 in the world but, as an analyst pointed out, there are no number 2, 3, 4, 5, etc. up to number 10 given the wide gap between the US and the second-ranked armed forces.[1] Recent articles have argued that the United States could easily destroy China's entire nuclear arsenal with a preemptive strike.[2] The United States also enjoys a unique and multi-layered connection with South Korea. The ROK and US militaries have been closely integrated for several generations. Many members of the South Korean elite have American academic degrees and tens of thousands of South Korean children, mostly the offspring of the upper classes, are in American high schools. 53,000[3] Korean students, often the nation's best, are studying in US universities. The Korean-American community is smaller than the Chinese-Korean population, but it includes a large number of well-educated members of the American upper class. Therefore, compared to China, the United States has a stronger, wider, and deeper connection with South Korea. On a strategic level, the United States is the only country which can provide the ROK with military protection against North Korea and reassure Korea about Japan thanks to Washington's ties with Tokyo.

Therefore, South Korea is America's to lose. Regardless of the dexterity of Chinese diplomacy, if the United States plays its cards well, it can retain its position as the pre-eminent power in South Korea. In a way, Roh Mun-Hyun's presidency was telling. His supporters included numerous foes of the American presence. He had severe disagreements with America and openly disliked American primacy. Yet, the US role in Korea survived, and to the extent that America's position suffered, it was due more to American decisions than to South Korean ones. In the near future, there are several ways in which America could precipitate its own eviction from South Korea.

One of these is a misreading of the North Korean problem. Washington, both in the Clinton and Bush-43 administrations, has put the North Korean weapons of mass destruction (WMD) question at the heart of its Korea policy. Consequently, there have been frequent clashes with South Korea, under the Kim Young-Sam, Kim Dae-Jung, and Roh Mun-Hyun presidencies. These will continue even if a Grand National Party (GNP) leader succeeds Roh. South Korea's geo-political outlook regarding the DPRK is by definition different from America's. If, however, the United States realizes that the real prize in Korea is the ROK, with its economy approaching the $1 trillion mark, and makes the DPRK WMD problem a subset of a broader ROK-centric vision, it will minimize conflicts with Seoul. If it remains over-focused on the nuclear and missile issues, it may further weaken the ROK–US alliance.

Another threat to American power in Korea is Southwest Asia. The more the United States depletes its resources in Iraq, engages on a confrontation with Iran, and otherwise invests in risky enterprises in the Greater Middle East, the fewer resources it has in East Asia. As Zbigniew Brzezinski argued in 2003, "While America is paramount it isn't omnipotent".[4] There is a point where the combination of the large military and diplomatic resources the United States is investing in Southwest Asia with the failures in Iraq and possibly in dealing with Iran, will weaken American power in Asia.

Finally, American concepts of what the former US Secretary of Defense, Donald Rumsfeld labelled "transformation". Though "transformation" is an ill-defined term, its consequences are greater investments in aerospace and electronic systems and a reduction in the importance of ground forces. There is, however, no substitute for a ground presence. As a result, the military and political influence of the United States in the region could decline as "transformation" advances.

Japan

The third issue is Japan. Japan's relationship with South Korea depends partly on domestic political developments in the ROK. Some South Koreans, mostly conservatives but also men such as former president Kim Dae Jung, think that stronger ties with Japan are essential for Korea. Others tend to view Japan as an unfriendly dangerous neighbour. In many cases politicians, both of the right and left, instrumentalize the "Japan issue" to portray their political opponents as un-patriotic Koreans who fail to stand up to the Japanese. Japanese policies also affect Korea–Japanese relations. The more Japanese leaders appear unable, as was Prime Minister Koizumi, to manage effectively the "history issue", the harder it will be to improve ties between the two nations. There are also strategic divergences regarding the North Korean nuclear and missile programmes and the abduction question. For Japan, the DPRK's rockets represent a grave danger, and the kidnapping of its citizens is an emotional issue. China is also seen as a threat in Japan. The Roh administration, however, tended to be much less concerned by the DPRK's WMD systems and unconcerned by the abductions of Japanese (and South Koreans) and took a much more benign view of China. As long as Tokyo and Seoul remain so far apart on these questions, it will be difficult for them to develop a strategic partnership. The closer Tokyo moves to the South Korean position, the greater its influence in South Korea will be.

The DPRK's future

The fate of North Korea is the fourth issue to take into account when analysing the ROK–China relationship. Our knowledge of the DPRK is imperfect. But we do know that there is a chance, perhaps very low but possibly quite significant, that it could collapse in the next five to ten years. The demise of the Kim patrimonial state would change everything for South Korea. Regime collapse in North Korea need not automatically lead to the end of the DPRK state. But as in the case of East Germany, the North Korean entity's whose separate existence from the rest of the nation is only legitimized by the political system. Thus, the separate North Korean state might not survive the fall of its leader. If this were to happen, South Korea would suddenly face the challenge of unification. The ROK cannot survive such a shock without massive foreign economic and political support. It is far less rich and stable than West Germany was when it absorbed the East. North Korea is in far worse economic, political, and medical, shape than the German Democratic Republic. East Germans had a standard of living probably not worse than that of many South Koreans in the early 1970s, whereas North Koreans know famine. Unlike East Germans, with easy access to Western television and radio and visits from West Germans relatives, North Koreans remain far more isolated. Consequently, unification will actually weaken the ROK, transforming it from a prosperous country with an advanced economy into a very vulnerable polity.

China

Finally, China's evolution will obviously affect South Korea's China policy. A China following the "stakeholder" model of former US Deputy Secretary of State Robert Zoellick can establish itself as an important partner of the ROK without causing major disruptions to the ROK–US and ROK–Japan relationship. But were China to launch an unprovoked attack on Taiwan or to resort to force to take the Sengakus (Daioyutai) from Japan, South Korea would have to choose between China and the US–Japan and could not remain on good terms with both.

China's attitude towards Korea in particular will also be of great importance. China assertions concerning Koguryo might lead to rising Sinophobia in South Korea. China's relations with the North are also relevant. If South Koreans believe that Chinese actions are compatible with the ROK's own goals, the relationship with Beijing will be far better than if Seoul perceives Chinese policy toward the North as clashing with its own national interest.

Asia

The evolution of the Asian international system as a whole will also have an impact on the ROK's policies towards China and the mainland in general. If the international environment in Asia is benign, closer involvement will not entail major risks nor will it necessarily call for downgrading the partnership with the United States. However, if Asia is the scene of numerous conflicts and crisis, then a closer relationship with China may be incompatible with the alliance with America. Such a situation would force the ROK to make a strategic choice between Washington and Beijing.

The outlook for Korea's China policy

In the realm of diplomacy and strategy, for the first decades of its post-1953 existence, the Republic of Korea was an insular state connected only to the United States. Foreign affairs meant, for all practical purposes, ties with America. Therefore, the challenge of managing relations with a multiplicity of nations, and with North Korea, is a new challenge. The domestic political environment has also evolved, from autocracy to liberal democracy.

Therefore, it is clearly impossible to predict the course of South Korea's China policy given the large number of ever-changing parameters. We can, however, make a few concluding comments which will help understand the question.

First, the domestic evolution of the ROK is the critical factor. There are nations where there is a broad consensus on the country's nature and objectives. In South Korea, however, there is a chasm not only concerning foreign policy but also regarding the fundamental nature of the country. For some South Koreans, the history of the ROK is one of a successful struggle against communism and poverty waged with the assistance of the United States. They are proud of the achievements of the Park Chung-Hee regime. For others, South Korea before democratization was a hateful dictatorship propped up by the United States. The traces of this era, including America's special position in Korea, must be cleansed from the body politic. The first group is wary of any moves, involving ties with North Korea or China, which could endanger the ROK–US Alliance. The others, however, welcome all opportunities to weaken the weight and influence of the United States in Korea. The struggle for the soul of the ROK is still going on. It is too early to say which side will win. It is also possible that a compromise will emerge between the two sides, as occurred, to some extent, in several western European nations.

Second, perceptions of North Korea in South Korea will affect the ROK's China policy. Seoul could reach the conclusion that unification is clearly undesirable (due to the cost) but is afraid that the DPRK's collapse might force a merger upon a reluctant South. Under such a scenario, China would assume a key role in ROK strategy as the country that can keep the North alive, even if this entails a partial "neo-colonial" control by Beijing over Pyongyang. If, on the other hand, South Koreans are determined to press for rapid unification, then they may see China as an obstacle to their cherished goal.

Third, as noted, the policies of South Korea's neighbours, and of the United States, will affect the ROK's China's policies. A combination of a "stakeholder" China with a United States retreating into partial post-Iraq isolationism and continued bad blood between Japan and Korea would leave a benign China in a dominant position. Under such a scenario, Seoul would look to China as its major economic and strategic partner. On the other hand, were the United States to regroup and re-focus effectively on Asia while internal socio-economic developments destabilize China, China may become a marginal factor in ROK policy.

Under the Roh administration, Seoul clearly made the choice of seeking a strategic relationship with China. Its motives included a belief that China was essential to the ROK's policy of engagement (or "peace and prosperity") with the North, an interest in taking advantage of China's economic growth, and the desire to end what it considered the South's over-dependence on the United States. China certainly helped the DPRK survive, though it may have been motivated primarily by its own interests in avoiding a collapse rather than by the state of the ROK–PRC relationship. South Korea's economy has benefited from China's development, though the same applies to nations such as Taiwan or Japan which have bad and non-existent relations with Beijing (Taiwan) or tense ones (Japan). China has helped South Koreans feel less dependent on the United States, though whether this is a positive or negative outcome depends on one's views of the ROK's national interest.

As noted, how South Korea evolves will depend on numerous factors which are, by definition, impossible to predict. The evolution of the past 15 years seems to indicate that South Korea is gradually being "re-Asianized" but this trajectory is in no way irreversible.

Notes

1 See Chapter 3 in Odom and Dujarric (2004).
2 See, for example, Lieber and Press (2006).
3 Institute of International Education, *Open Doors*, International Students in the US 2004/05 academic year, http://opendoors.iienetwork.org/?p = 69691 27 September 2006
4 28 October 2003, New American Strategies for Peace, Washington DC. http://www.prospect.org/webfeatures/2003/10/brzezinski-z-10-31.html 17 September 2006.

References

Lieber Keir A. and Daryl G. Press (2006), "The End of MAD? The Nuclear Dimension of U.S. Primacy", *International Security*, Vol. 30, No. 4, Spring, 7–44.
Odom, William E. and Robert Dujarric (2004), *America's Inadvertent Empire,* New Haven, CT: Yale University Press.

Index